SOCIETY FOR EXP

SEMINAR SERIES

BIOLOGICAL TIMEK

BIOLOGICAL TIMEKEEPING

Edited by

JOHN BRADY

Reader in Insect Behaviour, Imperial College, London

CAMBRIDGE UNIVERSITY PRESS

Cambridge

London   New York   New Rochelle

Melbourne   Sydney

Published by the Press Syndicate of the University of Cambridge
The Pitt Building, Trumpington Street, Cambridge CB2 1RP
32 East 57th Street, New York, NY 10022, USA
296 Beaconsfield Parade, Middle Park, Melbourne 3206, Australia

First published 1982

Printed in Great Britain at the University Press, Cambridge

Library of Congress catalogue card number: 81-15506

British Library cataloguing in publication data

Biological timekeeping.—(Society for Experimental
   Biology seminar series; 14)
   1. Biological rhythms—Congresses
   I. Brady, John II. Series
   574.19′1   QH527

ISBN 0 521 23307 0 hard covers
ISBN 0 521 29899 7 paperback

CONTENTS

Contributors ix   *Preface* xi   *Glossary* xiii

1   Introduction to biological timekeeping
John Brady   1

1.1   Biological timekeeping phenomena   1
1.2   Clock concepts   2
1.3   Biological clocks as oscillators   4
1.4   Biological clock literature   5

PART I: RHYTHMIC PHENOMENA

2   Circadian rhythms in animals and plants
Serge Daan   11

2.1   Introduction – the evolution of daily programmes   11
2.2   Endogenous oscillators for daily timekeeping   12
2.2.1   Some oscillator principles   14
2.2.2   Self-sustained oscillations   16
2.2.3   Oscillator precision   17
2.2.4   Homeostasis of oscillator frequency and temperature compensation 18
2.3   Entrainment   20
2.3.1   Photoreceptors – light meter and camera   21
2.3.2   Phase responses – staying on local time   23
2.3.3   Fast and slow clocks   27
2.4   The adaptive nature of circadian rhythms   28
2.4.1   Activity and rest   28
2.4.2   Circadian repertoires   29
2.4.3   The role of learning   30
2.5   Further reading and key references   31

3   Tidal and lunar rhythms in animals and plants
E. Naylor   33

3.1   Introduction   33
3.2   Basic environmental phenomena   33
3.3   Tidal rhythms   35
3.3.1   Endogenous control   35
3.3.2   Entrainment   36
3.3.3   Phase–response curves   40
3.3.4   Conclusions   41
3.4   Lunar and semilunar rhythms   42

3.4.1	Rhythms in reproduction	42
3.4.2	Rhythms of locomotor activity	43
3.4.3	Entrainment	45
3.4.4	Conclusions	47
3.5	Further reading and key references	47

4 Time-compensated celestial orientation
Klaus Hoffmann 49

4.1	Introduction	49
4.2	Light-compass orientation	49
4.3	Sun-compass in birds	50
4.4	Time-compensated sun orientation in other animals	56
4.5	Compass orientation by other celestial cues	57
4.6	Bi-coordinate navigation by celestial cues?	58
4.7	The annual clock and orientation	59
4.8	Concluding remarks	61
4.9	Further reading and key references	61

PART II: PHOTOPERIODISM

5 Photoperiodism in animals and plants
D. S. Saunders 65

5.1	Introduction	65
5.2	The photoperiodic response	67
5.2.1	The critical photoperiod	67
5.2.2	The nature of the clock mechanism	69
5.3	Night-interruption experiments – the central role of night-length	70
5.4	Hour-glass or circadian clock?	71
5.5	Some models for the photoperiodic clock	74
5.6	Photoperiodism and circannual rhythms	77
5.7	How valid are the differences between the various types of clock?	79
5.8	Further reading and key references	81

6 Photoperiodic physiology in animals
B. K. Follett 83

6.1	Introduction	83
6.2	Photoperiodic control of reproduction in vertebrates	84
6.2.1	Endocrine changes	86
6.2.2	Photoperiodic time measurement	88
6.2.3	Bird photo-neuroendocrine mechanisms	90
6.2.4	Mammal photo-neuroendocrine mechanisms	92
6.3	Photoperiodism in insects	94
6.3.1	Diapause	95
6.3.2	Aphid polymorphism	96
6.4	Conclusions	97
6.5	Further reading and key references	98

7 Phytochrome and photoperiodic physiology in plants
Daphne Vince-Prue 101

7.1	Introduction	101
7.2	The properties and functions of phytochrome	102
7.3	Phytochrome and photoperiodic induction	106

7.3.1	Problems associated with the need for light	108
7.3.2	Problems associated with dusk perception	109
7.3.3	Problems associated with night-break experiments	109
7.4	Induction under prolonged exposures to light	112
7.5	The action of phytochrome *via* circadian rhythms and membranes	114
7.6	Further reading and key references	116

PART III: CIRCADIAN PHYSIOLOGY AND CLOCK MECHANISMS

8 Circadian rhythms in animal physiology
John Brady — 121

8.1	Introduction	121
8.2	Cellular rhythms	121
8.3	Tissue rhythms	122
8.3.1	Endocrine rhythms	122
8.3.2	Excretory rhythms	124
8.3.3	Arthropod cuticle rhythms	126
8.4	Whole animal rhythms	127
8.4.1	Metabolic rhythms	127
8.4.2	Sensitivity rhythms	128
8.4.3	Developmental ('gated') rhythms	129
8.4.4	Behavioural rhythms	131
8.5	Sleep	136
8.6	Circadian organisation of animal physiology	138
8.7	Further reading and key references	140

9 Circadian rhythms in man
Jürgen Aschoff — 143

9.1	Introduction	143
9.2	Internal temporal order	143
9.3	Free-running rhythms	145
9.4	Entrainment by zeitgebers	146
9.5	Spontaneous internal desynchronisation	149
9.6	Transmeridian flight and 'jet-lag'	151
9.7	Shift work	153
9.8	Medical aspects	155
9.9	Further reading and key references	156

10 Biochemical rhythms in plants
Manfred Kluge — 159

10.1	Introduction	159
10.2	Energy metabolism	160
10.2.1	Rhythmic glycolysis in fermenting yeast	160
10.2.2	Endogenous rhythms in the energy metabolism of *Chenopodium rubrum*	163
10.3	Rhythmic bioluminescence in *Gonyaulax polyedra*	164
10.4	Rhythms of photosynthesis	166
10.5	Rhythmicity in crassulacean acid metabolism	167
10.6	Rhythmic movements of leaves – a biochemical problem?	171
10.7	Further reading and key references	171

viii   *Contents*

11   Circadian clock mechanisms
     Jon W. Jacklet   173

  11.1   Introduction   173
  11.2   The *Aplysia* eye clock – a model system   173
  11.3   Coupling concepts   174
  11.4   Clock sites and coupling in animals   175
11.4.1   Insects – optic lobes and brain neurosecretion   176
11.4.2   Vertebrates – pineal and suprachiasmatic nucleus   178
11.4.3   Coupling between primary clocks   179
  11.5   Cellular clock mechanisms   180
11.5.1   Clock genetics   181
11.5.2   The avian pineal cell clock   181
11.5.3   Identifying treatments which affect the clock itself   183
11.5.4   Chemically dissecting the *Aplysia* eye clock   183
11.5.5   Protein synthesis – the heart of the clock?   186
11.5.6   Membrane-based clocks?   186
  11.6   Further reading and key references   187

     Index   189

CONTRIBUTORS

Aschoff, J.
Max-Planck-Institut für Verhaltensphysiologie, D-8131 Andechs, Federal Republic of Germany.

Brady, J.
Department of Pure and Applied Biology, Imperial College of Science and Technology, London, S.W.7, UK.

Daan, S.
Zoölogisch Laboratorium, Rijksuniversiteit Groningen, Haren, The Netherlands.

Follett, B. K.
ARC Group on Photoperiodism and Reproduction, Department of Zoology, The University, Bristol, UK.

Hoffmann, K.
Max-Planck-Institut für Verhaltensphysiologie, D-8131 Andechs, Federal Republic of Germany.

Jacklet, J. W.
Department of Biological Sciences and Neurobiology Research Center, State University of New York at Albany, Albany, New York, USA.

Kluge, M.
Institut für Botanik der Technischen Hochschule, Darmstadt, Federal Republic of Germany.

Naylor, E.
Department of Marine Biology, University of Liverpool, Port Erin, Isle of Man, UK.

Saunders, D. S.
Department of Zoology, University of Edinburgh, West Mains Road, Edinburgh, UK.

Vince-Prue, D.
Glasshouse Crops Research Institute, Littlehampton, Sussex, UK.

PREFACE

This book is the outcome of the first really multidisciplinary meeting on biological clocks to be held in Britain – a one-day Seminar organised by the Society for Experimental Biology at Imperial College, London, on 26 March 1980. The papers presented were mainly concerned with broad reviews and recent scientific advances. The book, however, has gathered the same authors together specifically to write a student text ranging widely over the whole subject. It is thus aimed particularly at third-year undergraduates and those embarking on research into biological clocks. The former should find the basis for an excellent specialism essay in any one of our eleven chapters; the latter, by reading the book through, should gain a clear insight into the whole field. There are other introductory books, but none at this level that provides such a balanced and well-informed coverage of both plant and animal clocks.

Aiming at this target has led to some changes in the usual format of the Society's Seminar Series. Primarily, this has meant getting all the chapters written at a level which spends time explaining the background of each topic before outlining its present 'state of the art'. A further change has been the insertion of a cross-referencing system to interlink the wide-ranging aspects of the subject. This not only saves the different chapters from having to go over some of the same ground, but also leads the reader into the several parallel avenues of research that have arisen from the subject's multidisciplinary nature: plants and animals do the same kinds of timekeeping by different mechanisms. Finally, we have included a rather full Glossary which, if read from start to finish, would provide an adequate if indigestible introduction to the formal characteristics of biological clocks.

To my co-authors, I express sincere thanks for their indulgent cooperation in the slightly unusual editorial disciplines of producing a multi-author student text-book. Without their specialist inputs the book could not possibly speak with the broad authority it does. To Louise Sanders of the Cambridge University Press, we are all indebted for a painstaking removal of many infelicities of style; scientists, even those who think they can edit, really do not write English very elegantly.

John Brady
Imperial College at Silwood Park, Ascot

GLOSSARY

Terms and symbols commonly used in the literature of biological timekeeping. Note that though the examples given mostly refer to daily (24-h) rhythms, they are, by analogy, usually also used in the same context for tidal (12.4-h), semilunar (14.8-day), lunar (29.5-day), and annual rhythms.

Symbols and abbreviations
(terms in italic are defined elsewhere in the Glossary)

LD	Light:dark; as in LD 12:12 meaning a cycle of 12 h light:12 h darkness.
LL	Continuous light.
DD	Continuous darkness.
τ	('tau') The 'natural' period of a biological rhythm *free-running* in constant conditions (especially in DD or LL).
T	The *period* of a *zeitgeber* cycle; most commonly used when that is other than 24 h for *circadian* rhythms.
ϕ	('phi') A *phase* of a biological rhythm; e.g. daily onset of locomotor activity, daily peak of photosynthesis; especially used as ϕ_i to indicate the inducible phase of a circadian rhythm in *photoperiodic* induction (§5.5).
$\Delta\phi$	('delta phi') A *phase shift*, expressed in hours or degrees of *phase angle* (Fig. G.1).
ψ	('psi') A *phase angle* of one rhythm relative to another, especially to a *zeitgeber*; sometimes expressed as hours, but more correctly as degrees, with one full cycle of a rhythm = 360° (Fig. G.1).
CAM	Crassulacean acid metabolism; special photosynthetic mechanism in some succulent plants, much used for studying plant rhythms (see §10.5).
PRC	See *phase-response curve* (p. xv).
Q_{10}	Temperature coefficient; the change in rate of a process (expressed as a multiple of the initial rate) produced by raising the temperature 10 °C. Usually more than 2 for most physiological processes, but characteristically near 1.0 for most biological timekeeping – see *temperature compensation*, below, and Fig. 1.1.
SCN	Suprachiasmatic nucleus in the vertebrate hypothalamus – a 'clock' (see §11.4.2).

Terms

(*terms in italic are defined elsewhere in the Glossary*)

Aestivation; summer or dry season *diapause* or *dormancy*.

Amplitude; the peak to trough difference in a biological oscillation (Fig. G.1); in ideal physical oscillators the mean to peak difference.

Azimuth; the compass-bearing to the point on the horizon vertically below the sun, or moon, etc. (§4.4).

Biological clock; a term implying an underlying physiological mechanism that times the overt measurable rhythm or other form of biological timekeeping; see also *oscillator* (§1.2, 1.3).

Biological rhythm; a cyclical variation exhibited in a biological function; especially daily, tidal, monthly and annual rhythms (§1.1).

Circadian rhythm; a cyclical variation in the intensity of a metabolic or physiological process, or of some facet of behaviour, with a *period* (τ) of about 24 h when in constant conditions (the term 'circadian' is derived from the Latin for 'about a day'). It is often incorrectly applied to rhythms that have been measured only in natural or artificial 24-h day–night cycles. These may or may not persist in constant conditions (§2.2.2), and until it is known, or can be reasonably assumed, that they do, the term *diel* is the correct label.

Circatidal, also *circasemilunar*, *circalunar* and *circannual rhythms*; biological rhythms with periods of about 12.4 h, 15 days, 29 days, and 12 months when *free-running* in constant conditions.

Crepuscular activity; an activity mainly performed at dusk and/or dawn.

Critical photoperiod; that 24-h LD ratio at which 50% of the population under study is *photoperiodically* switched from one state to another, e.g. into flowering from non-flowering, or into development from *diapause* (§5.2.1).

Diapause; a period of arrested growth or reduced physiological activity, commonly induced by a seasonal change in *photoperiod* (i.e. day-length); a term used mainly for invertebrates, especially insects. Distinguished from mere *quiescence* by lasting for a fixed minimum length of time, usually several weeks or months, and by the *dormancy* not being broken immediately upon the return of equable conditions.

Diel rhythm; a rhythm that has been measured only in natural or artificial day–night cycles, and not yet known to persist in constant conditions – cf. *circadian*.

Diurnal activity; activity performed mainly during the daytime – cf. *nocturnal*.

Dormancy; a term used either more or less synonymously with *diapause*, but especially for plants, or to mean a period of *quiescence* caused directly by adverse conditions, and lasting only while they prevail.

Endogenous; of rhythms or other biological timekeeping controlled from within the organism by some kind of physiological '*biological clock*' (§1.2, 2.2, 3.3.1).

Entrainment; the synchronisation of one biological rhythm to another of closely similar frequency, especially to a *zeitgeber* cycle, e.g. a circadian rhythm entrained to exactly 24 h per cycle by LD 12:12 (§2.3).

Equinox; the day when the sun passes directly over the equator so that there is a 12-h day and 12-h night over the entire earth. The *vernal equinox* occurs on about 21 March and the *autumnal equinox* on about 21 September – cf. *solstice.*

Exogenous; of rhythms or other biological timekeeping that arise solely, or even mainly, as direct responses to environmental signals (e.g. *diel* 24-h rhythms) – cf. *endogenous.*

Free-running; of rhythms running at their own 'natural' frequency (see τ) in constant conditions, and which are therefore not *entrained* to a *zeitgeber* such as a day–night cycle.

Frequency; the reciprocal of the *period* of a rhythm, e.g. once per 24 h.

Gating; the timing of a biological function so that it occurs only during a limited space of time (the 'gate'); especially refers to the circadian timing of once-in-a-lifetime events such as hatching, and used most commonly for insect adult emergence (§8.4.3).

Hibernation; winter or cold season *dormancy* or *diapause*; especially in vertebrates – cf. *aestivation.*

Hour-glass; an interval-timer which does not oscillate (i.e. repeat its timing cycle) in constant conditions. It is used especially in relation to *photoperiod* measurement (§5.4).

Neap tides; the smallest tides of the 15-day, semilunar cycle (Fig. 3.1).

Nocturnal activity; activity performed mainly at night – cf. *diurnal.*

Oscillator; usually applied to the unseen, *endogenous* 'driving' oscillator (the *biological clock*) whose influence from within the organism causes the measurable changes seen as the overt rhythm.

Period; the length of one complete cycle of a rhythm (Fig. G.1); reciprocal of *frequency*; τ for a *free-running* rhythm.

Fig. G.1. (**A**) Some oscillator terminology illustrated with a pure sine wave. (**B**) The same oscillation illustrating a phase shift relative to **A**. See also §2.2.1.

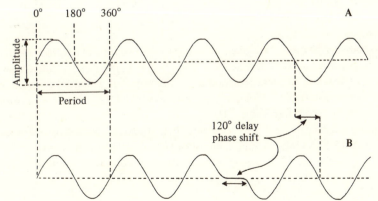

Phase; a particular reference point in the cycle of a rhythm, e.g. the daily onset of locomotor activity, or the light-to-dark transition in a *zeitgeber* cycle – see ϕ, above.

Phase angle; see ψ above (Fig. G.1).

Phase–response curve; the 24-h profile of an organism's *phase shifts* in response to environmental signals (Fig. 2.6).

Phase shift; a re-setting of a rhythm (Fig. G.1); either as an *advance shift* (i.e. forward, or earlier $= +\Delta\phi$), or as a *delay shift* (i.e. backward, or later $= -\Delta\phi$).

Photoperiodism; the seasonal day-length responses that cause altered physiological states such as flowering or non-flowering, diapause or development; the photoperiod is usually taken as the time between lights-on and lights-out in an artificial LD cycle (though many photoperiodic responses are in reality to changes in *night* length) – see *critical photoperiod* (§5.2.1).

Photophase; the light part of a LD cycle, usually used in a non-photoperiodic context.

Phytochrome; the plant pigment which is red/far-red light reversible and is involved in *photoperiodic* responses (§7.2).

Pulvinus; a specialised leaf or petiole joint which causes the so-called 'sleep' movements of leaves and leaflets in plants, especially in Leguminosae.

Rhythm; a function which oscillates at a regular *frequency*; biological rhythms (*circadian*, *circatidal*, etc.) are the overt, measurable activities whose periodicity is taken to reflect that of some internal *oscillator* (or 'clock') driving them.

Skeleton photoperiod; experimental photoperiod cycle consisting of one long light phase followed by darkness interrupted by a short light break, with the organism responding as if the interval between the first light-on and the second light-off marked a single photophase (§5.3).

Skotophase (or *scotophase*); the dark part of a LD cycle.

Solstice; the day when the sun reaches its furthest declination north or south, on about 21 June and 21 December, i.e. half-way between the *equinoxes*.

Spring tides; the largest tides of the 15-day, semilunar cycle (Fig. 3.1).

Synodic month; the lunar month of 29.5 days between new moons; it includes two complete *spring-tide* cycles of 14.8 days (Fig. 3.1).

Temperature coefficient; see Q_{10}.

Temperature compensation; the phenomenon (best known for τ in *circadian* rhythms) whereby biological timekeeping typically does not respond to different levels of constant ambient temperature in the way that would be expected if it obeyed normal physiological Q_{10} principles; it has Q_{10}s of around 1 instead of 2 or more (see Table 2.1).

Transients; unstable cycles which occur in a rhythm that has been subject to a large *phase shift*; for example, a *circadian* rhythm subjected to a reversal of its previous LD 12:12 *zeitgeber* cycle, usually takes a few days to stabilise at its new setting.

Zeitgeber; from the German for 'time-giver'. A periodic environmental signal that *entrains* some *biological rhythm*, for example a natural or artificial day–night cycle for a *circadian* rhythm (may also be a temperature cycle, or a social cycle) (see §2.2, 3.3.2, 9.4).

Zeitgedächtnis; from the German for 'time-memory'. Used mainly in reference to the time-sense in honey bees by which they can be trained to come to feed at particular times of day (§4.2, 4.4).

Zugunruhe; from the German for 'migration restlessness'. Describes the continually repeated, directionally biased hopping movements towards the migratory course that birds in a migratory 'mood' make when confined in a cage (§4.3).

JOHN BRADY

1 Introduction to biological timekeeping

1.1 Biological timekeeping phenomena

Many of the pressures placed on organisms by the environment arrive more or less arbitrarily – sudden death, meeting a rival, infection, cloud cover – but many more arrive quite predictably, in association with the appearance of daylight, low tide, full moon, onset of winter, and so on. The ability to anticipate these events in order to avoid their dangers and exploit their benefits must clearly be of great adaptive advantage (see e.g. §2.4, 3.3.1, 4.2, 6.1). It comes as no surprise, therefore, to find that apparently all organisms or at least all eukaryotes, have evolved various forms of time-keeping to gear their lives to fit this time-tabling of the environment. Nor is it a surprise that such timekeeping ability is usually built into the organisms' genome, and is inherited just like any other physiological characteristic (§11.5.1).

The ability to keep time demands the possession of some mechanism to measure it – a clock. What man-made clocks do is mark the passage of time against equal segments of some process occurring at a constant rate, for example the governed unwinding of a spring, the fall of a weight on a chain, the cycling of mains a.c. electricity, etc. For living organisms there are in principle two different ways of measuring time: either they can rely on the exogenous periodicity of the environment, using that as their clock so that they get up at sunrise, flower at mid-summer, hide under stones at low tide, and so on; *or* they can use some internal process to measure time, rather in the sense that a man-made clock does. There are examples of the former type of timekeeping in this book, a particularly clear one being discussed in §3.3.1, but for the most part the book concerns the much more intriguing second type. The basis for believing that these latter do represent endogenous physiological chronometry is argued in §2.2.

A clock can be used to do three kinds of timing.

(1) *Time-set*; set something to be 'on time' relative to environmental time, for example to be awake during daylight hours, lay eggs in spring, or hide under stones before low tide.

(2) *Measure duration*; time the length of something, for example the number of hours of light in a day in order to gauge the season, or, in a slightly different sense, time the duration of a longer period by adding up numbers of days.

(3) *Find local time*; for example in order to be able to navigate by celestial cues.

Biological systems can evidently do all of these things, and variants of them, by one means or another. The actual timekeeping occurs in five general forms.

(a) *High frequency physiological rhythms*; as in heart-beat, leaf fluttering, neurone spiking, etc.

(b) *Environmentally related rhythms*; that is those that follow the five basic environmental cycles of the 24-h day (Chapter 2), 12.4-h tides, 14.8-day spring tides, 29.5-day lunar month (Chapter 3), and the year (§4.7, 5.6).

(c) *Continuously consulted clocks*; of the kind needed to know what the time is at any given time of day, as used by bees visiting different species of flower that open at different times, or as used in sun-compass navigation by bees and migrating birds (Chapter 4).

(d) *Photoperiodism*; responses to seasonally changing day-length (Chapter 5).

(e) *Dormancy duration*; when seed dormancy, hibernation or diapause (§6.3.1) have a fixed minimum period of quiescence.

1.2   Clock concepts

The prime characteristic of a good clock is that it shall continue to measure time at the same rate under all conditions. For this reason man has expended considerable ingenuity in devising means to make mechanical clocks temperature-compensated, by using bimetallic curves on balance wheels, mercury columns in pendulum staffs, and so on. The point is that if circumstances change the basic rate constant of the process being used in the clock as a model of time (e.g. the unwinding spring, etc.), then the duration of the measured units of the process will vary relative to 'real', astronomical time.

It may be that biological clocks use high frequency physiological oscillations of the type (a) above as their basic time-dependent process, and some hypotheses for biological clock mechanisms explicitly invoke that possibility (§10.2.1), but there are real difficulties for this idea. The most important is that the rates at which these high frequency rhythms run is much affected by irrelevant physiological conditions, especially temperature (Fig. 1.1). The function of these rhythms, of course, is not to measure time; it is just that they happen to work by oscillating, so they do measure time in the sense of marking it out in units of equal length, but the speed at which they oscillate is in practice regulated not against external time but in response to internal physiological demand. They are not, therefore, true biological clocks any more than the clockwork motor of a toy car is a true mechanical clock.

These high frequency rhythms, type (a), are therefore not further considered as real clocks in this book, which concerns itself only with those biological processes that (1) measure time by some means, (2) do so in relation to environmental time-cues such as sunset, high tide, day-length, etc., and (3) use this temporal information to control the *timing* of the organism's biochemistry, physiology or behaviour. The dormancy duration type of biological clock, (e) above, falls within this definition, but its time-measuring mechanisms have been little studied and it is here only briefly touched upon (in Chapters 5, 6 and 7). That leaves us essentially covering environmentally-related rhythms (b), sun-compass type clocks (c), and photoperiodism (d).

Any clock, whether man-made or biological, consists in principle of five notional components.

(1) '*Hands*'; the overt, measurable processes that are regulated by the escapement.
(2) '*Mainspring*'; the source of energy that drives the system.
(3) '*Escapement*' (plus balance wheel or pendulum); the primary regulating oscillator, or pacemaker.
(4) '*Cogs*'; the coupling that links the 'escapement' to the 'hands'.
(5) '*Adjuster*'; the mechanism for shifting the 'hands' to entrain them to external astronomical time.

Fig. 1.1. The lack of constancy in high-frequency biological rhythms. (**A**) The effect of temperature on the rate of generation of spontaneous spikes in a nerve running to the eye muscle of the blowfly; between 15° and 30 °C the relationship is linear, with a Q_{10} of nearly 2. (**B**) The relationship between the heart rate of a fit middle-aged man and his rate of energy expenditure measured as Kg lifted 1 m min^{-1}. (After Brady, 1979.)

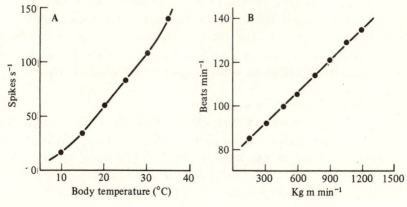

In terms of biological clocks, the 'hands' are all those rhythmic and other time-tabled phenomena that the organism exhibits overtly to the observer, such as locomotor activity, leaf movement, flowering, and dormancy. It is through these phenomena that the researcher must draw his inferences about the unseen driving oscillator (the 'escapement') within. They thus provide the same kind of information to him as does the sound of the heart-beat in a stethoscope to a doctor studying heart disease.

The 'mainspring' energy demands of biological clocks are apparently exceedingly small. Circadian (that is, about 24-h) rhythms, for example, though temporarily stopped by deep anoxia, re-emerge unchanged in phase when the animal or plant recovers. Virtually nothing else is known about the energy demands of clocks, though there are models which invoke energy metabolism as a basic component in plant circadian timing (§10.2.2).

The ultimate objective of much research is to discover the 'escapement' mechanism, that is, the underlying driving oscillator. So far, no such mechanism has been unequivocally identified, though there are certain strong hints as to the kinds of process that may be involved (Chapters 10 and 11). The much better understood component is the 'cogs' coupling the driving oscillator to the overt rhythm. For animals, at least, both hormonal and neural links occur (Chapter 11). The ability to synchronise with environmental periodicities is, of course, the vital adaptive function of biological clocks. The 'adjuster' which permits this re-setting, and thence entrainment of the clock to the environment, must operate at two levels, both as a receptor mechanism to detect the environmental time-signal (sunset, low tide, etc.), and as a system which couples that information to the driving pacemaker and shifts its oscillation appropriately towards the environment's (§2.3, 3.3.2).

It is common jargon to talk of '*the* clock' in discussions of biological timekeeping, but this short-hand is misleading. It disguises the fact that in all multicellular organisms there are probably as many clocks as there are cells. Since both protista and individual metazoan cells in culture keep time (§11.5.2), it is assumed that all five of the above components reside in each and every eukaryotic cell. 'The clock' in the metaphytan, and even more so in the metazoan, is thus in reality a unified complex of cellular and tissue-organised timekeeping, a hierarchy of clocks (§8.2, 11.3).

1.3   Biological clocks as oscillators

Three points are worth noting here. First, the evidence increasingly suggests that tidal rhythms, sun-compass clocks, and photoperiodism are all, or nearly all, based on the fundamental 24-h (circadian) rhythmicity of organisms (see also §5.7). It thus appears that the environmental effects of the earth's rotation about its axis have produced, by natural selection, a common internal chronometry of roughly 24-h periodicity in both animals and plants, and that this has subsequently been exploited for more sophisticated timekeeping. Second, one of the striking features about biological clocks is that even though they have presumably evolved independently many times, their *formal* characteristics are similar in widely different kinds of organism, from unicells to man. Their temporal features – responses to external time-cues, temperature compensation and so on – are all qualitatively the same, or nearly so. Third, these timekeeping abilities are apparently almost always driven by a clock that oscillates (i.e. by one that repeats the same physiological cycle approximately once per 24 h), rather than by using some non-oscillatory mechanism such as an hour-glass type of interval timer, or a process that counts high frequency events.

Just why so many biological clocks should work by oscillating is not immediately obvious, but the answer, or much of it, was supplied in 1976 by Pittendrigh & Daan in a classic series of papers (see §2.2.3, 2.3.3). The crux of the argument runs as follows. One of the prime characteristics of biological rhythms of the 24-h type (and incidentally one of the strongest bits of evidence for their being timed by internal clocks) is that when tested under constant conditions they persist at a frequency that differs slightly, but consistently, from 24 h per cycle; that is, they 'free run', usually within the range of 24 plus or minus *ca* 2 h; hence the term 'circadian' used to describe them (§2.2). The apparently obvious supposition that this rough 24-h periodicity was 'good enough' in natural circumstances because the environment always provided a final, corrective 24-h time-signal turns out to be too simple, however. What Pittendrigh & Daan have revealed is that both the 24-h oscillating nature of the underlying oscillators *and* their free-running departure from 24-h precision make them functional clocks. These two characteristics keep the timed behaviour and physiology in the correct phase relationship with environmental time and ensure, for example, that nocturnal animals remain inactive during the day despite the total darkness in their burrows (see also §2.3.3).

1.4   Biological clock literature

Biological clocks have been the target of several international symposia, the more important of which are listed chronologically below. These works, of course, collate current top-level research, and are quite unsuitable as an introduction to the subject. Rather fewer relevant student textbooks have been written; the more useful ones are also listed. In addition a few monographs on specific aspects of biological clocks have been written from time to time; they form the third list below.

The present volume is perhaps the first attempt at a semi-comprehensive introduction to all aspects of the subject, in both plants and animals. It is aimed primarily at final year biology undergraduates and those embarking on research in the area, but it is hoped that others, too, will find it useful as an introductory text; no other multi-author work has been prepared with these objects in mind. It makes no attempt to provide comprehensive coverage of the literature, but every chapter ends with a list of references that should provide access to all important sources.

The subject of biological timekeeping is littered with unavoidable jargon. Inevitably much of this is used throughout the book. To relieve the uninitiated reader, the book therefore starts with a full *Glossary* that explains the terms and abbreviations used. We recommend frequent reference to this.

Symposium volumes

1960 *Biological Clocks*, ed. A. Chovnick, *Cold Spring Harbor Symposia on Quantitative Biology*, **25**.

1965 *Circadian Clocks*, ed. J. Aschoff. Amsterdam: North-Holland.

1971 *Biochronometry*, ed. M. Menaker. Washington: National Academy of Sciences.

1976 *The Molecular Basis of Circadian Rhythms*, ed. J. W. Hastings & H. G. Schweiger. Berlin: Dahlem Konferenzen.

1976 *Biological Rhythms in the Marine Environment*, ed. P. J. De Coursey. Columbia: University of South Carolina Press.

1978 *Animal Migration, Navigation and Homing*, ed. K. Schmidt-Koenig & W. T. Keeton. Berlin, Heidelberg and New York: Springer-Verlag.

1979 *Cyclic Phenomena in Marine Plants and Animals*, ed. E. Naylor & R. G. Hartnoll. Oxford: Pergamon Press.

1979 *The Circadian System of Man*, ed. R. Wever. Berlin, Heidelberg and New York: Springer-Verlag.

1981 *Biological Rhythms – Handbook of Behavioral Neurobiology*, **4**, ed. J. Aschoff. New York: Plenum.

1981 *Biological Clocks in Seasonal Reproductive Cycles*, ed. B. K. & D. E. Follett. Bristol: John Wright.

Introductory general texts

Bierhuizen, J. F. (1972). *Circadian Rhythmicity*. Proceedings of the International Symposium on Circadian Rhythmicity, Wageningen, the Netherlands, 212 pp., no index. Wageningen: Centre for Agricultural Publishing and Documentation.

Brady, J. (1979). *Biological Clocks*. Studies in Biology, No. 104, 60 pp. London: Edward Arnold.

Bünning, E. (1973). *The Physiological Clock – Circadian Rhythms and Biological Chronometry*, 3rd edn, 258 pp. London: English Universities Press. New York, Heidelberg and Berlin: Springer-Verlag.

Palmer, J. D. (1976). *An Introduction to Biological Rhythms*, 375 pp. New York, San Francisco and London: Academic Press.

Saunders, D. S. (1977). *An Introduction to Biological Rhythms*, 170 pp. Glasgow and London: Blackie.

Monographs on specific aspects of biological clocks

Conroy, R. T. W. L. & Mills, J. N. (1970), *Human Circadian Rhythms*, 236 pp. London: Churchill.

Kendrick, R. E. & Frankland, B. (1976). *Phytochrome and Plant Growth*. Studies in Biology, No. 68, 68 pp. London: Edward Arnold.

Lofts, B. (1970). *Animal Photoperiodism*. Studies in Biology, No. 25, 64 pp. London: Edward Arnold.

Oswald, I. (1970). *Sleep*, 2nd edn, 157 pp. Harmondsworth, Middlesex: Penguin Books.

Palmer, J. D. (1974). *Biological Clocks in Marine Organisms*, 173 pp. New York and London: John Wiley.

Saunders, D. S. (1976). *Insect Clocks*, 279 pp. Oxford, New York, Toronto, Sydney, Paris and Frankfurt: Pergamon Press.

Schmidt-Koenig, K. (1975). *Migration and Homing in Animals*, 99 pp. Berlin, Heidelberg and New York: Springer-Verlag.

Smith, H. (1975). *Phytochrome and Photomorphogenesis*, 235 pp. London and New York: McGraw-Hill.

Sweeney, B. M. (1969). *Rhythmic Phenomena in Plants*, 147 pp. London and New York: Academic Press.

Vince-Prue, D. (1975). *Photoperiodism in Plants*, 444 pp. London and New York: McGraw-Hill.

PART I

Rhythmic phenomena

SERGE DAAN

2 Circadian rhythms in animals and plants

2.1 Introduction – the evolution of daily programmes

The earth has made some 15×10^{11} turns on its axis since the origin of life. Daily changes in light and temperature have thus accompanied evolution throughout its course, and the forces of natural selection must always have operated differentially across day and night. Inevitably, 24-h rhythmicity has become a nearly ubiquitous characteristic of life.

Profound as this influence may have been, its evolutionary history remains speculative. Fossil corals, it is true, have revealed that the earth rotated slightly faster in the distant past – the solar day lengthening by one second every five hundred centuries – but temporal patterns such as daily rhythms generally do not show in the geological record, and can only be inferred from what we know of organisms alive today. Photosynthesis, for instance, must always have been restricted to the hours of daylight, so growth and cell division in primitive algae were probably subject to daily rhythms just as they are in algae today. Likewise, primitive zooplankton grazing on such early algae were presumably faced with a daily periodicity in their food supply as a result of these rhythms. This may be why they evolved their present strategy of vertical migration, which involves sinking to deep and cold but empty waters in the morning to reduce metabolic expenditure while feeding conditions are suboptimal (Enright, 1977).

The problems became more severe for both plants and animals when they took to the land. The physical properties of air make for much larger daily fluctuations in temperature, water availability and light intensity than prevail in water. The first land animals were certainly restricted to high humidities, and were therefore probably all nocturnal. Primitive representatives of the two most successful groups, insects and tetrapod vertebrates (e.g. cockroaches and salamanders), are still predominantly nocturnal, as are virtually all terrestrial molluscs and Crustacea. Similarly, land plants presumably soon developed stomatal movements programmed on a daily routine, and in really arid environments this became coupled with biochemical rhythms that controlled water loss even further by keeping the stomata closed during photosynthesis (§ 10.5).

Competition among the early nocturnal grazers presumably put a premium on developing daytime activity. Once the primitive arthropods developed more efficient waterproofing, they could begin to occupy the vacant diurnal niche, just as the first waterproof tetrapods were doing the same thing (in the early Carboniferous). The abundance of plant food combined with heat from the sun made this step into daylight by the insects and reptiles one of the fabulous booms of evolutionary history. When the first mammals appeared a little later (in the Triassic), they remained, in contrast mainly nocturnal for a hundred million years, developing homeothermy and powerful olfactory abilities as adaptations to night life. In due course, however, they too conquered diurnal niches, just as some reptiles and birds, for example geckos and owls, reverted to the night.

The evolutionary choice between day and night has thus pervaded the entire behavioural, physiological and even morphological organisation of animals and plants. In plants, for instance, flowering co-evolved with the activity of insect pollinators; and the mode of attraction – vision in daytime, odour at night – determined the flowers' colour, odour and size. Throughout this chapter we will bear this complexity of life-style evolution in mind, examining the nature and function of daily rhythms while emphasising the unanswered questions as much as the answered.

2.2   Endogenous oscillators for daily timekeeping

The daily rhythms that one observes in plants and animals in nature commonly persist with no less vigour in the laboratory in constant conditions, which strongly implies that they originate endogenously, within the organism (see also §3.3.1). This was first seen by the French astronomer de Mairan in the leaf movements of *Mimosa* plants that he had placed in the continuous darkness of a cellar. The more crucial discovery, that the periodicity in such constant conditions deviates from 24 h, was made two centuries later in another plant, *Canavalia*, by Anthonia Kleinhoonte; one of her original records, redrawn in contemporary fashion, is presented in Fig. 2.1.

This record shows that when the plant was in constant light, its leaf movements oscillated spontaneously at about 25 h per cycle. No known geo-physical periodicity on our planet could generate this length of cycle directly, let alone also generate the cycles of, say, 22, 23 or 26 h that would be observed in other plants recorded at the same time. This difference between the unique 24-h periodicity of earthly environmental phenomena and the typically non-24-h periodicity exhibited in constant conditions by biological rhythms, is usually accepted as proof of the *endogeneity* of the latter – a proof now given for a multitude of daily rhythms in scores of animals and plants (and given similarly for tidal, lunar and annual rhythms – §3.3, 3.4, 5.6). The phenomenon may indeed even occur under natural conditions, when the light–dark (LD) cycle becomes too weak a signal to synchronise. Thus, woodmice in the arctic summer, and beavers under the ice in frozen lakes show such free-running 'drift' in their daily activity rhythms.

The issues involved are aptly summarised by Kleinhoonte's record. As long as a light–dark cycle was present, the rhythm ran in synchrony with that cycle (as on 13, 14 and 15 March in Fig. 2.1). A *phase* of the rhythm (i.e. the onset of upward leaf movement) occurred at a particular *phase* (i.e. time) of the LD cycle, and a shift in the LD cycle induced a shift in the plant's rhythm. When the LD cycle was eliminated on 18 March, however, the rhythm revealed its own natural, *free-running* properties, drifting relative to external 24-h solar time (see the Glossary).

Clearly the system employed by both plants and animals to adjust to environmental cycles due to the earth's rotation is that of an endogenous oscillation. This oscillation has a period of only approximately 24 h, however, and it therefore has to be *entrained* by (i.e. synchronised to) a periodic environmental signal, called the *zeitgeber* ('time-giver', German), such as the LD cycle in Fig. 2.1. By far the strongest and most reliable zeitgeber in nature

Fig. 2.1. Circadian leaf movement rhythm of *Canavalia ensiformis* in one of Kleinhoonte's original recordings. Black bars indicate the times in which the leaf moved upward; times of darkness are shaded (cf. Fig. 2.5).

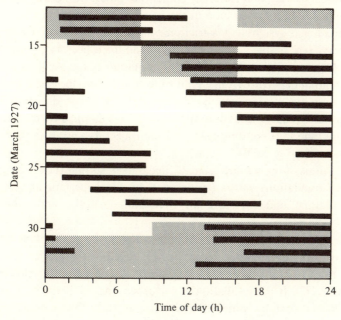

is the day–night cycle, and most organisms entrain readily to that – usually using either sunrise or sunset as the signal, sometimes both – but other periodic signals such as temperature cycles or social cues may also act as zeitgebers (§2.3; see also §3.3.2). The fact that daily rhythms free run in constant conditions (i.e. in the absence of a zeitgeber), and therefore 'lose' or 'gain' time relative to the environmental, precise 24-h day, has led to the term *circadian* used to identify them ('about a day', Latin; cf. circatidal in the Glossary).

Implicit in this concept of the endogeneity of actually measurable circadian rhythms – i.e. in leaf movement, running activity, and so on – is that the rhythm is *driven* from within the organism by some form of unseen pacemaker, a *self-sustained oscillator* that times the system. The physiological nature of such circadian pacemakers is examined in §8.6 and Chapter 11; the characteristics, entrainment and adaptiveness of the visible rhythms are examined in the present chapter.

2.2.1   *Some oscillator principles*

Any on-going process can be represented by a movement in at least two-dimensional space, that is, in a plane. For rhythms, this is commonly done as in Fig. G.1 (Glossary), in the form of an undulating graph with the state of the process (s) plotted against time. It is sometimes more helpful for understanding oscillations, however, if the rate of change in the process (r) is plotted against its state (s) at different points (i.e. times, or *phases*) in its cycle. The graph is then a closed loop in the *phase plane*, as in Fig. 2.2.

In an idealised linear system (e.g. a frictionless pendulum), the oscillation is a pure sine wave (i.e. simple harmonic motion) and the trajectory of r on s in the phase plane is a circle whose radius – the amplitude of the oscillation – depends on the initial departure from equilibrium (Fig. 2.2A) (the oscillation is 'linear' because its motion can be described by a linear differential equation). In a more realistic situation, the oscillation is damped by friction so that the amplitude falls continuously, and the trajectory spirals inwards towards $r = 0$, $s = 0$ (Fig. 2.2B).

Biological rhythms, however, are typically *un*damped, so that they belong to that class of oscillations called *limit cycles*, to which pertain all self-sustaining oscillators, and therefore all circadian, circatidal and other free-running rhythms.

A limit cycle, being undamped, can be represented in the phase plane by a system of vectors representing forces which together counteract any tendency (e.g. from friction) for the r, s trajectory to depart from its closed loop path (Fig. 2.2C). If the oscillation is perturbed, that is, if the cycle is driven off its normal path by some external stimulus, these forces return it, asymptotically, to that path. Any self-sustained oscillation is thus characterised in a particular phase plane by a singular path to which it returns after any departure. The rate of movement along the trajectory determines the cycling period and hence frequency.

In more concrete biological terms, this means that when, for instance, a circadian rhythm is perturbed by a light–dark signal, it will in due course return to its normal r, s limit cycle, even though its wave-form of s against time has exhibited an evident shift (as in Fig. G.1**B**). In practice, strongly phase-shifted biological rhythms often take more than one cycle to recover their normal trajectory, and the intervening unstable cycles, which may last several days, are called *transients*.

Some practical consequences follow from these principles. The first is that an agent which tends to push the oscillation away from its normal trajectory (e.g. a light–dark signal) must affect the rate of movement differentially at

Fig. 2.2. Phase plane representation of an oscillation in some function s and its rate of change r (see §2.2.1). (**A**) Harmonic oscillation; (**B**) damped harmonic oscillation; (**C**) non-linear, limit cycle oscillation; (**D**) accelerating and decelerating effects of the same stimulus applied at different phases. Large arrows on trajectory show direction of oscillation; small arrows indicate vector forces tending to keep oscillation on its limit cycle trajectory; broken arrows in **D** indicate the effects of an external, phase-shifting force at different points in the cycle.

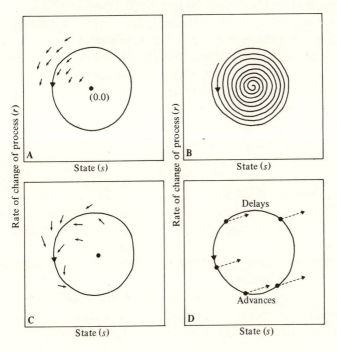

different points (phases) in the limit cycle (Fig. 2.2**D**). If the effect is to slow down the oscillation at one phase, it is likely to speed it up at another. This is an inherently stabilising feature of limit cycle oscillations (§2.2.4) and much affects the form of phase re-setting in response to zeitgebers (§2.3.2).

A second consequence arises from the theoretical necessity for there to be a central null point within the limit cycle where the vector describing the system's spontaneous motion is zero. Thus it should theoretically be possible to stop the oscillation by imposing a stimulus of just the right strength at just the right phase to move the system to this *singularity* point, as it is called. A driven pendulum in a clock can be stopped in this way by hitting it laterally with just the right force at just the right point in its swing. Although it may seem improbable that one should be able to do this with circadian rhythms, it has been done. The free-running emergence rhythm of *Drosophila* (Fig. 8.5) can be made arrhythmic by exposing the pupae to just 50 s of weak blue light at precisely 6.5 h through the circadian cycle (i.e. 6.5 h after the transfer to DD), and the circadian petal movement rhythm of *Kalanchöe* can likewise be stopped by a similarly delicate 'push' (Winfree, 1980).

2.2.2   Self-sustained oscillations

It is not immediately clear why evolution has usually chosen endogenous rhythmicity as an answer to the effects of the earth's rotation. The alternative would be to respond directly to a specific stimulus from the environment (e.g. dawn or dusk) by the initiation of the day's sequence of physiological and behavioural events. The significant difference lies in the re-initiation of the sequence in the absence of the stimulus. But since the stimulus may never be completely absent in nature, except perhaps in deep caves, the adaptive value of endogeneity is not obvious.

Daily rhythms in fact show a complete range from being totally dependent on exogenous stimuli to full endogeneity. When different rhythms are tested in constant conditions, some show immediate arrhythmicity, some show damped oscillations for a few cycles, and some show fully self-sustained persistent oscillations. Immediate arrhythmicity indicates that the rhythm arises exclusively as a direct response to the environment, persistence that it originates endogenously. However, a single function may remain rhythmic under one set of constant conditions, but become arrhythmic under another; and in a single individual one function may remain rhythmic while, simultaneously, another becomes arrhythmic (as occurs, respectively, in locomotor activity and feeding in starlings.

It has been proposed that self-sustained rhythmicity leads to the integrity of the physiological time-tabling of the various functions in the organism across the day and night. This hypothesis should be testable by studying physiological well-being in circumstances which lead to arrhythmicity. That seems not to have been investigated, although mortality in insects has been experimentally increased by keeping flies on light schedules that differ from 24 h per cycle (Pittendrigh & Minis, 1972; and also §5.5 final paragraph).

2.2.3 *Oscillator precision*

Even if the riddle of self-sustainment can be solved, one is still left with the problem of why some organisms have free-running circadian cycles that are typically shorter than 24 h, and others have cycles that are typically longer. Clearly, one cannot expect the accuracy of a quartz watch in a living system, but it turns out that these deviations from 24 h are neither arbitrary nor random. Changes in conditions such as light intensity and ambient temperature affect the circadian frequency in different organisms systematically. In humans kept in prolonged isolation, the sleep and wakefulness cycles of different individuals converge towards an average period of about 25 h (§9.3). Similarly, populations of *Euglena* cultured in constant light at 25 °C show synchronous cell division every 24.2 h. The function of such responses to external conditions can be sought only via their effect in the entrained situation, which is where natural selection operates. Let us first look, however, at the variability of non-entrained free-running circadian rhythms.

The variability from day to day in the period of a free-running rhythm defines its precision, which in homeothermic vertebrates is considerable. A classic example is the flying squirrel, *Glaucomys volans* (De Coursey, 1961). In constant darkness, the free-running period, as measured between the onsets of the daily activity peaks, varied for different individuals by standard deviations of only ±2 to ±15 min (i.e. 0.1–1.0% of their mean period lengths). Likewise in a large sample of laboratory mice, the average day-to-day variation was ±0.28 h (s.d.), or 1.2%. Furthermore, serial correlation analysis revealed that the underlying pacemaker oscillation was even more precise, since some of the variation was compensated for in successive cycles (i.e. if one cycle was short, the next tended to be longer (Pittendrigh & Daan, 1976)).

Why are circadian rhythms so precise? Is, perhaps, the precision of the free-running rhythm related to the accuracy generated during entrainment – that is, to the stability of the correspondence between rhythm and zeitgeber? Not necessarily. The effect of the daily re-set which corrects the rhythm's phase to that of the zeitgeber must create 'noise' in the organism's oscillating system, and this could be greater than the inherent variability of its free-running rhythm. This has not been studied directly, but De Coursey's record of *Glaucomys* in natural daylight suggests that the entrained activity rhythm was subject to day-to-day variations substantially greater than the average error of ± 5.8 min in the period of the free-running activity. Also, both the fact that there are pronounced seasonal changes in the sharpness of the natural day–night zeitgeber, and the fact that the most accurate entrained rhythms occur around the equinoxes, suggest that accuracy may indeed depend strongly on zeitgeber characteristics and hence on the oscillator interactions which occur during entrainment.

It is thus not clear if the precision of the endogenous rhythm restricts its accuracy in entrainment under natural conditions. Even if it does, one may ask why the precision evolved in the first place. Are not the environmental variations to which circadian rhythms are adaptive (i.e. those in temperature, humidity, predator behaviour, competitor activity, pollinator visitation, etc.) far more variable and less predictable than the rhythms themselves? The answer awaits a thorough study of the relationship between rhythm precision and environmental predictability.

Inquiry into rhythm precision can also be made in a physiological context. How are rhythms as precise as that of *Glaucomys* generated? One possibility is that precision may be improved by mutual coupling between a number of oscillating elements, and Enright (1980) has shown in a computer simulation that the standard deviation of cycle length is inversely proportional to the square of the number of contributing elements. Hence, a neuronal structure which contains thousands of elements, each relatively 'sloppy', should be able to produce a precise collective output, which may be how the *Aplysia* eye clock works (§11.2).

While this concept may be applicable to animals with localised circadian pacemakers, what about plants? They, too, show signs of considerable precision: *Mirabilis jalapa* is called the 'four o'clock plant' because its flowers open accurately at tea-time; and the flowers of a single passion-flower plant, *Passiflora foetida*, may pop open within 30 s of each other, with the flowers on different plants doing so within a few minutes (Janzen, 1968). Are centralised pacemakers also responsible for accurate timing in plants? There is little or no evidence for this, but auxin levels do vary across the day, and photoperiodic responses in some plants certainly depend on specific tissues (Fig. 7.1). In principle, the timing system might be localised in the very structures carrying out the rhythmic function. The pulvini (see the Glossary) at the leaf nodes that perform the circadian leaf movements in *Samanea*, for example, continue to be rhythmic even when leaves and stem have been cut away (see also §10.6).

2.2.4   *Homeostasis of oscillator frequency and temperature compensation*

The precision in the cycling of circadian rhythms from day to day is related to a more general homeostatic conservation of the oscillators' frequency (Pittendrigh & Daan, 1976). Circadian rhythms have a relatively narrow range of frequencies that they can be entrained to, typically only to zeitgeber cycles no shorter than about 18 h or longer than about 30 h. Moreover, their frequency is rather insensitive to the levels of ambient temperature and illumination, and with a few significant exceptions (see §11.5.5) the effects of drugs and chemicals on free-running rhythms are minor.

This homeostatic conservation of frequency has long been known particularly for the lack of effect caused by different steady levels of ambient temperature. Sudden changes in temperature may elicit considerable phase shifting, and circadian rhythms will indeed entrain to temperature cycles, but different *constant* levels of temperature have remarkably little effect on the free-running period. The Q_{10} of circadian rhythms, as of other biological timekeeping, is typically close to 1.0 (Table 2.1), in contrast with most other physiological processes which typically have Q_{10} values of around 2–3 (Fig. 1.1A). This stability in the face of different temperature levels is known as *temperature compensation* and it is evident that without it endogenous rhythms would be of little use as timekeepers. Man-made clocks are, of course, likewise temperature-compensated.

Another component of rhythm homeostasis arises from the nature of limit cycles. As we have seen (§2.2.1), an agent such as light or a temperature step which slows down the oscillation at one phase is likely to speed it up at

Table 2.1. *Examples, from various sources, of temperature compensation in the circadian rhythms of various organisms, calculated from the difference in the free-running period (τ) of the rhythms in constant darkness. The Q_{10}s are quoted for the differences in the rhythms' frequency at the two temperatures.* (See also Fig. 5.1**B** and p. 84).

Organism	Rhythm	Period at lower temperature °C	τ (h)	Period at higher temperature °C	τ (h)	Effective Q_{10} for frequency
Gonyaulax (dinoflagellate)	Luminescence	16	22.5	32	25.5	0.92
Phaseolus (bean)	Leaf movement	15	28.3	25	28.0	1.01
Drosophila (fruit fly)	Adult eclosion	16	24.4	26	24.0	1.02
Periplaneta (cockroach)	Activity	19	24.4	29	25.8	0.95
Lacerta (lizard)	Activity	16	25.2	35	24.2	1.02

another (Fig. 2.2**D**). Self-sustainment itself thus guarantees some compensation against accelerating and decelerating effects in different phases of the cycle. This feature may be highly relevant to the question raised earlier, of why there should be self-sustained oscillations at all. Perhaps the very nature of self-sustainment is crucial to the elimination of all sorts of environmental effects on biological timekeeping; and perhaps the increased complexity of circadian organisation of higher animals (see §8.6) creates stronger self-sustainment and thereby more accurate timing of the kind shown by *Glaucomys*.

2.3   Entrainment

Light is apparently the dominant stimulus in entrainment, and all the known centralised circadian pacemakers in animals are closely linked with photoreceptors – for example, as in the eye clock in *Aplysia*, the optic lobe in cockroaches and the suprachiasmatic nuclei (SCN) in rats (§11.4). The most precise visual information about local time is contained in the sun's azimuth (see the Glossary), but this is useful only when the sun is above the horizon and not overcast, and only for a diurnal animal with a sense of compass direction (§4.4). The daily changes in light intensity (Fig. 2.3), on the other hand, contain really clear information on time of day only around the twilights, but do not depend on the sun being visible. Organisms may therefore use light *intensity* to adjust their circadian clocks once or twice each day, and this is evidently quite sufficient to keep most rhythms in proper phase with the environment (see also §3.3.2).

Fig. 2.3. Daily changes in light intensity just after the vernal equinox in Europe (at Tübingen, Germany, latitude 49° N. (After Erkert, 1969.)

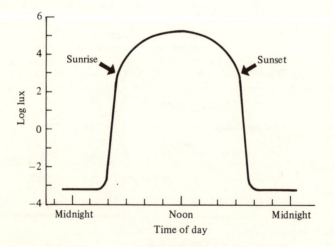

2.3.1 *Photoreceptors – light meter and camera*

How are these daily light intensity changes perceived? Animals, of course, have eyes, but the evolution of eyes for vision has led to features which are not conducive to light metering. Thus, for spatial resolution in a wide range of light intensities spanning 6–8 log units, the vertebrate eye shows marked adaptation by means of pupil contraction, pigment bleaching and neural inhibition. This greatly reduces the eye's ability to detect *temporal* changes in ambient light intensity. Furthermore, most animals have their eyes placed so that the central axis points a little above the horizontal and slightly forward, which is the direction where most relevant visual information normally comes from. The view above the animal is relatively empty, but that is exactly the direction in which one would point a light meter (i.e. towards the zenith) to record changes in general light intensity; and indeed many groups have developed two types of photoreceptor to overcome this conflict. They have eyes specialised for vision (e.g. insect compound eyes and vertebrate lateral eyes), as well as simple, non-image-forming eyes specialised as light meters (e.g. insects' dorsal ocelli and lower tetrapods' parietal or pineal eyes – Fig. 2.4). Perhaps these latter were the photoreceptors originally used for circadian entrainment.

The usual approach in the search for the relevant photoreceptors is to destroy or disconnect the candidate receptor and then observe whether the rhythm has been uncoupled from the LD zeitgeber so that it free runs in a light cycle. However, this may fail to identify the principal photoreceptor responsible since (1) the zeitgeber may still influence the rhythm via other, but normally redundant receptors, and (2) the removal of the zeitgeber input may change the oscillator's parameters (e.g. its free-running period) in such a way that the probability of entrainment is impaired even though the receptor tested is itself not responsible. These difficulties may be partially obviated by testing the selectively blinded animal with light pulses and quantitatively comparing the phase responses, though this has rarely been done.

The importance of the median rather than the bilateral photoreceptors for entrainment is indicated both for scorpions and grasshoppers (Truman, 1976), and for frogs and newts (Adler, 1976). On the other hand, other groups, for example cockroaches and mammals, employ only their lateral eyes. The evolution of light meters has, however, inevitably been subject to ecological constraints, and cockroaches typically lie up in fissures from which a dorsal-pointing light meter could not readily be used; whether their compound eyes nevertheless have any regional light meter specialisation in the ommatidia is unknown.

In the case of mammals, it seems that the retina contains ganglion cells specialised in collecting tonic information on light intensity at the expense of fine spatial resolution. These cells have dendritic connections covering a wide receptive field, and were found by Pickard (1980) who traced the axons back from the SCN which, at least in rodents, are the primary driving oscillators (§11.4.2, and see Fig. 6.6). Coincidentally, Groos & Mason (1980) showed that individual SCN cells respond tonically to continuous localised illumination of the retina over a similarly wide receptor field. Thus entrusting the retina with light meter function in mammals may have been the evolutionary consequences of the heavy skull, and the pelt that came with endothermy, as well as of the fossorial habit of mammals during the initial eons of their evolution.

Fig. 2.4. Spatial arrangement of photoreceptors shown in vertical transverse sections through the brains of (**A**) a housefly (compiled from Strausfeld, 1976) and (**B**) an embryo vertebrate (compiled from Eakin, 1973).

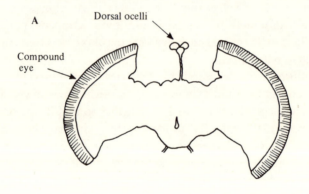

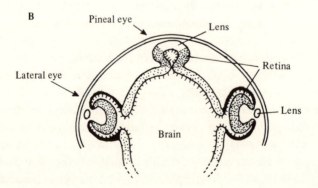

2.3.2 *Phase responses – staying on local time*

How is entrainment of circadian rhythms actually effected by light? What is the form of the oscillator system's responses? As we have seen, the main entraining responses in nature occur at dawn and dusk when the light changes are steepest (Fig. 2.3). The usual experimental protocol to elucidate the oscillator's phase responses to such lights-on and lights-out signals is to place the animal, or plant, in constant darkness (DD) and then expose it at different phases of its free-running rhythm to a short light pulse (usually < 1 h) and observe how the rhythm phase shifts. Since different organisms have widely different free-running periods, it is convenient to divide any given free-running cycle into 360° (see Fig. G.1) so that all comparisons are based on the same notional 'time' scale. (In entrainment to a 24-h LD cycle, 360° = 24 h). An alternative notation is to divide the free-running cycle into 24 circadian 'hours' and then to express events in terms of *circadian time* (see Fig. 5.5). It is conventional to use as a reference point the phase that would normally (i.e. in LD 12:12) coincide with the onset of darkness, and to call this phase 180° (or circadian time 12.00). The part of the cycle covering phases 0–180° is then called *subjective day*, and the part covering 180–360°, *subjective night*.

Now let us take a particular phase of the circadian cycle of a nocturnal rodent, e.g. 200°. In LD 12:12 this phase occurs slightly over 1 h after the onset of darkness. If, then, the animal sees light at this phase in its circadian system's cycle, it must mean that this has drifted forward relative to the LD cycle, and the appropriate response would be a correcting backwards shift, a *phase delay*. Similarly, the appropriate answer to light perceived at phase 340° (which should normally occur 1 h before dawn) would be a *phase advance*. Adaptively, therefore, different directions of phase shifting are to be expected in response to light signals given at different points in the circadian cycle, and experimentally that is exactly what is observed. Additionally, however, and less intuitively obvious, the magnitude of the phase shifts does not vary in simple proportion to the timing (i.e. phase angle) of the experimentally imposed light signal.

Fig. 2.5 shows three such responses in the common vole, *Microtus arvalis*. This vole is not exclusively nocturnal: it leaves its burrow not only at night for its main sessions of activity (indicated by the long bursts of wheel running in the figure), but also in the daytime for short feeding trips about every 2 h. In nature, it therefore receives a series of light pulses. Such pulses seen during the subjective day in constant darkness (i.e. between 0 and 180° of the free-running rhythm) elicit no phase response (Fig. 2.5C). It is now clear why

Fig. 2.5. Phase responses in the free-running locomotor activity rhythms of three voles (*Microtus arvalis*) to single light pulses of 20 min (at arrows); black blocks indicate times when the vole was active in its running-wheel. (**A**) around the time of activity onset the pulse produces a phase delay; (**B**) later in the activity period it produces a phase advance; (**C**) in the rest period ('dead zone') it produces no response. Records of three different individuals free-running in constant darkness. Dotted diagonal lines drawn to emphasise the phase setting of the onset of activity. As in Fig. 2.1, each day's record presented in succession down the page.

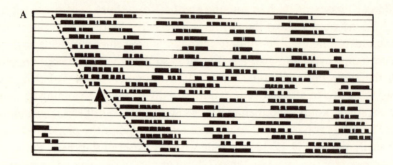

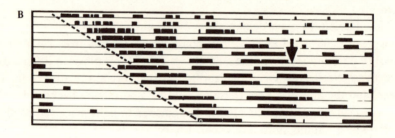

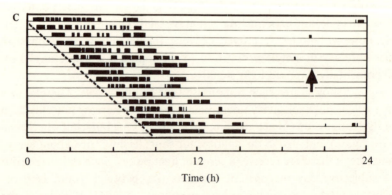

0   12   24

Time (h)

this is so: light seen by the vole in this phase of its cycle tells it that it is above ground but not what time of day it is.

It would be possible to scan the vole's entire circadian cycle with short light stimuli in this way in order to explore its responses at all circadian phases, and then draw a complete *phase–response curve* right across the 360°. This has not been done for *Microtus*, but it has been done for other nocturnal rodents, as well as for many other organisms, both plant and animal; examples are shown in Fig. 2.6 (see also Figs. 3.4 and 11.7). All agree in having delay responses in the beginning of the subjective night, advance responses in the late subjective night, and a prolonged dead zone of near insensitivity to light pulses during the subjective day. The magnitude of the responses varies to some extent with the strength of the stimulus (e.g. light intensity and pulse duration), but these generalisations remain qualitatively true. The transition from delay to advance phase shifts in the middle of the night may occur suddenly, with large delays changing within a few degrees to large advances, as in *Gonyaulax*, *Drosophila* and *Sarcophaga*. Alternatively, and especially in locomotor activity and other behavioural rhythms, the maximum shifts may be small and the changeover gradual, as in the rodents and the cockroach, *Nauphoeta*.

All this gives no clue as to the physiological mechanisms of entrainment, but it does describe the circadian timekeeping system in terms of the magnitude of its phase-shifting ability to particular LD zeitgebers at all points in its cycle. It also makes sense of the relationship between the direction of phase shifting in the first and second halves of the night, and the observation that entrainment in nature occurs at dawn and dusk. Indeed, the use of such experimentally determined phase–response curves does in fact permit fairly accurate prediction of the real relationship between the animal's circadian timekeeping and local time (Pittendrigh & Daan, 1976).

If the phase–response curve is therefore such a faithful respresentation of the underlying clock, where is it generated? Is it a feature of this pacemaker *per se*, or is it a function of the interaction of the photoreceptor and the pacemaker? As we have seen (§2.2.1), an alternation between delay and advance phase shifts as a reaction to standard stimuli is at least partly in the very nature of self-sustained oscillations. In addition, however, the photoreceptors may also be partly responsible for the form of the phase–response curve. In several nocturnal arthropods (e.g. scorpions and crayfish) and vertebrates (e.g. rabbits), retinal sensitivity varies across the circadian cycle (Fig. 2.7), and that must affect the strength of the zeitgeber input to the pacemaker. The possibility has not been investigated, but it would make sense if the phase of least retinal sensitivity corresponded with the dead zone in the phase–response curve during the subjective day. That way the vole's

Fig. 2.6. Phase–response curves in eight different organisms. The curves show the changing magnitude of the phase shifts in the various free-running rhythms in constant darkness, in response to light pulses given at several different phases in the circadian cycle, i.e. at various test points in its 360° shown on the abscissa (cf. Figs. 3.4 and 11.7). Delay shifts (shaded) are plotted downwards from each respective horizontal line, advance shifts upwards, with the ordinate scales in approximately the same relative units of *ca* 4 h between the horizontal lines. (Compiled from various sources.) For *Drosophila* rhythm see Fig. 8.5; for *Gonyaulax* see Fig. 10.4.

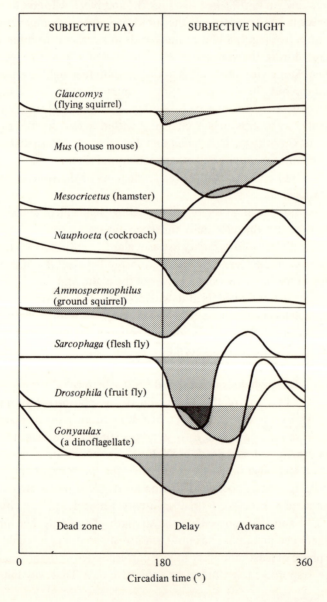

SUBJECTIVE DAY   SUBJECTIVE NIGHT

Glaucomys
(flying squirrel)

Mus (house mouse)

Mesocricetus (hamster)

Nauphoeta (cockroach)

Ammospermophilus
(ground squirrel)

Sarcophaga (flesh fly)

Drosophila (fruit fly)

Gonyaulax
(a dinoflagellate)

Dead zone   Delay   Advance

0   180   360

Circadian time (°)

circadian system, for example, would receive strong light stimuli only at those times of day when light intensity is a really relevant cue to local time – at dawn and dusk. The combined pacemaker–photoreceptor system would then seem optimally designed to keep to local time.

2.3.3 *Fast and slow clocks*

The length of the free-running, circadian period (τ, 'tau') in the absence of light (τ_{DD}) determines whether a light cycle will entrain the rhythm by daily phase delays or advances. If τ_{DD} exceeds 24 h, the rhythm must be re-set earlier, so that a daily advance is needed, and entrainment will be effected mainly in the morning. If τ_{DD} is less than 24 h, evening light will create the required phase delay. Many years ago, Aschoff noted a general difference between day-active and night-active animals in this respect. The former,

Fig. 2.7. Endogenous rhythms in retinal sensitivity in three nocturnal animals. The curves show the changing magnitude of the electrophysiological response to stimulation by regularly presented, standard flashes of light. For the crayfish, the peak to trough change in sensitivity is from *ca* 1500 to 3000 spikes per light flash; for the scorpion, from *ca* 0.1 to 0.5 mV in the eye's electroretinogram (i.e. its summed receptor potentials); for the rabbit, the cycle is measured in the cortical evoked responses, with the horizontal line at zero potential. (Compiled from Aréchiga, 1974; Fleissner, 1977; Bobbert, A. C., Brandenburg, J. & Krul, W. H., 1978.)

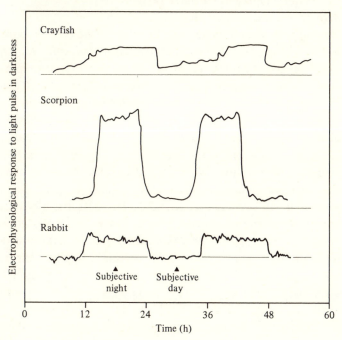

including man, typically have $\tau_{DD} > 24$ h, the latter, $\tau_{DD} < 24$ h, a tendency later confirmed in many mammals and birds, though not in insects (Aschoff, 1979). It ensures that nocturnal vertebrates are entrained mainly by sunset, while their diurnal fellows are entrained mainly by sunrise. Why this should be of particular significance to higher vertebrates is unclear and has been little researched. One suggestion is that daily confirmation of territorial occupancy is optimally scheduled as early as possible in the active period of the day or night, not only for songbirds with their dawn 'chorus', but also for nocturnal mammals in their chemical 'marking' (§2.4.2).

In any case, though it was once assumed that the 'circa' aspect of free-running rhythms merely indicated that evolution had produced no greater accuracy because that was unnecessary in the natural, entrained situation, it now seems clear that the departure of τ from 24 h may of itself by adaptive, assisting the stability of phase control in entrainment to a 24-h cycle (Pittendrigh & Daan, 1976; see also §2.2.3). It is also suggested that both the differences in τ between nocturnal and diurnal animals, and the phase angles they therefore maintain to their respective dusk and dawn zeitgebers, form the basis of what is known as 'Aschoff's Rule'. This is the generalisation that τ_{LL} is lengthened in many nocturnal animals and shortened in diurnal animals in proportion to the intensity of the constant light.

2.4   The adaptive nature of circadian rhythms

2.4.1   Activity and rest

We have examined much of the phenomenology of circadian rhythms – their endogeneity, entrainment, oscillator characteristics, and so on – but what is their adaptive meaning? Their role in timekeeping for sun-compass orientation and photoperiodism is discussed elsewhere (Chapters 4 and 5–7). The manifold uses to which daily behaviour patterns in animals can be put in order to fit the temporal pattern of the environment (Daan, 1981), and some resultant general questions that arise are considered here.

As we have seen, in most animals circadian rhythms generate gross patterns of locomotor activity alternating with rest or sleep (§8.5). In plants, the most conspicuous behaviour pattern is the circadian up-and-down movements of the leaves, especially in Leguminosae (Fig. 2.1). However, the survival value of these two rather generalised rhythms has not been firmly established. It has been suggested that plants fold down their leaves at night in order to reduce illumination by the moon of their upper surfaces, which carry their photoperiodic light receptors, and thereby avoid incorrect photoperiodic responses during moonlit nights. This hypothesis remains unsupported experimentally, however, and it seems unlikely that whole families of plants would have evolved the complex, mechanically active pulvini at their leaf nodes solely to suppress a maladaptive photoperiodic response. Nevertheless, in over two and a half centuries of research on leaf movements, no better suggestion for their adaptive significance has been advanced.

The function of the daily cycle of sleep and wakefulness in animals is scarcely better understood. Presumably, amongst other advantages, restricting activity to a part of the environment's 24-h cycle reduces competition by dividing habitats up temporally as well as spatially. However, that does not explain how sleep is of advantage throughout the remainder of the cycle. Meddis (1975) has argued that such enforced inactivity reduces the risks, particularly from predators, of being active at times of less than optimal behavioural performance. In this view sleep is a spontaneous, prolonged immobility, physiologically imposed and of as much behavioural significance as the phase of wakefulness. A more traditional view is that sleep restores body reserves, though it is unknown which. Its ecological significance would then be that it enables the animal to extend its activities when it is awake beyond what would otherwise be set by basic physiological limitations. We do not yet know the correct explanation, but it seems likely that the functions of sleep are as complex as its manifestations (see also Chapter 9 and §8.5).

2.4.2 Circadian repertoires

Circadian periodicity does not only generate 24-h fluctuations in general activity; it permeates much of animal and plant physiology. Animal behaviour is particularly profoundly affected (§8.4.4), often implying complex daily changes in 'motivational' state. Sometimes the adaptiveness of these changes in behavioural repertoire is fairly obvious, for example when they relate to prey availability, as in the tsetse fly (Fig. 8.6), but in others – especially in birds and mammals – the circadian organisation of behaviour is evidently much more complex, and its adaptiveness less easy to unravel. For example, Kacelnik (1979) came to the conclusion that the dawn chorus of songbirds is concentrated at a time of day when (a) the yield from foraging would be small due to low light intensity and invertebrate prey inactivity, (b) acoustic communication is efficient due to low wind speeds, and (c) the rate of territorial intrusion is at its daily peak.

A further complexity in such temporal ecological analyses is that behaviours which usually occur in a sequence and belong to a single motivational context may have optima at different times of day. The kestrel, for instance, hunts during the day when its prey (voles) is most readily available, but then caches the kill and does not eat it until just before nightfall. This strategy saves energy by reducing the costs of both hunting and thermoregulation, by delaying digestion to the coldest part of the 24 h.

In the timing of behavioural repertoires there is a recurring theme of synchronisation with other organisms: great tits sing in synchrony with the activity of territorial intruders, kestrels and tsetse flies hunt in synchrony with prey abundance, pollinating insects fly in synchrony with the opening of flowers, the activity of parasites is synchronous with that of their hosts, and vulnerable stages in a life cycle are synchronised with those of conspecifics in a population to reduce predation. Such daily synchronies are surely adaptive, and many must arise endogenously from circadian changes in motivational states. Less obvious is how much is innate in these circadian programmes and how much is due to individual experience of the time structure of the environment.

2.4.3   *The role of learning*
Early in this century, Semon (1905) defended the idea that daily rhythmicity was *learnt* by both animals and plants, with their experience of a cyclical environment being crucial to their subsequent expression of endogenous rhythmicity in constant conditions. This proposition became untenable as soon as it was shown that plants and animals raised in constant conditions from before the zygote exhibited unimpaired rhythmicity (as in Fig. 8.5**B**), and that animals raised in cycles of different frequency still had free-running rhythms with periods in the region of 24 h. The frequency of circadian rhythms is therefore innate, and moreover shows simple Mendelian inheritance (§11.5.1). On the other hand, with complex circadian behavioural programmes this does not necessarily mean that the temporal interdigitation of the various behavioural components is also innate. It may well be that some parts of the programme are fixed in the organism's genotype, while others are incorporated during the individual's life, in response to experience.

The evidence is too thin to be sure at the moment which is which, but the timing of some behaviours, particularly those of the once-in-a-lifetime sort such as adult eclosion in insects (§8.4.3), seem highly unlikely to be subject to learning. Other, repetitive behaviours, however, such as foraging and courtship, may well have their timing in the individual improved as a result of experience. This certainly occurs in honey bees foraging on flowers with temporally restricted nectar production (see §4.2), and it also seems to occur in the way that many animals on restricted feeding schedules come to 'anticipate' meal times (Daan, 1981). Moreover, experiments with rats have demonstrated that single, non-periodic experiences can affect task performance at circadian intervals.

The implication seems to be not only that circadian programming may be learnt, but also that learning itself has a circadian time base. Classical Pavlovian conditioning can evidently work this way, since rats show increases in digestive enzyme activity in association with a meal taken 24 h previously

(Suda & Saito, 1979). No doubt the more complex the circadian repertoire, the greater the potential for learnt phase settings. Perhaps the host of circadian physiological rhythms which create the temporal structure of the animal's internal environment also create daily changes in the animal's motivational levels for various behaviours. That would then cause daily changes in the level of reinforcement ('reward') for learning, and hence a correlation with the time course of the environment. This would make good adaptive sense as an answer to the predictable vagaries of living on a rotating planet, where today's sequence of circumstances is normally very similar to tomorrow's. Such possibilities await research.

Finally, one may ask whether this learning aspect of timekeeping is an advanced feature added late in evolution to the circadian rhythmicity of higher animals only, or whether some equivalent of it may occur in plants too? The answer cannot yet be given with any certainty but seems likely to be no. The incorporation of experience into temporal programming must surely be exclusive to behaviour coordinated by a sophisticated central nervous system.

2.5 Further reading and key references

Books and review articles are indicated by asterisks

Adler, K. (1976). Extraocular photoreception in amphibians. *Photochemistry and Photobiology*, **23**, 275–98.

Aréchiga, H. (1974). Circadian rhythm of sensory input in the crayfish. In *The Neurosciences; IIIrd Study Program*, ed. F. A. Schmitt, pp. 517–23. Cambridge, Massachusetts: Massachusetts Institute of Technology Press.

*Aschoff, J. (1979). Circadian rhythms: influences of internal and external factors on the period measured in constant conditions. *Zeitschrift für Tierpsychologie*, **49**, 225–49.

Bobbert, A. C., Brandenburg, J. & Krul, W. H. (1978). Seasonal fluctuations of the circadian changes in rabbit visual evoked potentials. *International Journal of Chronobiology*, **5**, 519–32.

*Daan, S. (1981). Adaptive daily strategies in behavior. In *Handbook of Behavioral Neurobiology*, **4**, ed. J. Aschoff, pp. 275–98. New York and London: Plenum.

De Coursey, P. J. (1961). Effect of light on the circadian activity rhythm of the flying squirrel, *Glaucomys volans*. *Zeitschrift für vergleichende Physiologie*, **44**, 331–54.

*Eakin, R. N. (1973). *The Third Eye*. Berkeley: University of California Press.

Enright, J. T. (1977). Diurnal vertical migration: adaptive significance and timing. I. Selective advantage: a metabolic model. *Limnology and Oceanography*, **22**, 856–72.

*Enright, J. T. (1980). *The Timing of Sleep and Wakefulness*. Berlin: Springer-Verlag.

Erkert, H. G. (1969). Die Bedeutung des Lichtsinnes für Aktivität und

Raumorientierung der Schleiereule (*Tyto alba guttata* Brehm). *Zeitschrift für vergleichende Physiologie*, **64**, 37–70.

Fleissner, G. (1977). Differences in the physiological properties of the medial and the lateral eyes and their possible meaning for the entrainment of the scorpion's circadian rhythm. *Journal of Interdisciplinary Cycle Research*, **8**, 15–26.

Groos, G. A. & Mason, R. (1980). The visual properties of rat and cat suprachiasmatic neurons. *Journal of Comparative Physiology*, **135**, 349–56.

Janzen, D. H. (1968). Reproductive behavior in the Passifloraceae and some of its pollinators in Central America. *Behaviour*, **32**, 33–48.

Kacelnik, A. (1979). The foraging efficiency of great tits (*Parus major* L.) in relation to light intensity. *Animal Behaviour*, **27**, 237–41.

Kleinhoonte, A. (1928). De door het licht geregelde autonome bewegingen der *Canavalia* bladeren. Ph.D. Thesis. Delft: W. D. Meinema, uitgever.

*Meddis, R. (1975). On the function of sleep. *Animal Behaviour*, **23**, 656–91.

Pickard, G. E. (1980). Morphological characteristics of retinal ganglion cells projecting to the suprachiasmatic nucleus: a horseradish peroxidase study. *Brain Research*, **183**, 458–65.

Pittendrigh, C. S. & Daan, S. (1976). A functional analysis of circadian pacemakers in nocturnal rodents. (Papers I to V in a series) *Journal of Comparative Physiology*, **106**, 223–355.

Pittendrigh, C. S. & Minis, D. H. (1972). Circadian systems: longevity as a function of circadian resonance in *Drosophila melanogaster*. *Proceedings of the National Academy of Sciences, USA*, **69**, 1527–39.

Semon, R. (1905). Ueber die Erblichkeit der Tagesperiode. *Biologisches Zentralblat*, **25**, 241–52.

Strausfeld, N. J. (1976). *Atlas of an Insect Brain*. Berlin, Heidelberg, New York: Springer-Verlag.

Suda, M. & Saito, M. (1979). Coordinative regulation of feeding behaviour and metabolism by a circadian timing system. In *Biological Rhythms and Their Central Mechanisms*, ed. M. Suda, O. Hayaishi & H. Nakagawa, pp. 263–72. Amsterdam: Elsevier/North-Holland.

*Truman, J. W. (1976). Extraretinal photoreception in insects. *Photochemistry and Photobiology*, **23**, 215–25.

*Winfree, A. T. (1980). *The Geometry of Biological Time*. Berlin: Springer-Verlag.

E. NAYLOR

3 Tidal and lunar rhythms in animals and plants

3.1 Introduction

It is now well established that many coastal marine organisms when kept in the laboratory, away from the influence of tides, exhibit endogenous rhythms of circatidal periodicity in the patterns of their physiology and behaviour. As with endogenous circadian rhythmicity (Chapter 2), the mechanism of this internal 'tidekeeping' ability has presumably been selected for and is inherited (see Williams *et al.*, in Naylor & Hartnoll, 1979; and §11.5.1). In nature such circatidal rhythmicity depends for its precision and entrainment upon the cyclical variations of tides and associated cycles of hydrostatic pressure, temperature, salinity, light and immersion. In this chapter we will briefly consider the evidence for circatidal (*ca* 12.4-h) rhythmicity in constant conditions, and then discuss in some detail its entrainment by environmental factors. In addition, we shall examine the question of circasemilunar (*ca* 14.8-day) and circalunar (*ca* 29.5-day) rhythms in plants and animals in the context of the spring/neap cycle of tides and monthly variations of moonlight.

3.2 Basic environmental phenomena

Tides are caused by the apparent movement of the moon around the earth, and to a lesser extent by the sun. The moon's gravitational force draws up a bulge in the sea lying beneath it, which is balanced by a reciprocal bulge in the sea on the opposite side of the earth. Since the moon's apparent time of revolution around the earth is 24.8 h, these two bulges of water cause high tides on average 12.4 h apart, although the precise timing varies according to local topography. In some parts of the world, the changing declination of the moon often causes the twice-daily tides to be of unequal height, a difference which may, in places, be so great that it produces effectively only one tide each day.

An additional complication is caused by the sun's gravity. This augments the pull on the sea when the earth, moon and sun are all in line, as they are twice a month at the full and new moons, thereby causing the large amplitude, so-called *spring tides* to occur. When the sun and the moon are at a right angle to each other in relation to the earth, during the first and last quarters of the moon, the gravitational pulls of the sun and moon somewhat counteract each other. At these times of the month the smaller amplitude *neap tides* occur. There are therefore two periods of spring tides and two of neap tides during each lunar (synodic) month of 29.5 days (Fig. 3.1).

Organisms inhabiting the intertidal zone are thus subject to several kinds of environmental periodicity, not only the 12.4-h tidal immersion and the 14.8-day semilunar variations in this, but also the 24-h daily cycle, the 29.5-day lunar cycle and, in temperate localities, the annual seasonal cycle as well. Among coastal organisms, those from the mid-tide level are primarily influenced by the 12.4-h periodicity, but those living above the level of mean high tides or below mean low tides are more acutely influenced by the 14.8-day periodicity, since they are immersed or exposed only at spring tides. Terrestrial organisms, of course, are primarily responsive both to the 24-h day–night cycle due to the sun, and to seasonal changes in photoperiod, but some terrestrial species, like some marine organisms, are also directly sensitive to lunar periodicity (§3.4.1).

Fig. 3.1. Generalised pattern of semi-diurnal tides (12.4-h intervals) over a lunar month. MHWS, mean high water spring tide level; MHWN, mean high water neap tide level; MTL, mid tide level; MLWN, mean low water neap tide level; MLWS, mean low water spring tide level; open circle, full moon; closed circle, new moon.

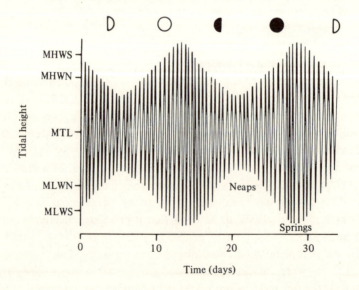

3.3   Tidal rhythms

3.3.1   *Endogenous control*

Tidal rhythmicity is of wide occurrence (Palmer, 1974; Enright, 1975; Naylor, 1976) and its endogenous control has now been described for a number of processes such as locomotor activity, respiratory ventilation, oxygen consumption and colour change, in a wide variety of animals and plants, from dinoflagellates and algae, through invertebrates, to shore fishes. Fig. 3.2 illustrates two examples of free-running circatidal rhythms expressed in the laboratory. Not uncommonly, such *ca* 12.4-h rhythms also show interaction with a circadian periodicity, as is slightly evident in Fig. 3.2**A**, where two alternate peaks (i.e. *ca* 24-h spaced) are higher than the others.

Fig. 3.2. Endogenous, free-running circatidal rhythms of locomotor activity in two species of intertidal crustaceans recorded in constant conditions in the laboratory. **(A)** *Carcinus maenas* walking rhythm recorded from three crabs in tilting box actographs. (After Naylor, 1963.) **(B)** *Eurydice pulchra* swimming rhythm, recorded as numbers (of five individuals) swimming past an infrared light source. (After Jones & Naylor, 1970.) Top trace shows concurrent tide position on the South Wales coast from which the animals were collected; the annual height range is 4 m (neaps) to 9 m (springs).

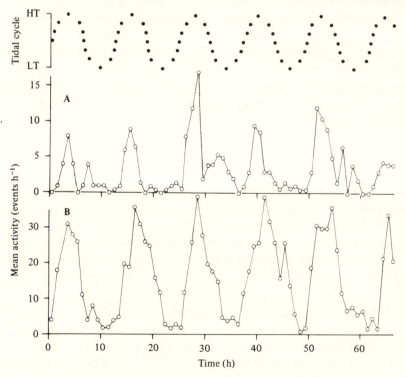

Also, as with circadian rhythms (§2.2), the activity peaks drift (i.e. free run) relative to the actual average tidal interval of 12.4 h.

The adaptive importance of this endogenous circatidal timekeeping is the anticipation of low tide that it provides. Thus the shore crab, *Carcinus maenas*, does not wait to be uncovered by the tide before seeking shelter both from avian predators and from desiccation; it ceases its foraging behaviour and secretes itself beneath stones long before low tide (Fig. 3.2A). Likewise, the sand-beach isopod, *Eurydice pulchra*, avoids being carried away with the falling tide by ceasing to swim and by burrowing in the sand before the tide has fully ebbed (Fig. 3.2**B**), thus maintaining its normal pattern of zonation on the beach. In contrast, some shore organisms, such as sessile barnacles which are structurally well adapted to withstand desiccation and to resist predators at low tide, appear not to make use of endogenous timing to control their behaviour; they simply close their shell aperture as a direct response to the falling tide (Naylor, 1976).

Nevertheless, many coastal organisms, particularly mobile ones, are found to exhibit endogenous circatidal and/or circadian patterning of their behaviour and physiology when they are tested in constant conditions in the laboratory. Such temporal patterns must clearly be taken into account in measurements of, for example, 'typical' behavioural responses and 'standard' respiratory rates. Furthermore, the rhythm patterns themselves vary in relation to factors such as season, actograph design, tidal amplitude and pattern, and the time of day at which low spring tides occur. All these factors are likely to be important when considering the adaptive value of endogenous tidal rhythmicity, or when assessing the role of environmental factors in entraining such rhythms (Naylor, 1976).

3.3.2   *Entrainment*

In attempting to identify which features of the tidal rise and fall are important zeitgebers for entrainment (see the Glossary), arrhythmic animals have been tested in cages placed between or below tidemarks, and attempts have been made in the laboratory to entrain tidal rhythmicity to each potential zeitgeber separately (see also §2.3). Fig. 3.3 illustrates successful entrainment of locomotor activity in previously arrhythmic *Carcinus* after exposure to cycles of temperature, hydrostatic pressure and salinity.

(a) *Temperature.* In the temperature experiment (Fig. 3.3A), peak activity occurred during the low temperature phase when the rhythm was entrained to a temperature cycle, and continued to peak at times of expected low temperature when free-running in a constant 13 °C. This behaviour is what would be expected of crabs during early summer when rhythmicity is first established following a winter period of inactivity below tidemarks. Alternate exposure to warm air and cold water evidently sets the rhythm. The temperature differential of the experiment (11 °C) is greater than would be experienced naturally, but a differential of only 4 °C will act as a zeitgeber, if it is combined with a 6:6 h cycle of immersion in water and exposure to air. It has also been shown that single temperature changes within the normal

Fig. 3.3. Mean hourly activity records during and after entrainment of endogenous circatidal locomotor rhythms using cycles of temperature, hydrostatic pressure and salinity in the shore crab, *Carcinus*. (**A**) Five crabs subjected to 120 h of 6:6 h cycles of 24°:13 °C, followed by 72 h recording at continuous 13 °C. (After Williams & Naylor, 1969.) (**B**) Six crabs subjected to 72 h of 6:6 h cycles of 1 atm.:1.6 atm., followed by 72 h at 1 atm. (After Naylor & Atkinson, 1972.) (**C**) Five crabs subjected to 36 h of 6:6 h cycles of 20‰:34‰ salinity, followed by 36 h at continuous 34‰. (After Taylor & Naylor, 1977.) Comparisons of raw data values for 'expected' high activity times (stippled) *versus* 'expected' low activity times in constant conditions after entrainment show highly significant differences ($P < 0.001\%$).

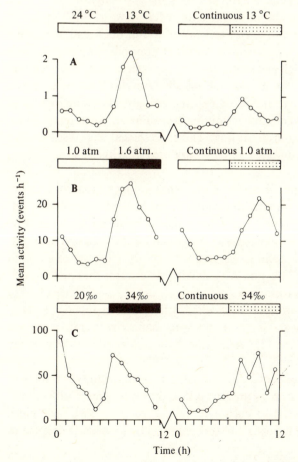

range for *Carcinus* result in transient changes in the phase and amplitude of subsequent activity peaks; temperature increases induce phase delays and amplitude reduction, in contrast to temperature decreases which induce phase advances and amplitude increase.

Another effect induced by low temperature is the re-establishment of tidal rhythmicity in arrhythmic animals. For example, exposure to 4 °C for at least 6 h restarts the rhythm in *Carcinus maenas*, with peak activity occurring at *ca* 12.4-h intervals from the end of chilling, irrespective of its duration (Naylor, 1963). Similar observations have been reported for shore fishes and the isopod, *Eurydice pulchra* (Jones & Naylor, 1970). This response has proved useful in physiological studies of tidal clock mechanisms (Williams *et al.*, in Naylor & Hartnoll, 1979).

(b) *Pressure*. Entrainment by pressure cycles equivalent to hydrostatic pressure changes on the shore has been demonstrated in both *Eurydice* and *Carcinus*. In *Carcinus* (Fig. 3.3 B), increases of less than 0.1 atm induce locomotor activity, and the imposition for a few days of 6:6 h cycles of 1.0:1.6 atm (equivalent to the rise and fall of a 6-m tide) readily entrains rhythmicity, which then free runs at constant atmospheric pressure, with peaks at the expected high pressure times. The persistence of this free-running rhythm depends upon the number of entraining cycles that the crab has experienced (up to a maximum of 6). Interestingly, the crabs are most responsive to pressure entrainment during late summer, when temperature differences between sea and air are least. This suggests that there is seasonality in the extent to which different variables are used as zeitgebers.

(c) *Salinity*. Until recently there was no evidence to suggest that the changes of salinity which occur on estuarine shores might be used as zeitgebers, but Taylor & Naylor (1977) have now shown this to be so for *Carcinus* (Fig. 3.3 C). An apparatus in which water circulated continuously at constant temperature and under continuous aeration was used to expose crabs to alternate 6-h phases of 34‰ and 20‰ salinity. Afterwards the crabs showed a free-running rhythm with peaks occurring at the expected times of 34‰ (= ambient seawater), irrespective of whether they were maintained at 34‰ or 20‰ after entrainment. Similar results were obtained with crabs entrained in 6:6 h cycles of 34‰ and 48‰ salinity, with the peaks again at the expected 34‰ times.

The striking difference between experiments involving salinity entrainment and those using temperature or pressure is that, during treatment with salinity cycles, activity is induced at each salinity change (Fig. 3.3 C, left half). Although the response to repeated exposure to 34‰ is evidently coupled to the endogenous clock, which it entrains, the 6-hourly peaks occurring at the salinity changes are not, because they do not free run in constant salinity. These 6-hourly peaks are probably best interpreted as exogenously induced responses which in nature permit the crabs to move to more favourable salinities. At low tide crabs may find themselves in pools where salinity decreases by freshwater inflow or increases by evaporation, and the salinity response improves their chances of avoiding such conditions. It is presumably the predictability of the sea's 34‰ salinity at high tide which leads to 34‰ acting as the effective zeitgeber. Other salinities occur more arbitrarily and are therefore less suitable time-signals for entraining the biological clock.

(d) *Mechanical disturbance.* Another tidal variable which has been shown to entrain endogenous rhythmicity is disturbance by wave action, simulated in the laboratory by artificial cycles of mechanical agitation. This is particularly apparent in species which spend one part of their lives buried in intertidal sand and another part foraging on the surface at low tide or swimming in the water at high tide. The first evidence for mechanical disturbance as an entraining agent for a locomotor rhythm was given by Enright (1975) for the sand-beach isopod, *Excirolana chiltoni* (see also the chapter by Klapow, in De Coursey, 1976). Intermittent swirling of water for a 6-h period every 12 h, particularly in the presence of sand, strongly entrained the rhythm. Similar results have been reported for a related sand-beach isopod (*Eurydice pulchra*), two East African crabs (*Uca urvillei* and *U. annulipes*), a sand-beach amphipod (*Talorchestia quoyana*) and the zooxanthellae-bearing turbellarian, *Convoluta roscoffensis*, which rises to the surface of sandy beaches at low tide (Neumann, in De Coursey, 1976).

(e) *Light.* The role of light in controlling the behaviour of coastal organisms is primarily related to the synchronisation of circadian components of behaviour which are often superimposed upon circatidal rhythms (see §3.3.1). This is most clearly illustrated in species which occur naturally in both tidal and non-tidal localities. In a non-tidal harbour adjacent to tidal coasts, *Carcinus maenas* shows a locomotor rhythm with two large nocturnal peaks every 24 h. This is entrained in the harbour to exactly 24 h by the day–night cycle, but it presumably reflects an underlying circatidal pattern, since, in the laboratory, cooling to 4 °C for 6 h (see §3.3.2a) induces a free-running circatidal rhythm. *Carcinus* from the relatively tideless Mediterranean, on the other hand, shows only single-peaked, circadian rhythmicity which does not revert to a circatidal rhythm after chilling. Similarly the brown shrimp, *Crangon crangon*, which exhibits weak endogenous circatidal locomotor rhythmicity on the tidal coasts of Britain, exhibits only circadian (i.e.

single-peaked) periodicity in the virtually tideless Baltic Sea (Al-Adhub & Naylor, 1975).

High shore organisms such as the strandline amphipod, *Talitrus saltator*, and subtidal forms such as the Norway lobster, *Nephrops norvegicus*, also show only circadian rhythms primarily entrained by light. Perhaps not surprisingly, therefore, the light–dark changes induced by tidal rise and fall also entrain circa*tidal* rhythms in some species. Darkening at high tide, due to dense suspended material, certainly appears to phase the circatidal swimming rhythm of the intertidal prawn, *Palaemon elegans*, in turbid estuaries. This species often inhabits high pools which are reached by the sea on only a few days every two weeks, at the times of spring tides (see Fig. 3.1). Tested at such times in constant conditions in the laboratory, *Palaemon* shows an endogenous circatidal swimming rhythm, with peaks at the times of high tide on the shore from which they were collected. Darkening of the pools by the turbid water of spring tides appears to be an important zeitgeber, since when prawns are collected at neap tides the circatidal rhythm is no longer expressed with peaks at the times of high tide. Instead, the rhythm is then entrained to the times of dusk and dawn.

There is also a light-modulated, tidal rhythm of vertical migration in sand in *Amphidinium herdmaniae*, a beach-dwelling dinoflagellate (Eaton & Simpson, in Naylor & Hartnoll, 1979). This rhythm is behaviourally similar to that reported in the diatom, *Hantzschia virgata*, and in other diatoms and euglenoids, but differs from them in that their rhythms are basically circadian (see Palmer, 1974).

3.3.3   Phase–response curves

Phase–response curves have been demonstrated for many circadian rhythms, the phase of a rhythm being advanced or delayed in response to the timing of, say, a light pulse (§2.3.2). In contrast, there has been little similar work done on the phase responses of circatidal rhythms. Virtually the only example is Enright's study of the tidal swimming rhythm of *Excirolana chiltoni*, which is re-set by 2-h exposures to simulated wave action (Enright, in De Coursey, 1976). Exposure before an expected activity peak produces phase advances, whilst exposure during or shortly after a peak produces phase delays (Fig. 3.4). The bimodality of this phase–response curve (cf. Fig. 2.6) would be readily understandable if the basic period of the endogenous rhythmic system were circatidal (i.e. *ca* 12.4 h). However, despite the economy of that hypothesis, Enright suggests that the underlying oscillation is more likely to be circadian, with the circatidal peaks appearing as expressions of alternate primary and secondary peaks of a circadian rhythm. If so, that raises the question of why phase–response curves of all other circadian rhythms tested are apparently unimodal over a 24-h time-base.

The *Excirolana* curve reveals that the underlying oscillator (§1.2) must be fairly stable, since the maximum advance or delay which could be produced was of the order of 2 h per day. This means that under field conditions the isopods' rhythm would be relatively immune to irregularly timed environmental stimuli which might arise during severe storms. Indeed, the multiplicity of potential time-cues in coastal environments, and the great variability in factors such as temperature, wave action and light, plus the seasonal changes in the animals' use of them as zeitgebers (§3.3.2), suggest that phase shifting by short experimental pulses of these variables will in general be unlikely.

3.3.4   Conclusions

It is clear that many intertidal organisms exhibit circatidal rhythms of behaviour and physiology which may or may not be modulated by superimposed circadian rhythms. These circatidal rhythms are entrained by one or more of the tide-related environmental variables operating on a shore, combinations of which can act synergistically, with some becoming more important than others at different times of the year.

The degree of expression of endogeneity of tidal rhythmicity tends to vary with season, tidal amplitude and pattern, tidal phase in the home locality, and with the adaptive advantage of endogenous rhythmic behaviour for the species concerned. Weakly expressed rhythms may possibly be the outcome of random processes (Lehmann, in De Coursey, 1976), but more strongly

Fig. 3.4. Phase–response curve of the circatidal swimming rhythm of the sand-beach isopod, *Excirolana chiltoni* (cf. Fig. 2.6). Points indicate the phase delay or advance in the swimming rhythm induced by 2-h periods of exposure to simulated waves at various times relative to the times of the primary tidal (time zero) and secondary tidal (time 12.4 h) activity peaks. Closed circles, results based on groups of animals; asterisk, mean of several experiments with single animals; open circles repeat some of the closed circle plots. (After Enright, in De Coursey, 1976.)

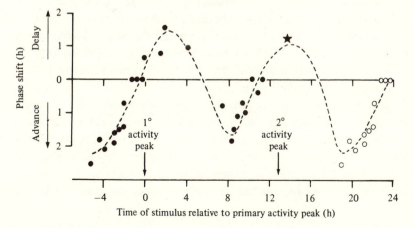

expressed circatidal rhythms are clearly under the control of endogenous, physiological oscillators. The alternating primary and secondary peaks in the tidal rhythm of *Excirolana* have prompted Enright (in De Coursey, 1976) to postulate that the basic oscillator in that 'tidal' rhythm is essentially circadian in period. Other authors too have discussed the possible derivation of tidal rhythms from crepuscular circadian cycles, with peaks at dusk and dawn. Nevertheless the bimodality of the phase–response curve of *Excirolana* seems more readily understandable on the basis that its driving oscillator is circatidal.

3.4   Lunar and semilunar rhythms
3.4.1   *Rhythms in reproduction*
The first well-analysed example of lunar rhythmicity was probably that of the polychaete, *Platynereis dumerilii*, by Hauenschild (1960). At sexual maturity in this species, males and females transform into 'heteronereis' forms which swarm at the sea surface to spawn and eventually die. In natural light–dark cycles in the laboratory, cultures spawned as in the sea, with maxima at new moon. In continuous bright light, spawning occurred uniformly throughout the month, but endogenous free-running circalunar rhythmicity could be re-initiated by subjecting the worms to six cycles of 12 h dim light (equivalent to moonlight):12 h bright light every two weeks. Evidently moonlight can serve as the monthly zeitgeber, a possibility also suggested for the fortnightly release of gametes in the brown alga, *Dictyota dichotoma* (Müller, in Palmer, 1974), and the lunar spawning rhythm of the sea urchin, *Centrostephanus coronatus* (Kennedy & Pearse, 1975).

Among early anecdotal accounts of lunar and semilunar rhythms, the well-known springtime semilunar spawning of the grunion fish, *Leuresthes tenuis*, high on California beaches, is still in need of experimental study to determine whether or not the rhythm is endogenous. Similarly awaiting experimental analysis is the spectacular synchronous spawning of the Pacific palolo worm, *Eunice viridis*, on the day of the last quarter of the moon in late October. Some aspects of this rhythm and the similar spawning pattern of the Atlantic palolo, *E. fucata*, have been studied (Naylor, 1976) but there is as yet no demonstration that they free run in constant conditions.

Moon-related rhythmicity might also, of course, be expected to occur in freshwater and terrestrial organisms, and a few examples are recorded. For instance, the mayfly, *Povilla adusta*, widely distributed in Central and Southern Africa, shows a lunar rhythm of emergence in Uganda (Hartland-Rowe, 1955). The adult swarms appear only around the times of full moon, with the greatest number of swarms on the second night after the full moon. Such observations require further study, as does the case of a terrestrial example concerning the breeding behaviour of the Sooty or Wideawake Tern, *Sterna fuscata*, reported by Chapin & Wing (1959). Nesting records of this tern on Ascension Island (latitude 7° 57'S, longitude 14° 22'W) show a remarkable correlation between the birds' breeding and the lunar cycle (Fig. 3.5). The birds return to the island around the time of each tenth full moon, and lay their eggs about six weeks later. It is difficult to avoid the conclusion that, where it breeds so near to the equator, this species may use the full moon as its 'circannual' reproductive cue, rather than the annual change of day-length, which it uses in more temperate localities (see §5.2).

3.4.2   Rhythms of locomotor activity

The best-studied endogenous semilunar or lunar modulations of locomotor activity are in intertidal crustaceans. The sand-beach isopods, *Excirolana* (Enright, and Klapow, in De Coursey, 1976) and *Eurydice*, and the amphipod, *Talitrus*, show spontaneous lunar or semilunar rhythms of activity often correlated with the spring/neap changes in the distribution of populations on the beach from which they came (Fig. 3.6). One possible function of such activity patterns is that they maintain the zonation of an intertidal organism by preventing individuals from becoming stranded above the level of high water during neap tides.

Fig. 3.5. Breeding pattern of Sooty Terns on Ascension Island during the years 1941–1958. Bars indicate periods when birds were present on the island; diamonds denote the dates on which eggs were first reported during each breeding period; open circles indicate the date of every tenth full moon. (After Chapin & Wing, 1959.)

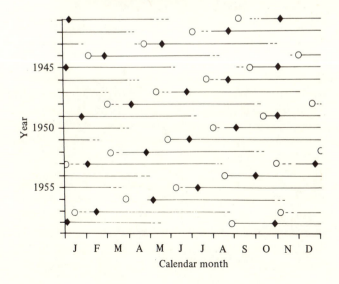

Fig. 3.6. Endogenous circasemilunar rhythms of locomotor activity in two
sand-beach crustaceans over 1.5 lunar cycles in the laboratory. (**A**) Total
daily activity of eight *Talitrus saltator* exhibiting a free-running circadian
rhythm in constant darkness from the time of collection on day zero. (After
Williams, in Naylor & Hartnoll, 1979.) (**B**) Daily maximum numbers of
Eurydice pulchra emerging from sand and swimming at 'expected' high tide
on the home beach, using 40 freshly collected isopods every 48 h throughout
the experiment, and maintaining them in LD 12:12 in the laboratory. (After
Alheit & Naylor, 1976.) Tidal heights illustrate spring/neap cycles of high
tides on the beaches from which the animals were collected at the times when
the experiments were carried out. Lunar cycle: open circles, full moon; closed
circles, new moon.

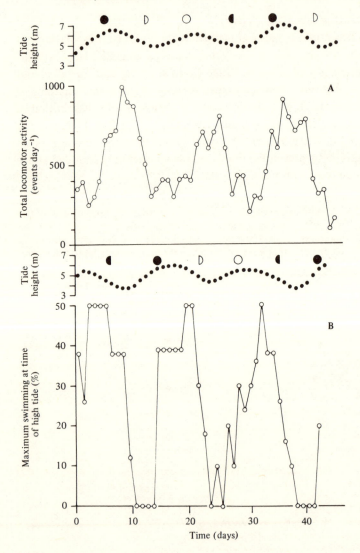

At least in *Excirolana* and *Talitrus*, moulting and hatching are also correlated with the semilunar activity rhythm. This is presumably because the risk of desiccation is reduced by ensuring that freshly-emerged animals appear only during spring tides, when most of the beach is traversed by the sea. Endogenous tidal and semilunar swimming rhythms have also been shown in two species of estuarine amphipods, *Gammarus zaddachi* and *G. chevreuxi* (Dieleman, in Naylor & Hartnoll, 1979). Peak swimming occurs at the times of spring tides, and endogenous control ensures that activity is minimal at neaps when downstream transport by river flow would be hazardous. Swimming occurs mainly during flooding spring tides, which ensures position maintenance of the populations in their preferred habitats.

It has been suggested that semilunar and lunar rhythms arise as 'beat' phenomena generated by the interaction of underlying endogenous circadian and circatidal oscillations. However, this idea is not supported by observations such as those of Williams (in Naylor & Hartnoll, 1979), who demonstrated a free-running circasemilunar activity rhythm in *Talitrus* without any sign of a tidal component modulating the underlying circadian rhythm. It is likely that in this and several other organisms, semilunar periodicity is driven by a true endogenous oscillator of approximately 14.8-day periodicity. Certainly this would seem to be the case in terrestrial species, for example in homing pigeons, which show an apparent lunar rhythm in the day-to-day variations in their initial bearings during orientation behaviour (Larkin & Keeton, 1978).

3.4.3 *Entrainment*

Extensive studies of entrainment by moonlight have been carried out by Neumann (1978, and in De Coursey, 1976) on the intertidal midge, *Clunio marinus*. The larvae and pupae of this insect are restricted to the lowest levels of the intertidal zone and are therefore exposed to air only at spring tides (see Fig. 3.1). Since both copulation between the winged males and wingless females, and all subsequent egg-laying, must take place in air, the emergence of adult flies from the pupae takes place only at low spring tides, and hence at semilunar intervals. Cultures of the midge kept in LD 12:12 exhibit only 24-h rhythmicity in their emergence, but cultures exposed to simulated moonlight (0.3 lux) during a run of four nights every month, show a circasemilunar emergence rhythm. Even one sequence of three 'moonlit' nights is sufficient to re-establish the rhythm, thus confirming that it is truly endogenous.

In the European populations of *Clunio*, entrainment to moonlight occurs only in the southern races. From about Normandy northwards, moonlight is apparently an unreliable zeitgeber, owing to irregularities of cloud cover, and there the daily light–dark cycles plus a tidal factor combine to entrain the rhythm (Fig. 3.7). The tidal factor is not hydrostatic pressure, nor change in light intensity (see §3.3.2), but some aspect of water agitation (Neumann, 1978). Different populations of *Clunio* also show genetic adaptation of their endogenous clock to local tide patterns. Races from Helgoland and Normandy both show maximum emergence during low water of spring tides, but there is a 2-h difference in the timing of low tide in these two localities which suggests that the phase relationships of entrainment should be different in the two populations. This proves to be so, since, when entrained in the laboratory to the same combined cycle of light–dark plus wave simulation, the semilunar rhythms of the two races show a phase difference of three days. This difference corresponds well with the time difference of afternoon spring low tides in the two localities (Neumann, 1978).

Thus, in relatively non-tidal localities and where moonlight is a reliable

Fig. 3.7. Numbers of Helgoland *Clunio* midges emerging daily in cultures exposed to artificial tidal cycles of 12.5 h in LD 12:12 over 42 days. **(A)** Influence of tidal cycles with alternating hydrostatic pressure, light intensity and water turbulence; **(B)** same tidal programme but without alternating water disturbance; **(C)** imposed pattern of light and dark (boxed), and onset of time of artificial tide (broken lines). (After Neumann, 1978.) Note that the cultures had been exposed to the experimental entraining programme for 30 days before these recordings began.

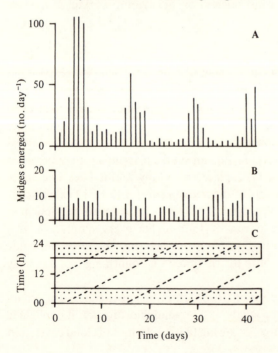

synchroniser, organisms can couple their semilunar or lunar periodicity to that variable. In strongly tidal localities, however, and where moonlight is an unreliable synchroniser, the interaction of wave turbulence and light as a semilunar synchroniser is not surprising, particularly in view of the importance of these as zeitgebers in tidal rhythms (see §3.3.2). The coupling of semilunar rhythms to factors associated directly with the spring/neap tide cycle is a possibility which has not been fully investigated.

Another potential semilunar zeitgeber is the 14.8-day cycle of surface temperature which occurs in some intertidal sediments. This is caused by the same fortnightly interaction of the tide cycle and the daily cycle of the sun's heating of the beach, which is least when high tides occur around midday. During the summer in Holland, this can cause semilunar differences in mud temperatures of up to 5 °C (de Wilde & Berghuis, in Naylor & Hartnoll, 1979). It has been suggested that such temperature cycles may entrain the semilunar rhythm of high shore amphipods (see the chapter by Williams, in Naylor & Hartnoll, 1979). However, such phenomena are likely to vary regionally, presumably having greatest influence in localities where low spring tides occur around midday and where the beach is very flat.

3.4.4 *Conclusions*

Further investigation of the mechanisms of entrainment of tidal, lunar and semilunar rhythms would clearly be worthwhile. Present models of tidal rhythmic systems and their entrainment are still inadequate (Enright, in De Coursey, 1976), and this is even truer for lunar and semilunar rhythms. Our understanding of the mechanisms and temporal patterning of organisms' perception of the environmental variables they use as zeitgebers, and the nature of the transducers coupling these to the endogenous oscillators is also incomplete. The amount of information on the phenomenology of tidal, semilunar and lunar rhythms is now considerable, however, and the framework that this provides poses a number of challenging behavioural and physiological questions; the answers to these require the development of further critical formulation of hypotheses and rigorous experimental analyses.

3.5 Further reading and key references

Books and review articles are indicated by asterisks

Al-Adhub, A. H. Y. & Naylor, E. (1975). Emergence rhythms and tidal migrations in the brown shrimp *Crangon crangon* (L.). *Journal of the Marine Biological Association, U.K.*, **55**, 801–10.

Alheit, J. & Naylor, E. (1976). Behaviour basis of intertidal zonation in *Eurydice pulchra. Journal of Experimental Marine Biology and Ecology*, **23**, 135–44.

Chapin, J. P. & Wing, L. W. (1959). The wideawake calendar 1941–1958. *Auk*, **76**, 153–8.

*De Coursey, P. J. (Ed.) (1976). *Biological Rhythms in the Marine Environment*, 283 pp. Columbia: University of South Carolina Press.

*Enright, J. T. (1975). Orientation in time: endogenous clocks. In *Marine Ecology*, **II**, ed. O. Kinne, pp. 917–45. London: Wiley.

Hartland-Rowe, R. (1955). Lunar rhythm in the emergence of an ephemeropteran. *Nature*, **176**, 657.

Hauenschild, C. (1960). Lunar periodicity. In *Biological Clocks. Cold Spring Harbor Symposia on Quantitative Biology*, **25**, 491–7.

Jones, D. A. & Naylor, E. (1970). The swimming rhythm of the sand beach isopod *Eurydice pulchra*. *Journal of Experimental Marine Biology and Ecology*, **4**, 188–99.

Kennedy, B. & Pearse, J. S. (1975). Lunar synchronisation of the monthly reproductive rhythm in the sea urchin *Centrostephanus coronatus* Verrill. *Journal of Experimental Marine Biology and Ecology*, **17**, 323–31.

Larkin, T. & Keeton, W. T. (1978). An apparent lunar rhythm in the day-to-day variations in initial bearings of homing pigeons. In *Animal Migration, Navigation and Homing*, ed. K. Schmidt-Koenig & T. W. Keeton, pp. 92–106. Berlin, Heidelberg and New York: Springer-Verlag.

Naylor, E. (1963). Temperature relationships of the locomotor rhythm of *Carcinus*. *Journal of Experimental Biology*, **40**, 669–79.

*Naylor, E. (1976). Rhythmic behaviour and reproduction in marine animals. In *Adaptation to Environment: Essays on the Physiology of Marine Animals*, ed. R. C. Newell, pp. 393–429. London: Butterworths.

Naylor, E. & Atkinson, R. J. A. (1972). Pressure and the rhythmic behaviour of inshore marine animals. *Symposia of the Society for Experimental Biology*, **26**, 395–415.

*Naylor, E. & Hartnoll, R. G. (Ed.) (1979). *Cyclic Phenomena in Marine Plants and Animals*, 477 pp. Oxford: Pergamon Press.

Neumann, D. (1978). Entrainment of a semi-lunar rhythm by simulated tidal cycles of mechanical disturbance. *Journal of Experimental Marine biology and Ecology*, **35**, 73–85.

*Palmer, J. D. (1974). *Biological Clocks in Marine Organisms*, 173 pp. New York: John Wiley & Sons.

Taylor, A. C. & Naylor, E. (1977). Entrainment of the locomotor rhythm of *Carcinus* by cycles of salinity change. *Journal of the Marine Biological Association, U.K.*, **57**, 273–7.

Williams, B. G. & Naylor, E. (1969). Synchronization of the locomotor tidal rhythm of *Carcinus*. *Journal of Experimental Biology*, **51**, 715–25.

KLAUS HOFFMANN

4   Time-compensated celestial orientation

4.1   Introduction

One of the most spectacular aspects of biological clocks is their participation in celestial orientation. Such orientation was first discovered about 70 years ago. At the turn of the century many investigators had marvelled at the 'unfailing' sense of direction in ants. Several hypotheses were formulated to account for this performance, including the idea that the animals possess a very exact kinaesthetic memory, recording and evaluating all their twists and turns on the outward journey, and making the correct calculations from these data to find home on the way back. Another suggestion was that the ants possessed some mystical sense of direction which defied physiological explanation.

4.2   Light-compass orientation

In 1911, however, by some simple but ingenious experiments, Santschi demonstrated that ants use the sun to find and maintain their direction. When he shielded ants which were on their way back to the nest from the direct light of the sun, and reflected the rays of the sun using a mirror, the animals altered their course, predictably (Fig. 4.1); and when they were again exposed directly to the sun they resumed their original direction. Several such experiments conclusively showed that the sun was the orienting stimulus. In the following years a similar mode of orientation was found in a wide variety of animals: in other insects, as well as in spiders, polychaetes and gastropods. The animals were shown to be able to maintain their direction with the help of the sun, the moon, or an artificial light source. Since a light source provided the reference direction, like the needle of a compass, this behaviour is called 'light-compass', or more commonly, 'sun-compass' orientation.

Such an orientation will suffice if the animals have to maintain the direction for only a brief time. For instance, if an ant wants to find its way back to the nest it could do so by remembering the angle to the sun on the way out and then adopting the opposite angle on return. However, since the sun moves in the sky by an average of some 15° h⁻¹, if the whole journey takes several hours, reliance on the angle to the sun would be highly misleading. The difficulty could be overcome if the animals made allowance for the passage of time and compensated their angle accordingly. Though Santschi mentioned this as a possibility, it was considered too implausible at the time, and later findings in ants and bees seemed to contradict it. However, Beling showed, in 1929, that bees have a good 'time sense' in the form of the ability to come to a feeding place at any time of day that has been fixed by former training.

It was in 1950, nearly 40 years after Santschi's original discovery, that time-compensated sun-compass orientation was demonstrated simultaneously and independently by Kramer in birds and by von Frisch in bees. These discoveries greatly stimulated further research on biological clocks, as evidenced, for example, by the Cold Spring Harbor Symposium on the topic in 1960 (Chovnick, 1960). The clock component of sun-compass orientation has, in the event, been best analysed in birds; we shall therefore look at them in most detail. Schmidt-Koenig has reviewed the whole subject of animal navigation in two recent, succinct books (1975, 1979).

4.3   Sun-compass in birds

Even when in captivity and confined to cages, birds may show *zugunruhe* ('migratory restlessness', see the Glossary), during the appropriate seasons. Kramer observed that caged starlings kept in an outside aviary exhibited zugunruhe that was not random but was oriented roughly in the

Fig. 4.1. Track of two ants (**A, B**) returning to the nest. The broken parts of the line indicate times when the direct light from the sun was shaded and the sun's image projected by a mirror (m). (After Santschi, 1911.)

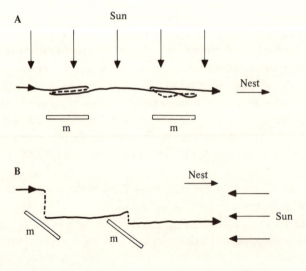

Fig. 4.2. Choices of starlings (trained to feed in particular directions) when their view of the sky was restricted to four windows. (**A**) Sun directly visible; (**B**) and (**C**) light from the sun deflected by mirrors. The open semicircles symbolise the 12 feeding bowls; each black dot represents one attempt to find food. The solid centripetal arrows give the training direction, the centrifugal arrows the mean direction of choices. The broken arrows show incidence of light from the sky.

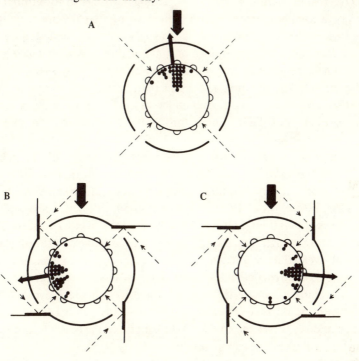

Fig. 4.3. Mean direction of choices of a starling trained to feed in the east in the morning (**A**) and tested at other times of day (**B**) and (**C**). Note that the bird's change of angle with the sun(s) corresponds to the time of day. (From Hoffmann, 1971, after Kramer, 1952.)

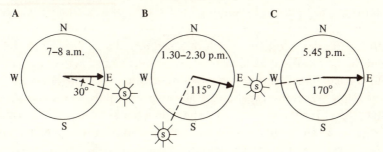

birds' normal migratory direction. By restricting the birds to small circular cages, in which the sight of landmarks was excluded, he was able to show that the sun was the guiding cue. Since the birds maintained the same direction for several hours, and did so at different times of day, he concluded that they must be able to compensate for the movement of the sun.

These results were confirmed by training starlings to look for food in a particular compass direction, and then showing that the direction in which they looked changed predictably if the sun's rays were deflected by mirrors (Fig. 4.2). If the birds were trained only at one time of day, and tested at other times, when the sun was in quite different positions, they searched for food in the correct compass direction rather than keeping a constant angle to the sun (Fig. 4.3). They also oriented under an artificial sun, shifting their angle relative to a fixed light source throughout the day by the appropriate *ca* 15° h^{-1} change of angle (Kramer, 1952).

Starlings can thus evidently find compass directions with the help of the sun, and can also compensate for its daily motion. To do this, however, they need information about the time of day. The artificial sun experiments showed that this information did not depend upon celestial cues, and it was hypothesised that it might be provided by an internal clock instead. Since the change between night and day is both the most reliable and the most obvious external cycle that might synchronise such a clock to local time (§2.3), experiments were carried out to re-set starlings' clocks, and thereby shift their food-searching direction, by exposing them to light–dark cycles 6 h out of phase with the normal day (Hoffmann, 1954, 1975). Fig. 4.4 illustrates the change in direction expected for a bird trained to the south if its clock is 6 h late; Fig. 4.5 gives the actual results.

After 12 to 18 days in the shifted light cycle, the direction in which the starlings searched for food was changed correspondingly (Fig. 4.5 **B**), and when the birds were then returned to natural conditions, the original training direction was again preferred in due course (Fig. 4.5 **C**). This demonstrated that the clock mechanism underlying the sun-based direction finding of starlings can be re-set by shifting the light cycle, a finding since confirmed in several other bird species. Homing pigeons, for example, show similar predictable deviations as a result of experimentally-induced clock shifts, not only in their learnt directional food responses, but also in their initial homing flight orientation when released some distance from their loft (Schmidt-Koenig, 1975, p. 57). Such experiments have proved powerful tools in testing hypotheses for the mechanisms which underlie bi-coordinate navigation of the kind shown in homing – that is 'true' navigation in which the animal takes the correct direction home regardless of where it is starting from, as opposed to simple compass orientation in which the animal merely takes a fixed direction regardless of where that leads to (see §4.6).

All these findings clearly established that sun-compass orientation of birds involves compensation for the sun's motion based on some kind of internal clock regulated by the change of night and day. No information as to the nature of the mechanism was revealed, however. One possibility was an interval-timer, or hour-glass which, once set in motion by each dawn or dusk, ran on for about 24 h. The main alternative possibility was an endogenous circadian oscillation which was entrained to local time by the daily light cycle (§2.2). To find out which hypothesis was correct, further experiments were performed with the artificial day abruptly advanced by 6 h, and the direction then tested daily. As Fig. 4.6 shows, the birds changed their direction gradually rather than abruptly, taking several days to reach the final direction. This ruled out the hour-glass mechanism and suggested instead that an internal circadian clock was gradually drawn into phase by the external cycle.

Final proof for this hypothesis was provided by training starlings to look

Fig. 4.4. Expected change of direction of a bird trained to feed to the south if its clock has been shifted 6 h late by exposure to an artificial light–dark cycle 6 h behind the natural day (as indicated in **C**). (**A**) and (**B**) Expected angle to the sun before the light cycle change; (**D**) after the change. LT, local time; AT, artificial time; s, sun; solid arrow, original training direction; open arrow, expected direction after clock shift. The black or hatched areas in **C** indicate darkness. (From Hoffmann, 1954.)

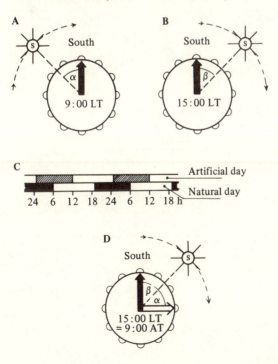

for food in specific compass directions, and maintaining them first in a light–dark regime corresponding to the natural day, and then in constant dim illumination, while recording their perch-hopping activity at the same time (Hoffmann, in Chovnick, 1960). There was a well-marked daily rhythm of the locomotor activity in the light cycle (Fig. 4.7, left), and this free ran in the con-

Fig. 4.5. Change of direction in two starlings (G and R) after exposure to artificial days 6 h behind local time (cf. Fig. 4.4). (A) Direction during training in natural day; (B) after 12–18 days in shifted day; (C) 8–17 days after return into natural day. Note change of direction in B and return to original direction in C. Each dot represents one critical choice (without reward) (from Hoffmann, 1971). For further explanation see Figs. 4.2 and 4.4.

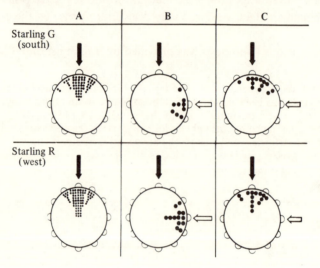

Fig. 4.6. Change of direction in starlings after a shift of light cycle 6 h forward. Centrifugal arrows indicate mean directions before (A), during re-entrainment (B–D) and after (E) the birds' clocks were shifted. Solid centripetal arrows indicate training direction; open centripetal arrow, direction predicted for the 6-h clock shift. Experiments with three birds combined. (From Hoffmann, 1971.)

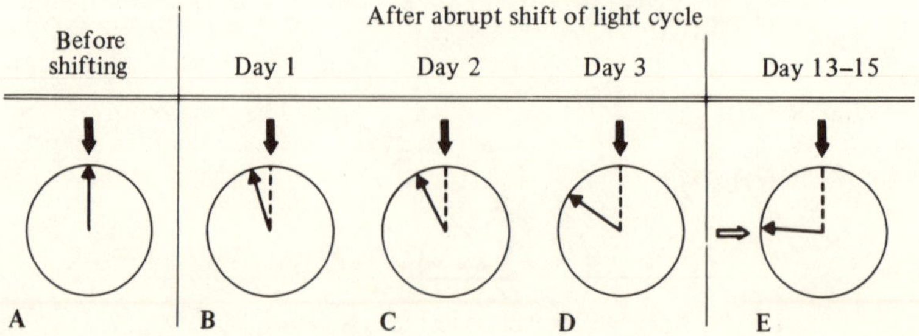

stant light, with the onset of activity advancing each day (that is, the birds' rhythm ran faster than the earth's rotation). On the ninth and tenth day of this free-running situation, the directional choice was tested under the natural sun (Fig. 4.7 **B**). It deviated from the original training direction by an amount corresponding to the state of the circadian clock as indicated by the rhythm of perch-hopping activity. When an artificial light–dark cycle in phase with the local day was re-established, and the birds were tested 17 days later, they again chose the original training direction, so their clock had evidently been re-entrained (Fig. 4.7 **C**).

This experiment thus definitely established that the timekeeping mechanism underlying the compensation for the sun's motion throughout the day is an endogenous circadian clock which is normally entrained by the environmental day–night cycle, but which can free run in constant conditions at its own circadian frequency. In fact this kind of clock can be consulted at any time of day or night, as was revealed by experiments with starlings in the arctic (Hoffmann, 1959).

Fig. 4.7. Rhythm of locomotor activity (left) and direction chosen (right) of two starlings, N and W, kept in constant light and temperature. Note that in LL the rhythm of activity advanced about 0.5 h per day and that when tested at **B** the direction chosen changed correspondingly. Left: the hatched areas indicate darkness; onsets of activity are given by the circles (open for starling N, solid for starling W); black squares mark the test times corresponding to **B** and **C** at the right. Right: (**A**) orientation during training; (**B**) after 10 and 11 days in constant conditions; (**C**) in a light–dark cycle corresponding to natural day; LL, constant light; LD, light–dark cycle; centrifugal arrows give mean direction of critical choices (without reward). (From Hoffmann, in Chovnick, 1960.)

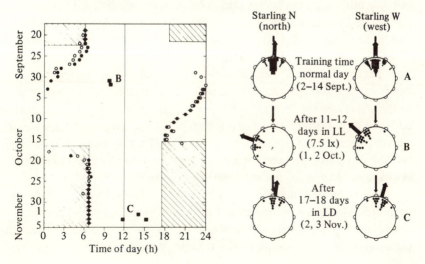

4.4   Time-compensated sun orientation in other animals

While Kramer was discovering time-compensated sun orientation in birds, von Frisch was working on the same problem in honey bees. In his first experiments he trained bees to come to a feeding station west of the hive in the evening, and during the night moved the hive to a new site. When he tested the bees the next morning, the majority still visited the station west of the hive, though they now had to fly away from the sun rather than towards it as they had during training. This, and further experiments on foragers's dances in the hive, firmly established that bees can compensate for the sun's motion (Von Frisch, 1967).

An interesting feature of these bee dances is that in the total darkness of the hive, the dancer transposes the horizontal sun angle of her flight to the food source that she is indicating, to an equivalent angle to gravity on the vertical surface of the comb. Particularly striking is the performance of so-called 'marathon' dancers, who sometimes dance off and on for many hours without leaving the hive. While they do this they continuously compensate for the sun's movement, even at night, when their dancing has to allow for movement of the sun on the other side of the earth. The compensation is not perfect, but in general it is accurate to well within $\pm 5°$ (von Frisch, 1967, p. 350). The bees apparently correct their dance angle whenever the interval between successive dances is ten minutes or more, which implies an amazing precision in their ability to 'read' the time from their circadian clock.

After Kramer and von Frisch had published their results, time-compensated sun orientation was found in an ever-increasing number of animals, not only in other birds and insects, but also in crustaceans, spiders, fish, amphibians, reptiles and mammals (see Jander, 1963; Hoffmann, 1965, 1971, 1975; von Frisch, 1967; Wallraff, 1981). The basic features seem to be the same in nearly all cases. An internal clock, based upon a continuous circadian oscillation and synchronised with local time by the change of day and night, allows compensation for the sun's movement. Whenever the light–dark cycle is shifted, the direction chosen is correspondingly shifted, and in most instances correct orientation continues as predicted when the circadian oscillation free runs in constant conditions. Furthermore, in bees and some other arthropods, the sun need not be seen directly; its position can be derived from the polarisation pattern of the sky (von Frisch, 1967).

The work carried out on the sandhopper, *Talitrus saltator*, illustrates well both the biological significance of this type of orientation and the methods developed to analyse its mechanism. *Talitrus* lives on beaches near the high-water line. It is mainly active at night, spending the day buried in the sand (see also Fig. 3.6). If the animals are exposed to dry air, they flee in a direction perpendicular to and down their home shoreline, thus avoiding desiccation. By using mirrors, Pardi & Papi demonstrated that sandhoppers use the sun as the guiding stimulus (Pardi, in Chovnick, 1960). As in birds, the direction taken could be predictably changed by shifting the light cycle. Moreover, when Papi (1955) collected sandhoppers from the west coast of Italy, sent them (in constant darkness) to Argentina, and there tested their orientational course, the sandhoppers showed the same angle to the sun that the control group showed in Italy at the same universal time. Their clock was apparently still running on Italian time.

Accurate orientation with the help of the sun involves not only a clock, but also a knowledge of the rate of change of the sun's azimuth (see the Glossary) during the course of the day. This differs widely at different latitudes, and also varies with the seasons. For example, at the poles it is uniformly *ca* 15° h^{-1} during the summer, whereas at the equator during the equinoxes, when the sun passes overhead, it is effectively 0° h^{-1} except at noon when it changes rapidly through the whole 180°. In addition, the azimuth moves clockwise in northern latitudes and counter-clockwise in southern latitudes.

The question of which factors or mechanisms provide animals with their local knowledge of these daily changes in azimuth angle has not yet been thoroughly investigated, but there is evidence in some birds, fish and crustaceans that at least a rough compensation of the sun's motion exists in animals that have never before seen the sun move (Hoffmann; Pardi; Braemer; in Chovnick, 1960). On the other hand, honey bees and ants (Jander, 1963) have to learn the sun's motion before they can use a time-compensated sun-compass accurately. There are also species differences both in the influence of the sun's altitude, and in the way the sun's invisible motion at night is compensated for (see Wallfaff, 1981).

4.5 Compass orientation by other celestial cues

Orientation with the help of the moon or the stars has been described in some animals. The only aspect of this that is directly relevant to biological timekeeping is whether time compensation for the movement of the celestial bodies occurs, and if it does, on what mechanism it is based.

Sandhoppers, it has been found, not only use sun-compass orientation during the daytime, but also use lunar direction-finding at night (Papi & Pardi, 1963; Enright, 1972). As with the help of the sun during daylight, at night, with the help of the moon, the animals maintain a direction more or less perpendicular to the local coastline. They do so, moreover, not only when they are tested immediately after capture, but also if they are collected several days before the experiment and are kept in constant darkness until tested. Though there is some deterioration with time, it is clear that they are still able to compensate for the moon's motion.

On the basis of these experiments, Papi suggested that in addition to the circadian clock which accounts for the compensation of solar movement, the animals might possess a second clock whose period is equal to the lunar day, that is, *ca* 24 h 50 min. Which clock mechanism underlies lunar orientation in amphipods has been much discussed (see also §3.3.4), and the problem has still not been rigorously resolved, but one thing is clear from Papi's and Enright's work: the assumption of an hour-glass mechanism set in motion by dusk or by moonrise can be ruled out (see Hoffmann, 1965; Enright, 1972; Wallraff, 1981).

In several bird species that migrate at night, the use of stellar cues for direction finding is well documented. Kramer made the first contributions to this field, using the method he employed to demonstrate sun-compass orientation, that is, observation of the direction of zugunruhe in caged birds (§4.3). Under the artificial sky of a planetarium, Sauer (1957) was able to show conclusively that several warbler species use configurations of fixed stars for determining their direction. Since then orientation by stars has been found in many other birds, nearly always by Kramer's method, though often with refinements such as recording rather than directly observing the birds' preferred direction (Hoffmann, 1965; Keeton, 1974; Emlen, 1975).

The question that has to be asked is whether finding compass directions by stars involves any form of time compensation. In principle, no clock need be involved, since without any information on time of day or season it should be possible to orient, given some knowledge of star configurations. Further, without even this knowledge it should be possible to determine the centre of the apparent rotation of the sky (i.e. around the pole star) and thus the celestial pole. By contrast, due to the different azimuth velocities of the different stars, time-compensated orientation would be much more complicated than with the sun or the moon. Some early experiments of Sauer & Sauer (in Chovnick, 1960) suggested that compensation for elapsed time might be involved in stellar orientation, but later work in other laboratories has failed to confirm this, and the evidence for the participation of a clock mechanism in stellar orientation is weak.

4.6   Bi-coordinate navigation by celestial cues?

In many experiments with birds, and in particular with pigeons, homing in a directed manner over hundreds of kilometres of unknown territory has been clearly established. Once direction finding by the sun and the stars had been described, it was natural to speculate that birds might use such celestial cues just as man does, for true bi-coordinate navigation – that is, for knowing the direction home by knowing in effect the latitude and longitude of where they are at any given moment. This would involve not only a high degree of precision in measuring the altitude of celestial bodies, but also a very stable and precise clock maintaining the local time of the home area. This cannot be the clock normally involved in sun-compass orientation, since that has to meet much less stringent criteria, and its ready shiftability would anyway render it quite unsuitable.

Though some early experiments supported the idea that birds might use the sun and stars for bi-coordinate navigation (Matthews, 1968; Sauer & Sauer, in Chovnick, 1960), later findings have not supported that hypothesis. The overwhelming consensus is that, though sun and stars can be used as a compass, they are not involved in true bi-coordinate navigation (Hoffmann, 1965, 1975; Keeton, 1974; Emlen, 1975; Wallraff, 1981). In particular, clock-shift experiments with displaced homing pigeons indicate that celestial bodies provide information on direction only. In nearly all cases when such birds are released away from home, their initial direction deviates from that of control birds as predicted by the assumption of simple compass orientation.

In 1953 Kramer formulated a concept that complete homing orientation consists of two independent steps, one establishing the geographical position of the release site relative to home, the other making use of a compass to steer in the required direction (the 'map and compass' concept). In general, the results of clock-shift experiments are consistent with this concept, but it is now clear that in addition to sun- and star-compasses, a compass based on the detection of the earth's magnetic field exists in birds, and this compass of course needs no time compensation (Wiltschko & Wiltschko, 1972; Keeton, 1974).

On the other hand, the physiological basis for the first step in Kramer's concept, that of establishing the geographical position of the release site (the 'map') remains an enigma. It is also not clear why birds whose clock has been shifted, and which, when tested, should therefore get conflicting information from their sun-compass and from the magnetic field, nearly always choose the former cue for orientation unless the sight of the sun is obscured by heavy overcast.

4.7 The annual clock and orientation
We have already examined in depth the question of whether internal timekeeping underlies animals' exploitation of celestial cues for orientation. A further problem concerns the seasonal changes that occur in the direction of migrating animals. Many birds from the northern hemisphere, for example, migrate south in autumn and then return northwards in spring. This

twice-yearly reversal of migratory direction suggests that it might depend upon the internal physiological state of the birds.

In many species, the annual cycle of gonadal and other functions is controlled photoperiodically (§5.2, 6.2). Emlen (1969) therefore tested the relationship between seasonal physiology and migratory direction in indigo buntings, by advancing their annual cycle by photoperiodic manipulation so that they were in autumn condition in spring. When their orientation was tested under the spring sky of a planetarium, their zugunruhe was oriented south, while control birds in phase with the season oriented northward. Evidently the direction taken depends upon the phase of the annual physiological clock.

An even more sophisticated change in preferred direction with season was found by Gwinner & Wiltschko (1978, 1980) in the garden warbler. This species reaches its winter quarters in Africa by flying first in a south-westerly (SW) direction across the Straits of Gibraltar and later changing towards south or south-east (SE); in spring, however, the birds migrate due north, straight across the Mediterranean (Fig. 4.8 A). When young birds were maintained in captivity under a permanent photoperiod of LD 12:12, and their zugunruhe direction was determined in an orientation cage, they showed the same SW to SE change in direction as autumn progressed, and in the following spring oriented directly north (Fig. 4.8 B). The change of direction thus depends upon the stage of the annual cycle. Moreover, this cycles endogenously, free-running in the absence of environmental cues (see Gwinner, 1981).

Fig. 4.8. (A) Migratory direction of garden warblers (*Sylvia borin*) during autumn and spring migration. Hatched area, wintering quarters. (B) Average direction of migratory restlessness (zugunruhe) of 11 birds tested in circular orientation cages in (a) early, and (b) late autumn, and (c) in spring. Note change of direction from early to late autumn and reversal in spring. *n*, number of individual test-nights during which zugunruhe was recorded; arrows show means of these values. (After Gwinner, 1981.)

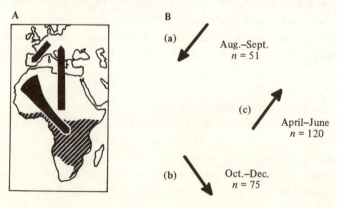

4.8 Concluding remarks

This review has been largely historical, most of the pertinent work having been done some years ago. This is not due to lack of activity in the field of orientation, however; on the contrary, that has become increasingly active in recent years. The situation simply reflects the general attitude that celestial orientation provides cues only for direction finding, and is not the basis for true bi-coordinate navigation – and hence that clock mechanisms are not involved in the map aspect of Kramer's homing concept. The analysis of clock mechanisms has thus been developed much further by workers in other fields, as evidenced by the rest of this book.

4.9 Further reading and key references

Books and review articles are indicated by asterisks

Beling, I (1929). Über das Zeitgedächtnis der Bienen. *Zeitschrift für vergleichende Physiologie*, **9**, 529–38.

*Chovnick, A. (1960). Ed. *Biological Clocks, Cold Spring Harbor Symposia on Quantitative Biology*, **25**.

Emlen, S. T. (1969). Bird migration: influence of physiological state upon celestial orientation. *Science*, **165**, 716–8.

*Emlen, S. T. (1975). Migration: orientation and navigation. In *Avian Biology*, **5**, ed. D. S. Farner & J. R. King, pp. 129–219. New York: Academic Press.

Enright, J. T. (1972). When the beachhopper looks at the moon: the moon compass hypothesis. In *Animal Orientation and Navigation*, ed. S. R. Galler *et al.*, pp. 523–55. Washington, D.C.: National Aeronautics and Space Administration.

Frisch, K. von (1950). Die Sonne als Kompass im Leben der Bienen. *Experientia*, **6**, 210–21.

*Frisch, K. von (1967). *The Dance Language and Orientation of Bees*. Cambridge, Massachusetts: Harvard University Press.

*Gwinner, E. (1981). Rhythms and Time Measurement. In *A New Dictionary of Birds*, 2nd edn., ed. Sir A. Landsborough Thompson, London and Edinburgh: Thomas Nelson.

Gwinner, E. & Wiltschko, W. (1978). Endogenously controlled changes in migratory direction of the Garden Warbler, *Sylvia borin. Journal of Comparative Physiology*, **125**, 267–73.

Gwinner, E. & Wiltschko, W. (1980). Circannual changes in migratory orientation of the Garden Warbler, *Sylvia borin. Behavioral Ecology and Sociobiology*, **7**, 73–8.

Hoffmann, K. (1954). Versuche zu der im Richtungsfinden der Vögel enthaltenen Zeitschätzung. *Zeitschrift für Tierpsychologie*, **11**, 453–75.

Hoffmann, K. (1959). Die Richtungsorientierung von Staren unter der Mitternachtssonne. *Zeitschrift für vergleichende Physiologie*, **41**, 417–80.

*Hoffmann, K. (1965). Clock mechanisms in celestial orientation of animals. In *Circadian Clocks*, ed. J. Aschoff, pp. 426–41. Amsterdam: North Holland.

*Hoffmann, K. (1971). Biological clocks in animal orientation and in other functions. In *Circadian Rhythmicity*, ed. J. F. Bierhuizen, pp. 175–205. Wageningen: Centre for Agricultural Publishing and Documentation.

*Hoffmann, K. (1975). Circadian rhythms in animal orientation. In *Physiological Adaptation to the Environment*, ed. F. J. Vernberg, pp. 435–50. New York: Intext Educational.

*Jander, R. (1963). Insect orientation. *Annual Review of Entomology*, **8**, 95–114.

*Keeton, W. T. (1974). The orientational and navigational basis of homing in birds. *Advances in the Study of Behavior*, **5**, 47–132.

Kramer, G. (1950). Weitere Analyse der Faktoren, welche die Zugaktivität des gekäfigten Vögels orientieren. *Naturwissenschaften*, **37**, 377–8.

*Kramer, G. (1952). Experiments on bird orientation. *Ibis*, **94**, 265–85.

Kramer G. (1953). Wird die Sonnenhöhe bei der Heimfindeorientierung verwertet? *Journal of Ornithology*, **94**, 201–19.

*Matthews, G. V. T. (1968). *Bird Navigation*, 2nd edn. Cambridge and London: Cambridge University Press.

Papi, F. (1955). Experiments on the sense of time in *Talitrus saltator* (Montagu) (Crustacea-Amphipoda). *Experientia*, **11**, 201.

Papi, F. & Pardi, L. (1963). On the lunar orientation of sandhoppers (Amphipoda Talitridae). *Biological Bulletin*, **124**, 97–105.

Santschi, F. (1911). Observations et remarques critiques sur le mecanisme de l'orientation chez les fourmis. *Revue Suisse de Zoologie*, **19**, 303–38.

Sauer, F. (1957). Die Sternenorientierung nächtlich ziehender Grasmücken (*Sylvia atricapilla, borin* and *curruca*). *Zeitschrift für Tierpsychologie*, **14**, 29–70.

*Schmidt-Koenig, K. (1975). *Migration and Homing in Animals*, 99 pp. Berlin, Heidelberg, New York: Springer-Verlag.

*Schmidt-Koenig, K. (1979). *Avian Orientation and Navigation*, 180 pp. London, New York, San Francisco: Academic Press.

*Wallraff, H. G. (1981). Clock-controlled orientation in space. In *Handbook of Behavioral Neurobiology*, **4**, ed. J. Aschoff, pp. 299–309. New York and London: Plenum Press.

Wiltschko, W. & Wiltschko, R. (1972). Magnetic compass of European robins. *Science*, **176**, 62–4.

PART II

Photoperiodism

D. S. SAUNDERS

5 Photoperiodism in animals and plants

5.1 Introduction

Man must have been aware of seasonal cycles of flowering, fruiting, reproduction and migration ever since he became aware of his environment; an awareness which assumed an increased importance when he became an agriculturalist and stockbreeder. Indeed, some of man's earliest scientific accomplishments were in astronomy and related mathematics, generally acquired with a view to calculating and predicting the seasons from an accurate knowledge of planetary movements. Seasonal cycles in animals and plants were undoubtedly taken as inbuilt 'rhythms of life' – direct responses to their physical environment, particularly to changes in temperature or precipitation. It is only in the last hundred years or so that man has asked the 'hows' and 'whys' of seasonal periodicity, prompted no doubt by observations that plants and animals may frequently anticipate the seasons.

Apart from the centuries-old Japanese custom of Yogai in which songbirds were brought to an early maturity, and therefore musical activity, by artificially extending day-length, most of the early progress was made with plants. It was Henfrey, for example, in his book *The Vegetation of Europe* (1852), who reminded us that day-length is a function of latitude, and that this factor might be responsible for the natural distribution of plants. Later, with the advent of artificial light sources, several investigators found that the sexual maturation of some horticulturally important species could be accelerated, like that of the Japanese songbirds, by augmenting natural day-lengths, a practice which became known as 'electro-horticulture'. Before the First World War, Tournois demonstrated that *Humulus japonicus* (hop) and *Cannabis sativa* (hemp) could be made to flower by *excluding* daylight for all but six hours per day, whereas Klebs showed that *Sempervivum funkii*, normally flowering in June, could be made to bloom in the winter by increasing day-length. Klebs also distinguished the 'nutritive', that is, photosynthetic, role of light from its 'catalytic', that is, photoperiodic, role, and Tournois suggested that night-length, rather than day-length, might be important.

These pioneer studies were followed by the outstanding investigations of Garner & Allard (1920) who first adequately described the effects of day-length on a variety of plants, including tobacco, soy bean, radish, carrot and lettuce. They introduced the terms photoperiodism, photoperiod (day-length), short- and long-day plants, and the notion of the critical photoperiod (§5.2). They showed that the Maryland Narrowleaf variety of tobacco (*Nicotiana tabacum*) and the Biloxi variety of soy bean (*Glycine max*), like hop and hemp, were short-day plants, only flowering when days were shorter than a critical value. Other species were long-day plants, only flowering when days exceeded the critical photoperiod; still others were apparently indifferent to photoperiod, or were 'day-neutral'. It was thus realised that plants may respond to the precise and 'noise-free' environmental signals of day-length (or night-length) to regulate their seasonal cycles of growth and reproduction.

Although Schäfer suggested in 1907 that day-length and its seasonal change might be a controlling factor in the migration of birds, as well as in their annual gonadal growth, it was Marcovitch (1923) who produced the first experimental evidence for photoperiodism in animals. Working with the strawberry root aphis, he found that the autumnal sexual forms, bearing wings and laying eggs, could be produced in the spring merely by curtailing the photoperiod to about 7–8 h per day. Conversely, long exposure to artificial light in September inhibited the sexual forms and induced viviparous reproduction. Photoperiodic control of diapause and non-diapause development in insects was then demonstrated in a number of other early papers, Kogure's (1933) extensive work with the short-day commercial silk moth, *Bombyx mori*, becoming a classic of its type.

Modern experimental work with vertebrates began with the observations of Rowan (1926) on gonadal growth and migration in the snow bird, *Junco hyemalis*, in Alberta, where it was shown that artificial lengthening of the days caused maturation and a tendency to migrate northwards, even in the coldest part of the year, whereas shortening of the photoperiod led to gonadal regression and a southerly movement (see also §4.7). Similar early work on mammalian breeding cycles had been carried out by the early 1930s. Photoperiod effects on a wide array of physiological processes are now known, particularly in those terrestrial or freshwater organisms living in temperate regions where seasonal changes in climate and availability of food pose a real challenge to survival. In this chapter, however, discussion of the phenomenon will be limited to the four groups – flowering plants, insects, birds and mammals – for which most information is currently available.

5.2 The photoperiodic response

It would be surprising indeed if a complicated phenomenon such as the photoperiodic response were identical in such disparate organisms as the four groups considered here. Although the same basic 'clockwork' *may* be used (see below), the phenomenon is undoubtedly a product of natural selection and has either evolved on many occasions in slightly different forms, that is, has a polyphyletic origin, or has undergone extensive radiation from a single or monophyletic source. Photoperiodism may thus appear in different forms. Organisms may respond to absolute day- or night-lengths, to naturally-changing photoperiods, or to sequences of short-to-long, or long-to-short day-lengths at different stages of their development. All such responses, however, imply that the organism is able to measure time, either from the length of the day or the length of the night or perhaps in some other way.

5.2.1 *The critical photoperiod*

For the sake of simplicity, the present discussion will be limited to responses to stationary photoperiods, a selection of which are shown in Fig. 5.1. Whether long- or short-day species, all show a more-or-less well-marked *critical photoperiod* which separates the two appropriate seasonal pathways, for example, flowering *versus* vegetative growth, diapause *versus* development, gonadal growth *versus* regression. If the entire range of photoperiods, from continuous darkness to continuous light, is examined, regimes outside those occurring in the organism's natural environment may show intermediate responses. In insects, for example, the incidence of diapause frequently declines in very short day-lengths (Fig. 5.1B), and these reactions, although of no ecological significance, must be explained in physiological terms.

Fig. 5.1. (**A**) Photoperiod–response curves for diapause induction in the flesh fly, *Sarcophaga argyrostoma* (after Saunders), and testis growth in the quail (after Follett). (**B**) Photoperiod–response curves for diapause induction in the cabbage butterfly, *Pieris brassicae*, at three temperatures (after Danilevskii, 1965).

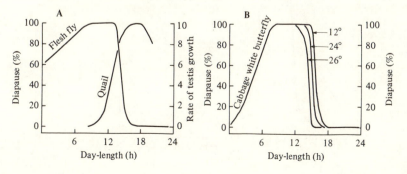

Since day-length varies with latitude as well as with season, local popula-tions frequently differ in their critical photoperiods and consequently in their dates of starting and finishing seasonal activity; and perhaps also in the number of generations accomplished during the favourable, or 'growing', season. Fig. 5.2 shows examples for insects. In the knot grass moth, *Acronycta rumicis*, a population from the Black Sea coast of the Soviet Union at 43° N shows a critical day-length of about $14\frac{1}{2}$ h per 24, whereas populations at latitudes 50° N, 55° N and 60° N show critical values of $16\frac{1}{2}$, 18 and $19\frac{1}{2}$ h, respectively (Danilevskii, 1965).

These data indicate that the critical day-length changes by about $1\frac{1}{2}$ h with every 5° of latitude, and suggest a continuous latitudinal cline. In the cabbage

Fig. 5.2. The effects of latitude on the photoperiodic response for two species of insect in the Soviet Union. (**A**) *Acronycta rumicis* (knot grass moth) at: (1) Sukhumi, latitude 43° N; (2) Belgorod, latitude 50° N; (3) Vitebsk, latitude 55° N; (4) Leningrad, latitude 60° N. (**B**) *Pieris brassicae* (cabbage white butterfly) at: (1) Sukhumi; (2) Belgorod; (3) Brest-Litovsk, latitude 52° N; (4) Leningrad. (After Danilevskii, 1965.)

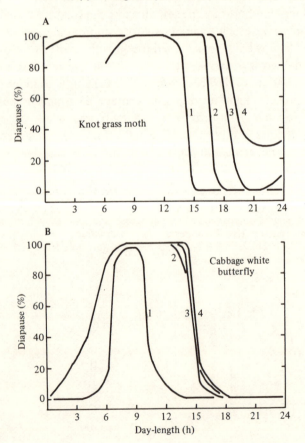

white butterfly, *Pieris brassicae*, however, two distinct geographical races seem to exist (Fig. 5.2**B**): a southerly race (Black Sea) with a critical day-length of about 10 h per 24, and a more northerly population, occurring from latitude 50° to 60° N, with a critical value of about 15 h per 24. The selective advantage of this is clear. The insects at higher latitudes compensate for the longer summer day-lengths but earlier onset of winter with an earlier diapause threshold. Southerly populations, on the other hand, are able to exploit the longer growing season by delaying the onset of diapause with a shorter critical photoperiod.

Similar phenomena also occur in vertebrates. In ducks and geese, for example, this is obvious in the dates of egg-laying in birds held captive at the Wildfowl Trust, Slimbridge (near Bristol, England, at latitude 51.5° N). The Hawaiian né-né (*Branta sandvicensis*), which in the wild is exposed to photoperiods ranging from 11 to 13.5 h, breeds much earlier (in February) than any other *Branta* or *Anser* goose. Mid-latitude Greylag geese (*Anser anser*), whose breeding ranges lie between latitudes 50° and 56° N, lay eggs at the end of March when days are longer than 14 h. The high-latitude geese which breed in the Arctic and are exposed to continuous light from April onwards, lie at the other extreme. At Slimbridge, where the days barely reach 17 h, some of these species can only just reproduce; the median date of egg-laying in the white-fronted goose (*Anser albifrons*), which has a natural range at about latitude 73° N, is mid May (Murton & Westwood, 1977).

5.2.2 *The nature of the clock mechanism*

The word 'photoperiod' implies that the clock mechanism involves reactions to light, 'photo', and, in addition, contains a timing component, 'period'. It also involves the relevant physiological effector mechanism that ultimately leads to the controlled event of flowering, diapause, etc. The first and last of these processes will receive only a brief treatment here. A response to light suggests the involvement of pigment systems to absorb light energy. Suffice it to say that these pigments, where known, are very different in different organisms.

In plants the leaves are the photoreceptors and the pigment is phytochrome with its two forms, one absorbing in the red, the other in the far-red (see §7.2). Light absorption by chlorophyll, leading to photosynthesis, is not involved. In animals there is nothing equivalent to phytochrome with its red/far-red reversibility, and photoperiodic light effects are apparently mediated by pathways which are quite distinct from those involved with vision (Fig. 8.9). Thus, in insects and birds light is absorbed directly by the brain, and in mammals, although retinal photoreception is involved, the signals pass along the retino-hypothalamic tract rather than the optic nerve proper (§11.4.2).

The ultimate effector pathways are also different in the four groups, as one might expect. In plants the photoperiodic effect is passed from the leaves to the buds, and a so far undiscovered hormone, 'florigen', has been proposed (§7.5). In insects and vertebrates the clock is in the CNS, and it switches the appropriate endocrine centres on and off (§6.2, 6.3).

In spite of these differences, which are not unexpected, in photoreceptor and effector systems, the different kinds of organisms contain clocks which look extraordinarily alike, at least at the formal level. Whether this similarity represents anything more than the fact that the phenomenon in all organisms can be described by the same mathematical and topological language, based on oscillator theory (§2.2.1), remains to be seen when the concrete nature of the clocks is discovered. At the moment, however, the phenomenon of photoperiodism in plants, insects, and vertebrates *can* be compared to advantage in a formal way, thus providing us with one of the few areas of biological enquiry where a truly integrated approach may be made. It is these formal properties of the response which will be examined here.

5.3   Night-interruption experiments – the central role of night-length

Formal analysis of the photoperiodic clock treats the organism as a 'black box', varying the input (the light–dark regime) on the one hand, and noting the output (the photoperiodic response) on the other. Apart from simply varying the hours of light (and hence the hours of darkness) within the 24-h period, some of the earliest formal approaches involved the interruption of the dark period of the cycle with a supplementary pulse of light. These experiments are known as *night-interruption* or *light-break* experiments, and the main 'day' plus the supplementary light-break is considered as enclosing a so-called *skeleton photoperiod* (see also §7.4).

In plants, short light pulses in the dark period frequently reverse the short- or long-day effects of the 'main' photoperiod, with pulses as short as a few minutes sometimes being effective. Similar work on birds produces essentially the same results, short and therefore non-physiologically inductive days becoming inductive if the middle of the long night is interrupted by a pulse of light. In such experiments, the non-inductive short-day regime and the inductive light-break regimes often contain the same total amount of light; it is therefore concluded that it is the length of the *dark* period (i.e. the night-length) that is of central importance. In early work with arthropods the supplementary light pulse was also placed in the middle of the night, but, unlike that which induced responses in plants and birds, had limited effect. When long-day effects *were* obtained they were interpreted as evidence that though the length of the dark period was more significant than that of the light, the 'light reaction' developed more slowly than in plants or birds.

Subsequently, the systematic pulsing of ·the dark period in nights of different lengths has provided a second piece of information: the timing of the interruption is of crucial importance. In plants (e.g. in *Kalanchöe blossfeldiana*, Fig. 5.3 A) and most birds, such experiments reveal a single point of long-day effect, but in insects there are commonly *two*. In the pink bollworm moth, *Pectinophora gossypiella*, for example (Fig. 5.3 B), the second point (**b**) was found to be about the same interval after dusk (9.5–11 h) as the first point (**a**) was before dawn. This observation has played an important part in the development of one of the most useful models for the photoperiodic clock (§ 5.5).

5.4 Hour-glass or circadian clock?

The first theories to explain the workings of the photoperiodic clock likened it to an 'hour-glass' set in motion at dusk. If dawn then arrived early (i.e. before the end of the critical night-length), short-night (or long-day) effects were produced, whereas if dawn arrived late (i.e. after the end of the critical night-length) the dark period was read as a long night. This simple linear system had to be largely independent of temperature to account for the thermostability of the critical night (see Fig. 5.1 B and also § 2.2.4), and often incorporated a dependence on a certain range of accompanying light values. Such theories survive today in various forms, by far the most convincing being that for the aphid, *Megoura viciae* (Lees, 1973).

Fig. 5.3. (**A**) Flower formation in *Kalanchöe blossfeldiana* in response to 5-min light breaks in the dark portion of an 8 h light: 16 h dark cycle (LD 8:16) (solid line) compared with the circadian rhythm of petal movement (broken line, arbitrary units). (After Bünning, 1960.) (**B**) Incidence of pupal diapause in the pink bollworm moth, *Pectinophora gossypiella*, in response to 1-h light breaks in the dark portion of an LD 10:14 cycle, showing the bimodal response (**a** and **b**) common in insect night-interruption experiments. (After Adkisson, 1964.) The abscissae indicate the basic light cycles, with each circle in the curves showing the response in one batch of *Kalanchöe* or *Pectinophora* given this basic cycle plus a light break ('pulse') at the time in the dark phase (black) which the circle falls vertically above.

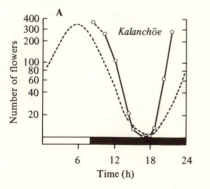 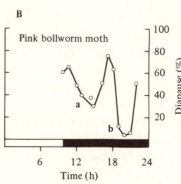

A quite different proposition was advanced in 1936 by Erwin Bünning. This equated night-length measurement in plants with the circadian rhythms (see the Glossary) known to provide timing for a multitude of daily phenomena (see Chapter 2). Bünning's proposal was that each 24-h cycle consisted of two half-cycles, differing in their sensitivity to light (Bünning, 1960). The first 12 h constituted the 'photophil' or light-requiring half-cycle, and the second 12 h the 'scotophil' or dark-requiring half-cycle. Short-day effects were produced when the daylight was restricted to the photophil, but long-day effects when it extended into the light-sensitive scotophil. This model for the clock, therefore, was an oscillator as opposed to an hour-glass, and served to focus attention on the many similarities between classical photoperiodism and the overt diurnal rhythms of behaviour and physiology. This model has become known as *Bünning's Hypothesis.*

Like many original and rather revolutionary ideas, Bünning's hypothesis received scant attention (and frequent disbelief) for the next twenty years or so, except in Bünning's own laboratory. This reluctance to accept the model was compounded by the then general scepticism as to the reality of circadian rhythms themselves. However, unequivocal evidence has now been produced to show that photoperiodic time measurement in plants, birds, mammals and insects is indeed a function of the circadian system; in that sense at least, therefore, some form of Bünning's general hypothesis is valid.

Whilst experimental protocols were restricted to cycles of 24 h, the circadian or hour-glass nature of the clock could not be tested. Attention was therefore turned to two types of experiment using light cycles whose periods were greater than the natural solar day. In the first, the night-interruption technique was extended to 48- and 72-h cycles; in the second, now called *resonance* experiments, a short photoperiod (e.g. 12 h) was coupled in different experimental groups to different lengths of darkness to give abnormal light:dark cycles from, say, 20 to 72 h or more. Once again these experiments were first conducted with plants (see Bünning, 1960; Hamner, 1960) and only later with birds, mammals and insects. Examples are given in Figs. 5.4, 6.3, and 7.5.

In the long-day plant, *Hyoscyamus niger*, 2-h light breaks applied systematically in the 'night' of a 9 h light:39 h dark cycle revealed maxima of flowering 16 and 40 h after dawn, that is, 24 h apart; and in *Kalanchöe blossfeldiana*, a short-day plant, maintained in 48- and 72-h cycles, flowering was again induced when the pulses fell at 24-h intervals in the dark (cf. Fig. 7.5). Resonance experiments were performed by Hamner and his associates (Hamner, 1960) on short-day plants including the Biloxi variety of soy bean and the Japanese morning glory (*Pharbitis nil*). In both cases flowering was maximal when cycle lengths were close to 24, 48 or 72 h, but minimal when close to 36 or 60 h. In both types of experiment, lights come on at different times in the extended dark periods, and the sensitive points at 24-h intervals are readily equated with Bünning's 'scotophil', recurring at circadian intervals. These results are therefore powerful evidence in favour of the circadian basis for the phenomenon.

Remarkably similar results, once more underlining the *formal* similarities between our four groups of organism, have also been recorded for birds (Fig. 6.3), mammals and some insects (Fig. 5.4). In other insects, however, including the aphid *Megoura viciae* (Lees, 1973) and the European corn borer, *Ostrinia nubilalis*, identical experimental methods have produced no clear evidence for a circadian component, and the hour-glass model seems more appropriate. We will attempt to resolve this untidy dilemma later (§5.7).

Long-period night-interruption and resonance experiments provide additional information about the clock which we should note here before proceeding. In experiments using different 'main' light periods, the peaks of

Fig. 5.4. (**A**) Flower formation in the soy bean, *Glycine max*, in response to 30-min light breaks in a cycle of 8 h light:64 h dark (circles), compared with the circadian rhythm of leaf movement (wavy solid line, arbitrary units). (After Bünning, 1960.) (**B**) Incidence of pupal diapause in groups of flesh flies, *Sarcophaga argyrostoma*, maintained in resonance experiments (see §5.4) using either a 12-h (solid line) or a 16-h (broken line) photoperiod in cycles up to 72 h in length. Note that the oscillation is apparently timed from lights-off. (After Saunders, 1978 a.) The long dark phases of the experimental cycles are black on the abscissa bars. (See also Figs. 6.3, 7.5**B**.)

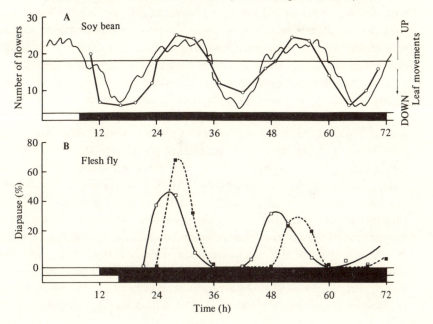

long- or short-day effect frequently recur at characteristic intervals (i.e. in multiples of 24 h) after the lights-out (Fig. 5.4 **B**). This suggests that once the light period exceeds a certain value, the photoperiodic oscillation starts anew each dusk at a particular phase, and then free runs (see the Glossary) in darkness. The significance of this observation in models for the clock will become apparent in the next section.

5.5   Some models for the photoperiodic clock

Apart from the hour-glass schemes and the generalised Bünning hypothesis outlined above, several more explicit models have been proposed. The best of these are based on known properties of the circadian system, particularly the entrainment of that system by the light (and temperature) cycles encountered by the organism in its natural (and laboratory) environment (§2.3).

Most work on plant photoperiodism has followed Bünning's idea that the circadian system includes a particular light-sensitive phase which achieves different phase relationships to the light cycle as photoperiod changes. One valuable research technique contributed by the Bünning school is the measurement of some *overt* circadian rhythm in the organism under investigation in order to investigate the entrainment of its covert photoperiodic system. Bünning refers to these overt systems as the hands of the clock (see §1.2). In plants, circadian movements of the leaves or the petals (Bünning, 1969) are often used as such hands. The close parallelism between leaf movements and flower induction in *Glycine max* is apparent in Fig. 5.4. In the short-day plant, *Colias frederici*, the light-sensitive phase has a fixed phase relationship to leaf movement, occurring about 5 h after the minimum position of the leaves. These and other studies encourage the belief that, not only is the photoperiodic response circadian in nature, but the same oscillation drives both photoperiodism and overt rhythmicity.

The use of overt indicator rhythms has also been pursued by Pittendrigh and his associates in their study of insect photoperiodism. This part of the story starts with the apparently perplexing results obtained by Adkisson (1964) for night-interruptions in the pink bollworm moth, *Pectinophora gossypiella* (Fig. 5.3 **B**), which shows two points, rather than one, of sensitivity (diapause reversal). Did this mean that this insect, and others like it, had two inductive phases in the night; or if there was only one, was it at **a** or at **b**? Recognition of the extraordinary parallels between this type of response and the entrainment of the circadian pupal eclosion rhythm in the non-photoperiodic insect, *Drosophila pseudoobscura*, to similar light regimes is due to Pittendrigh (1965, 1966). Apart from proposing to use the overt rhythm of eclosion as the hands of the clock, Pittendrigh noted the dual action of light in Bünning's general hypothesis – (1) entrainment of the circadian system, and (2) photoperiodic induction – and suggested that a knowledge of entrainment was essential to our understanding of the clock. The outcome of this approach was a more modern version of Bünning's hypothesis, which Pittendrigh called *external coincidence*.

In its most recent form (Pittendrigh, 1966), the external coincidence model incorporates much of what is known about entrainment of such rhythms as pupal eclosion (see Figs. 2.6 and 8.5). It is proposed that the photoperiodic oscillation, like that governing eclosion, is re-set to a characteristic phase at the end of light periods in excess of about 12 h, and re-starts its motion at the onset of darkness. For an organism such as *Pectinophora*, a light-sensitive, or photo-inducible, phase (called ϕ_i) is located about 9 to $9\frac{1}{2}$ h through the dark part of the cycle (at the end of the critical night-length). Consequently, when nights are long, ϕ_i falls in the dark and the short-day autumnal physiological response is induced (diapause, for example), whereas when nights are short, dawn occurs earlier in the cycle so ϕ_i falls in the light, and the long-day summer response (non-diapause) occurs (Figs. 5.5 A, **B**). The model was called 'external' coincidence both to distinguish it from other possible schemes (see below), and to draw attention to the temporal coincidence between ϕ_i and the external or environmental light. One thing is immediately clear: although the clock is circadian, and free runs in extended dark periods, it measures night-length in natural or 24-h light–dark cycles as if it were an hour-glass. We shall return to this important point later.

It is in night-interruption experiments of the type shown in Fig. 5.3 that the parallels between photoperiodism and its overt hands become most apparent (Fig. 5.5 C, **D**). Thus, as with the eclosion rhythm in *D. pseudoobscura* (Pittendrigh, 1965), light pulses falling early in the night cause phase delays in the underlying oscillation, whilst those falling late in the night cause phase advances, as shown by the phase–response curve (see §2.3.2). After an early pulse, therefore, ϕ_i is delayed until (at point **a** in Fig. 5.3 **B**) it crosses the dawn threshold of the main light component and diapause is eliminated. After a late pulse, on the other hand, ϕ_i is advanced until it coincides directly with the scanning light pulse, again eliminating diapause (and producing point **b** in Fig. 5.3 **B**). Pulses of light falling between **a** and **b**, where the phase jump occurs, are not responded to and diapause incidence remains high. The model states, therefore, that ϕ_i is at **b** and not **a**.

The model has been criticised for apparently failing to explain some of the characteristics of insect photoperiodism, such as the decline in diapause incidence in very short photoperiods (Fig. 5.1 **B**), and the performance of the clock in continuous darkness. It has, however, been applied successfully to the flesh fly, *Sarcophaga argyrostoma*, (Saunders, 1978 a, 1979) with many of

Fig. 5.5. The 'external coincidence' model for the photoperiodic clock, as applied to the flesh fly, *Sarcophaga argyrostoma*: (**A**) in a 12 h light: 12 h dark (LD 12:12) cycle; (**B**) in LD 16:8. The underlying circadian oscillation, shown here as the phase–response curve to 1-h light interruptions, is re-set to a specific phase of its cycle ('Ct 12') at the end of each 12- or 16-h day. (Ct 12 = 'circadian time' 12 'h' through the *ca* 24-h cycle of the underlying oscillation – see §2.3.2). Light pulses falling when the curve is below the horizontal line re-set the rhythm to later (delays); pulses when the curve is above the line re-set it to earlier (advances) – as shown on the ordinate scale in **A** (see also Fig. 2.6). Consequently, with a short night, as in **B**, the photo-inducible phase (ϕ_i) falls in the light, giving short-night responses, whereas with a long night, as in **A**, it falls in the dark and gives a long-night response. **C** and **D** show the model as it could operate with 1-h light interruptions falling in the night of LD 12:12 cycles; **C** with the interruption 3 h into the night, i.e. at the phase point in the underlying circadian clock's cycle that is 3 h on from Ct 12 (= Ct 15); **D** with the interruption 8 h into the night (at Ct 20). In **C**, the light-break at Ct 15 causes a phase delay, re-setting the clock back to about Ct 12 so that it starts its cycle again 4 h late, and ϕ_i then falls in the light of the next day. In **D**, the light-break at Ct 20, which falls on ϕ_i, causes a phase advance and thus has the same effect as an early dawn. Both early and late interruptions therefore produce the physiological response of a short night (low incidence of diapause), equivalent to points **a** and **b** in Fig. 5.3**B**.

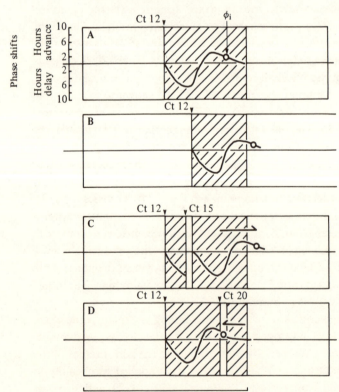

the above-mentioned difficulties eliminated by the application of entrainment theory.

Several alternatives to external coincidence have been proposed, most of them incorporating two (dawn and dusk) components and a mutual interaction. A consequence of such models is that light is seen to have but a single role, that of entrainment, as opposed to the duality (entrainment *and* induction) demanded by external coincidence and the Bünning hypothesis.

Pittendrigh (1972) proposed two such schemes, noting that complex multicellular organisms possess several, if not many, independent or loosely-coupled circadian pacemakers (see §8.6, 11.3). In particular, the locomotor activity rhythms of rodents, birds, lizards and other vertebrates are clearly composed of separate 'morning' and 'evening' oscillators which, under certain circumstances, may 'split' and assume quite different mutual phase relationships (§11.4.3). Using this theoretical reasoning Pittendrigh proposed the *internal coincidence* model, a clock consisting of at least two circadian components; one coupled to dawn and the other to dusk. This attractive proposition suggests, perhaps, the bringing together in time of short-lived metabolic reactants whose product is required for the next step in an inductive sequence.

Another line of reasoning, again based on the concept of a multi-oscillator circadian system, is behind the so-called resonance model (Pittendrigh, 1972). This argues that circadian organisation might be involved in photoperiodic induction, but not necessarily in time measurement *per se*. The theoretical background for the model rests on the observation that plants and animals do better if in resonance with the driving light cycle (see §5.4). It notes that generalised aspects of physiology, such as fitness, survival and rates of development are better in LD cycles close to the natural 24 h of the solar day, and hence to the endogenous circadian period. The model suggests that whatever the actual mechanism for night-length measurement (be it oscillator or hour-glass), time-measurement, like other generalised aspects of physiology, is more effective, in, say, cycles of 24, 48 or 72 h, than in cycles of 36 or 60 h (see Fig. 5.4), presumably because the former cycles encourage internal synchrony between the constituent oscillators, whereas the latter may bring about temporal disorder (see also p. 17).

5.6 Photoperiodism and circannual rhythms

Classical photoperiodism, involving measurement of night-length or its changes, is not the only way in which organisms obtain calendar information. Particularly in long-lived organisms there occurs an alternative, which has the formal properties of an endogenous year-long rhythm. Like circadian rhythms, these so-called *circannual* rhythms appear to be temperature-compensated and to free run in constant darkness, constant light, *or* in unchanging 24-h light–dark cycles, with a period close to a year, commonly between 40 and 50 weeks. In nature they are apparently entrained to the exact astronomical year by the seasonal changes in day-length. It must be stressed, however, that these striking parallels to circadian rhythmicity are only formal properties, and we know next-to-nothing about their concrete physiology.

Circannual rhythmicity was probably first observed when European species of trees and livestock were transported to equatorial regions where the day-length was virtually unchanging across the year. Deprived of their normal seasonal cues, the yearly cycles of leaf unfolding, fruiting and reproduction were seen to persist with a near-annual periodicity, but in many cases to lose strict synchrony with both seasons and other individuals in the population. These rhythms are now known in plants, birds, mammals, insects, and even coelenterates. They are particularly important to transequatorial migrants such as the willow warbler and the chiffchaff, which fly from areas with a decreasing photoperiod to areas with an increasing photoperiod through tropical regions devoid of reliable photoperiodic clues, and still need to maintain annual cycles of reproduction, moulting and migration (§4.7, Fig. 4.8).

The beetle, *Anthrenus verbasci*, provides one of the earliest-known examples (Blake, 1959). Its larvae are found in dried animal remains (frequently in old bird's nests) and take one, two or three years to complete their development, depending on the temperature. Each winter the larvae enter diapause and then become re-activated in the spring. Following the spring of their pupation, the adults emerge and may be found feeding on flower heads. When maintained experimentally in continuous darkness, at a series of constant temperatures, pupations are observed to occur in peaks, about 42–46 weeks apart (Fig. 5.6 A). This rhythm is comparable to the circadian rhythm of eclosion in fruit flies and flesh flies, differing only in period. It is a circannual rhythm partitioning the population into approximately annual peaks or 'gates' (see the Glossary). The endogenous period of the rhythm (42 to 46 weeks) is temperature-compensated, but can be lengthened by exposure to the decreasing day-lengths of autumn; in this way the innate calendar is entrained or synchronised to the astronomical year, and pupation occurs at the appropriate season.

Circannual rhythms of breeding, antler development and pelt changes are well-known in vertebrates. In ground squirrels, rhythms of hibernation and activity, body weight, and core temperature, persist in laboratory conditions, with a circannual period (Pengelley & Asmundson, 1969). In the starling, *Sturnus vulgaris*, the annual testicular cycle in an unchanging LD 12:12 begins with testis growth in December, and reaches average spermatogenesis by mid-January; the testes then become quiescent by June, only to recommence a second cycle in the following October or November (Fig. 5.6**B**). The free-running cycle is therefore about 9 to $9\frac{1}{2}$ months. Circannual rhythms in avian reproduction, like pupation in *Anthrenus*, seem to be synchronised by seasonal changes in photoperiod (Gwinner, and Schwab, in Menaker, 1971) (see also Fig. 3.5).

5.7 How valid are the differences between the various types of clock?

The responses of plants and animals to seasonal changes of photoperiod are many and varied. They range from clocks which seem to measure night-length like a non-repetitive hour-glass, to oscillatory mechanisms with a period close to a year. Between the two are various clocks based on circadian rhythmicity, which seem to distinguish long nights from short nights by radically different means, and more complicated devices which are either able

Fig. 5.6. (**A**) Circannual rhythm of pupation in a mixed-age population of the beetle, *Anthrenus verbasci*, in continuous darkness. (After Blake, 1959.) Populations at high temperature pupate in a single 'annual' peak, 30 to 40 weeks after oviposition; those at lower temperatures utilise sequentially later 'gates' (see the Glossary) at intervals of 42 to 46 weeks. The dotted distribution indicates the position of the 'missing' gate, presumed to lie at about 110 weeks. (**B**) Circannual rhythm of testicular growth of the starling, *Sturnus vulgaris*, in an unchanging photoperiod of LD 12:12. (After Schwab, in Menaker, 1971.)

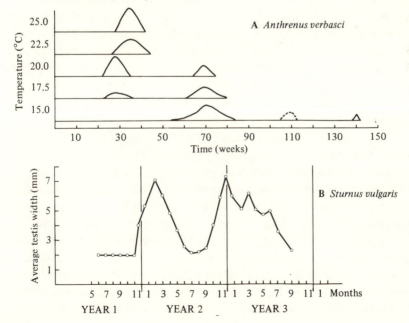

to distinguish lengthening from shortening nights, or to perceive sequences of night-lengths at different stages of development. Such an array is to be expected in the rich diversity of plant and animal life. Nevertheless, one of the aims of the comparative physiologist must be to examine the differences between the various clocks, as they are described, and to resolve and rationalise anomalies.

This is a difficult task until more is known about the concrete physiological processes behind these photoperiodic and circannual clocks. A useful starting point might be a suggestion that these timekeeping devices, like good man-made clocks, are oscillators, either circadian or circannual, or both. These oscillators possess formal properties which predispose them for the job: a regular clock-like periodicity close to either a day or a year; an accuracy which is homeostatically buffered against adventitious changes in temperature or chemical milieu; and a period which is synchronised by more-or-less discrete phase shifts to a meaningful phase relationship with the daily or annual cycles of the sun. How then are these clock properties manifested in the photoperiodic mechanisms known to us today?

Hour-glasses differ from oscillators only in that they fail to re-set themselves in the absence of repeated light cycles: the hour-glass of *Megoura viciae* (Lees, 1973) seems to differ from the circadian clock of *Sarcophaga argyrostoma* (Saunders, 1978b, 1979) only in this respect. The aphid hour-glass is set in motion at the dusk transition and measures night-length. The photoperiodic oscillator in the flesh fly is re-set to a characteristic phase at the end of the light; it too measures night-length in natural or 24-h light–dark cycles as if it were an hour-glass. Although it persists or free runs in extended nights (see Fig. 5.4B), there is evidence that it, too, gradually damps out over the next few cycles if not reinforced by further light pulses. Similar phenomena have been described in plants (Bünning, 1969). It is therefore tempting to suggest that hour-glasses are merely rapidly damped circadian oscillators, and that these two mechanisms are only evolutionary variations on a theme.

It is thus possible that all photoperiodic clocks are oscillatory in nature. Furthermore, they may all comprise a population of oscillators, and mutual synchrony, as envisaged by the resonance model (§ 5.4), might be of paramount importance for accurate time measurement (cf. §2.2.2). A valid distinction within these oscillator clocks may be whether they rely on environmental light (or temperature) for both induction and entrainment (= external coincidence), or whether induction is a consequence of the changing phase relationships between, say, dawn and dusk components (= internal coincidence). Satisfactory experimental distinction between these two is still wanting, but the former seems appropriate for plants and some insects (Saunders, 1978b), whereas the latter is perhaps more appropriate for vertebrates (Pittendrigh

& Daan, 1976). This says nothing about the *nature* of these oscillations: they might either be fundamental aspects of cellular organisation, or involve metabolic products such as hormones (see e.g. §6.2).

What of photoperiodism and circadian rhythmicity in relation to circannual rhythms? Some authors have suggested a causal relationship between the two, presumably by some sort of counting mechanism, and have described circannual cycles of circadian cycles. Others, however, have suggested that the two are really independent phenomena, daily light cycles and endogenous daily rhythms being as relevant to circannual rhythmicity as the heart-beat is to a circadian rhythm. Light *cycles* are certainly irrelevant in some organisms since circannual rhythms of some insects and some birds may persist in their absence. However, many long-lived organisms displaying circannual rhythms are also photoperiodic in the classical sense. Testis growth in the starling and the sparrow, for example, may be induced by long days, but only at certain seasons. Photoperiodic stimulation is possible in the spring, but by midsummer the birds enter a photo-refractory phase when gametogenesis cannot be induced or maintained by these same long days, until a sequence of short days has been experienced. Similar phenomena may be observed in mammals, and to some extent in plants and insects, and serve to prevent breeding at inappropriate seasons. These phenomena look remarkably like circannual rhythms, and suggest some sort of interaction between circannual rhythmicity and photoperiodism.

5.8 Further reading and key references

Books and review articles are indicated by asterisks

*Adkisson, P. L. (1964). Action of the photoperiod in controlling insect diapause. *American Naturalist*, **98**, 357–74.

Blake, G. M. (1959). Control of diapause by an 'internal clock' in *Anthrenus verbasci* (L.) (Col., Dermestidae). *Nature, London*, **183**, 126–7.

*Bünning, E. (1960). Circadian rhythms and time measurement in photoperiodism. *Cold Spring Harbor Symposia on Quantitative Biology*, **25**, 249–56.

*Bünning, E. (1969). Common features of photoperiodism in plants and animals. *Photochemistry and Photobiology*, **9**, 219–28.

*Danilevskii, A. S. (1965). *Photoperiodism and Seasonal Development of Insects*, first English edition. Edinburgh and London: Oliver and Boyd.

Garner, W. W. & Allard, H. A. (1920). Effect of the relative length of the day and night and other factors of the environment on growth and reproduction in plants. *Journal of Agricultural Research*, **18**, 553–606.

*Hamner, K. C. (1960). Photoperiodism and circadian rhythms. *Cold Spring Harbor Symposia on Quantitative Biology*, **25**, 269–77.

Kogure, M. (1933). The influence of light and temperature on certain characters of the silkworm, *Bombyx mori*. *Journal of the Department of Agriculture, Kyushu University*, **4**, 1–93.

Lees, A. D. (1973). Photoperiodic time measurement in the aphid *Megoura viciae*. *Journal of Insect Physiology*, **19**, 2279–316.

Marcovitch, S. (1923). Plant lice and light exposure. *Science*, Washington, **58**, 537–8.

*Menaker, M. (Ed.) (1971). *Biochronometry*. Washington: National Academy of Sciences.

*Murton, R. K. & Westwood, N. J. (1977). *Avian Breeding Cycles*. Oxford: Clarendon Press.

Pengelley, E. T. & Asmundson, S. M. (1969). Free-running periods of endogenous circannian rhythms in the golden-mantled ground squirrel, *Citellus lateralis*. *Comparative Biochemistry and Physiology*, **30**, 177–83.

*Pittendrigh, C. S. (1965). On the mechanism of entrainment of a circadian rhythm by light cycles. In *Circadian Clocks*, ed. J. Aschoff, pp. 277–97. Amsterdam: North-Holland.

*Pittendrigh, C. S. (1966). The circadian oscillation in *Drosophila pseudoobscura* pupae: a model for the photoperiodic clock. *Zeitschrift für Pflanzenphysiologie*, **54**, 275–307.

Pittendrigh, C. S. (1972). Circadian surfaces and the diversity of possible roles of circadian organization in photoperiodic induction. *Proceedings of the National Academy of Sciences, U.S.A.*, **69**, 2734–7.

Pittendrigh, C. S. & Daan, S. (1976). A functional analysis of circadian pacemakers in nocturnal rodents. V. A clock for all seasons. *Journal of Comparative Physiology*, **106**, 333–55.

Rowan, W. (1926). On photoperiodism, reproductive periodicity and the annual migration of birds and certain fishes. *Proceedings of the Boston Society for Natural History*, **38**, 147–89.

*Saunders, D. S. (1974). Circadian rhythms and photoperiodism in insects. In *The Physiology of Insecta*, 2nd edn, **II**, ed. M. Rockstein, pp. 461–533. New York and London: Academic Press.

Saunders, D. S. (1978*a*). An experimental and theoretical analysis of photoperiodic induction in the flesh-fly, *Sarcophaga argyrostoma*. *Journal of Comparative Physiology*, **124**, 75–95.

Saunders, D. S. (1978*b*). Internal and external coincidence and the apparent diversity of photoperiodic clocks in the insects. *Journal of Comparative Physiology*, **127**, 197–207.

Saunders, D. S. (1979). External coincidence and the photoinducible phase in the *Sarcophaga* photoperiodic clock. *Journal of Comparative Physiology*, **132**, 179–89.

B. K. FOLLETT

6 Photoperiodic physiology in animals

6.1 Introduction

Clear adaptive advantages exist in restricting parts of the life cycle to the optimal time of the year, a fact particularly true in temperate regions where the climate changes markedly. To survive winter, insects enter diapause, many mammals hibernate and change their coats, whilst birds often migrate to warmer parts of the world. In contrast, spring and summer offer an abundance of food and so animals usually reproduce at these times. What is not so obvious is that animals *anticipate* the arrival of winter or spring. This is a necessity because the relevant physiological changes do not take place instantly: fur cannot be changed overnight, nor can gonad growth and reproduction be compressed into less than about two months in any vertebrate, and in insects autumnal acclimatisation to low temperature takes several weeks.

To effect this seasonal anticipation, animals use environmental factors as cues, natural selection ensuring that the factor chosen is predictable and stable from year to year. In middle and high latitudes, this requirement is most readily met by the annual change in day-length, and many processes in many species are thus photoperiodically regulated (§ 5.1, 7.1). Long-day responses include breeding in both vertebrates and insects, spring moulting, and, especially in birds, migration to higher latitudes (§4.7). The shortening days of autumn induce breeding in other species, a second moult, return migration, hibernation, and in invertebrates, diapause.

Photoperiodism can be considered as involving two sets of components. First, there is a photoperiodic clock mechanism which includes both a photoreceptor to detect light and a clock to measure its duration, the clock being constructed so that it can distinguish 'long' from 'short', since what constitutes a long day for one species may not be so for another. The critical day-length is highly adaptive, and in any one species is usually related to the latitudinal range of the habitat, as illustrated, for example, both by the onset of diapause in the geographical races of the moth, *Acronycta rumicis*, and by breeding seasons of ducks and geese (§5.2.1 and see Murton & Westwood,

1977). The second component includes the neural and endocrine mechanisms that cause the physiological response that is actually observed, for example, diapause, breeding, moult, etc. These responses are evidently linked to the clock but are not part of it and can function quite independently (see also §5.2.2).

Despite the dominant role of photoperiod in seasonal physiological adjustment, it should be realised that other environmental factors, especially temperature, may have key modifying actions. Temperature differences, for example, though having little effect on the critical photoperiod (Fig. 5.1**B**), often markedly affect the intensity of the photoperiodically-induced response. Thus the critical day-length for diapause in the flesh fly (*Sarcophaga*) is 14 h at all temperatures from 15 to 25 °C, but whereas 100% diapause occurs in this photoperiod at 15 °C, at 20 °C the maximum response is in 80% of pupae, and at 25 °C in only 10%. Likewise, cold weather in the spring can delay egg-laying in the great tit (*Parus major*) by some weeks.

In only a few species is much known about the physiology of photoperiodism. Most work has been carried out on reproduction in higher vertebrates, and this is considered in some detail below, not least because it exemplifies the diversity of photoperiodic mechanisms and reminds one that convergent evolution is a pervasive force. At the end of the chapter the physiology of photoperiodism in insects and some commercial aspects of the subject are considered.

6.2   Photoperiodic control of reproduction in vertebrates

In most vertebrates living outside tropical regions, the annual breeding cycle is regulated by photoperiod. Virtually all birds are long-day species (p. 66), and this applies also to many smaller mammals such as mice, voles and ferets. In mammals like the sheep and red deer, which have longer gestation periods, the shortening days of autumn trigger breeding, the young being born the following spring. The horse, with a pregnancy of nearly one year, uses long days to initiate ovarian development. Amongst lower vertebrates, long days are important in many fish (e.g. stickleback, catfish, minnow) and in some reptiles. Trout, on the other hand, are typical winter breeders and for them short days are important in inducing spawning.

Fig. 6.1 shows the various phases in the annual cycle of the white-crowned sparrow, a highly photoperiodic species that has been intensively investigated by Farner and his colleagues (Wingfield & Farner, 1980). After the vernal equinox (see the Glossary), the lengthening days on the wintering grounds in California not only induce gonadal growth but also cause a hyperphagia that results in the laying down of fat (for migration), a pre-nuptial moult, and migratory behaviour. The birds arrive on the breeding grounds in Alaska in May and by mid-June the young are fledged. One important extra adaptation then appears. Despite the days being extremely long, the gonads suddenly collapse: the birds have become refractory to photostimulation. This device of refractoriness has been evolved in virtually all birds and mammals (see Farner & Follett, 1979; Follett & Robinson, 1980) and ensures that breeding stops before environmental conditions deteriorate. In mid-July another moult occurs, followed by a bout of pre-migratory fattening, the birds leaving Alaska in late August and arriving in California a month later. The short days of autumn dissipate the refractory state so that the birds can again respond to the lengthening photoperiods in the new year.

This is a fairly complicated example of an annual cycle but it is not atypical. The precise times of gonadal growth and the duration of the breeding period vary from species to species, but the pattern remains similar. For example, the rook breeds early in the year and has a single clutch, so that it has functional gonads for only six weeks beginning in late February; it then becomes refractory. In contrast, a multi-brooded species like the quail has large gonads for four months and only ceases breeding in late August. Such protracted seasons are also found in long-day rodents which produce several litters (for example, the bank vole, *Microtus agrestis*) and in the horse. The

Fig. 6.1. The annual cycle of the white-crowned sparrow, *Zonotrichia leucophrys*. See text for explanation. (From Farner & Follett, 1979.)

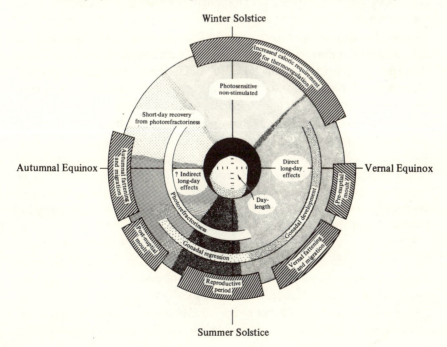

converse situation exists in short-day breeders, of course, but oestrous cycles can occur every 18 days from October until March in red-deer hinds so long as pregnancy is prevented. In sheep, there is much variation between commercial breeds, but in the Suffolk breed oestrous cycles of the ewes begin in August and end about six months later.

At a physiological level these seasonal cycles have been investigated in species that take readily to captivity and in which the photoperiodic responses can be mimicked artificially. Most information has come from the investigations on about a dozen birds (Galliformes – Japanese quail and grouse; Passeriformes – white-crowned sparrows, house sparrows, canary and starling; Anseriformes – domestic ducks, the mallard and green-winged teal; Columbiformes – pigeon and ring-dove), four long-day mammals (golden and Siberian hamsters, vole and ferret) and the short-day sheep (Suffolk and Soay breeds).

6.2.1   *Endocrine changes*

The primary effect of photoperiod is to alter gonadotrophin secretion from the pituitary gland. This is seen most readily when animals are exposed to an abrupt change in day-length; Fig. 6.2 (cf. Fig. 5.1A) shows results for male Japanese quail, and Soay sheep rams. In both cases, FSH (follicle-stimulating hormone) secretion increases many-fold following the change in photoperiod, and this causes rapid testicular growth and spermatogenesis. As the testes mature, FSH secretion diminishes to a level about five times higher than in the sexually immature animal. This decrease is necessary to stop further testicular growth, and since it does not occur in castrates, the feedback agents responsible for damping down FSH output must be gonadal in origin. Sex steroids, for example testosterone, are certainly involved, but there may also be an action by inhibin, a hormone which is thought to depress FSH secretion preferentially. The changes in LH (luteinizing hormone) secretion are also marked. In quail, the level increases ten-fold during the first week but then remains relatively constant. LH acts upon the testicular interstitial cells to stimulate testosterone secretion and in turn this is involved in triggering sexual behaviour, the growth of secondary sexual characters, spermatogenesis, and in controlling LH (and FSH) secretion by negative feedback onto the pituitary gland complex.

Similar changes in LH secretion occur in Soay sheep transferred to short days, although the manner in which LH is secreted in large mammals means that the alterations in overall levels are not as obvious as in quail (Fig. 6.2). LH is not secreted continuously but periodically in bursts lasting for a few minutes. It has been shown that under stimulatory short days the frequency of this episodic LH secretion is increased, leading to enhanced testosterone output (Fig. 6.2). This suggests that photoperiod acts by altering the frequency at which the hypothalamic neurones release Gn-RH (gonado-trophin-releasing hormone) into the portal vessels running from the median eminence to the pituitary. There may well be a hypothalamic timer that causes a brief discharge of Gn-RH at regular intervals, and day-length may alter the rate at which this operates. Whether species like the quail exhibit similar frequency modulation of Gn-RH release is not clear. Indeed, LH is high at

Fig. 6.2. Changes in follicle-stimulating hormone (FSH), luteinizing hormone (LH) and testosterone in the blood (plasma levels), and testicular size, in Japanese quail (**A**) and Soay sheep (**B**) transferred from non-stimulatory to photostimulatory day-lengths, and back again. LD, long days; SD, short days. See text for explanation. (Adapted from Follett, 1978.)

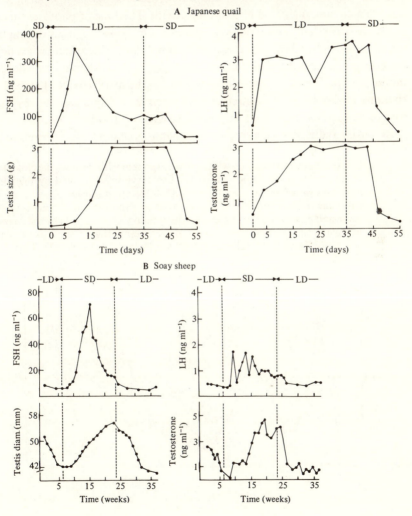

all times in photostimulated quail, suggesting that the effect is to increase the steady-state secretion of Gn-RH rather than to alter the rate of episodic secretion.

Apart, therefore, from the obvious difference in time – 28 days in quail, 120 days in sheep – there are remarkable similarities between the photo-periodically-induced changes in gonadotrophin secretion in birds and mammals.

6.2.2   *Photoperiodic time measurement*

Many birds and mammals monitor the seasonal change in day-length by using their circadian system (see the Glossary) as a photoperiodic clock. The best-known model of how this might occur supposes the animal to possess a circadian rhythm in photosensitivity. The time of photosensitivity is species-dependent but in long-day animals is imagined to occur during the night, 12–24 h after dawn. Photoperiodic stimulation occurs if and when light coincides with this phase of photosensitivity (ϕ_i; the 'external coincidence' model (§5.5)). The experiments used to test for the involvement of circadian rhythms in day-length measurement are complicated because the rhythms cannot be measured directly; they are discussed in detail in §5.3.

In birds, induction is a rapid event and gonadotrophin secretion is

Fig. 6.3. An experiment on white-crowned sparrows that shows the circadian rhythm in photoperiodic sensitivity. The curve was obtained by releasing sparrows ($n = 198$) on day 1 from LD 8:16 into darkness. At each of 21 subsequent times the rhythm was assayed by exposing birds to an 8-h light pulse and measuring the degree of induction (on a scale 0 to 1) by the change in plasma LH. The number of birds at each point ranges from 6 to 16; bars, $\pm$ s.e. (Redrawn from Follett, Mattocks & Farner, 1974.) (See also Figs. 5.4, 7.5**B**).

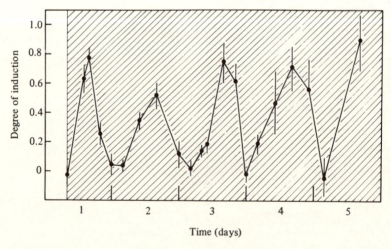

increased at the end of the first long day (Follett, Davies & Gledhill, 1977). This speed of response allows various experiments, two of which will be mentioned. First, it permits a simple test of the hypothesis that animals measure day-length using a circadian clock. In one experiment, white-crowned sparrows were held on short days and then placed in continuous darkness to allow any circadian rhythms to free run (Fig. 6.3). At a different time over the next five days each bird was exposed to a *single* 8-h light pulse. This light tested whether or not the bird was photoperiodically sensitive at the time when the pulse was given, any elevation in the level of plasma LH 6 h after the pulse indicating induction. In effect, the light pulse was being used as a probe to assess the status and position of the circadian photoperiodic rhythm. As Fig. 6.3 indicates, there seems little doubt that photoperiodic sensitivity is circadian based, the rhythm free ran for five cycles in darkness and showed no signs of damping out.

A second type of experiment directly measures the time course of hormonal output triggered by the circadian clock. Individual quail were moved from short days of 8 h light:16 h dark (LD 8:16) to long days of LD 20:4 and blood samples were taken every few hours (Fig. 6.4). During the first day,

Fig. 6.4. Plasma LH levels (see Fig. 6.2) in two male quail during the first two days of exposure to long days (LD 20:4; darkness shown by bars). (From Follett *et al.*, 1977.)

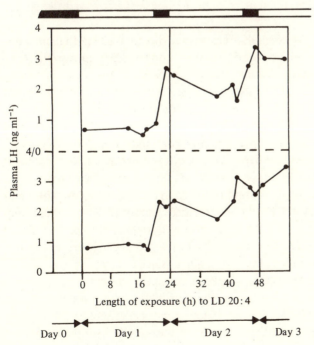

LH levels were low until about hour 18 when they rose abruptly. Secretion then remained steady until another rise occurred at the same time on the second day. It appears that the rises are a direct expression of the photoperiodic clock, reflecting a decision taken at about hour 16 that the day is long, which leads to rises in LH and FSH secretion at the same time on successive long days. The photosensitive phase (ϕ_i) in quail seems to last for about 4 h each day (12–16 h after dawn), light during this period triggering gonadal growth but not being inductive at other times. A dramatic example of this occurs in night-break experiments. Treating quail with a schedule of LD 6:18 which also includes a 15 min light pulse 13 h after dawn, causes nearly as rapid testicular growth as does LD 13:11, but if the pulse is located 17 h after dawn there is no growth.

The finding that birds, rodents and possibly sheep use a circadian timing mechanism (see Fig. 5.4) points to another similarity between the photoperiodic mechanisms of higher vertebrates but, as the next section shows, this does not extend to the photo-neuroendocrine machinery in the brain.

6.2.3   *Bird photo-neuroendocrine mechanisms*

The differences between birds and mammals can be readily appreciated when it is realised that birds use a non-retinal photoreceptor to detect light for the photoperiodic response whereas mammals use their eyes, and that the pineal organ has quite different roles in the house sparrow and the golden hamster.

Selective destruction of small areas within the quail's hypothalamus has pin-pointed three regions as essential for the photoperiodic response (Fig. 6.5). The functions of these regions are still unclear, but several intriguing possibilities exist. The first relates to the photoreceptor. It is 45 years since Benoit showed the eye to be unnecessary for seasonal gonadal growth in ducks, and since then it has been firmly established that the primary light receptor for a range of photoperiodic processes, including gonadal growth, migratory behaviour and fat deposition, is extraretinal. A simple experiment by Menaker, Roberts, Elliott & Underwood (1970) makes the point.

One group of sexually immature house sparrows (testicular weight 6 mg) had the feathers plucked from the skin on their skulls whilst in another group Indian Ink was painted over the skull surface. Both groups were then placed on long days of dim light. After six weeks the testes in the bald group weighed 323 mg, those in the Indian Ink group 8 mg. Since the eyes were present in both groups the difference must have been due to the amount of light passing directly through the skull to reach the non-retinal photoreceptor. Later, Oliver & Baylé (1976) in France placed micropellets ($600 \times 200 \ \mu$m) of radio-luminous paint in different parts of the quail's hypothalamus and discovered that implants in the posterior tuberal hypothalamus, but not in the anterior region (see Fig. 6.5), caused testicular growth. This suggests that the light receptor lies within the tuberal hypothalamus, but as yet no structure has been found in this area with the characteristics of a photoreceptor. Possibly, the receptor is some type of light-activated protein lying in the cell membrane.

The location of the photoperiodic clock in birds remains puzzling. Various experiments have shown the pineal to be important and capable of regulating other clock functions, notably circadian periodicity, via the rhythmic secretion of melatonin (§ 11.4.2, 11.5.2). However, its removal has little effect on the photoperiodic response, arguing that the photoperiodic clock itself must lie elsewhere in the brain. Lesions in both the anterior and posterior hypothalamus (Fig. 6.5) can upset circadian functions, but the effects are not dramatic and it is difficult to believe that lesions in this area block photo-induced growth by stopping the quail's capacity to measure day-length (Fig. 5.1A). It must be remembered, of course, that the Gn-RH cell bodies (§6.2.1) also lie in the hypothalamus, and their destruction would inevitably stop gonadal growth. At the moment there is evidence for them occurring in both the anterior and tuberal hypothalamus.

To summarise: birds detect light with non-retinal photoreceptors, some of which lie in the tuberal hypothalamus; photoperiod duration is measured by the circadian system; if the day is long, increased Gn-RH secretion occurs and hence LH and FSH secretion.

Fig. 6.5. Sagittal section through the quail's brain (bird looking left) showing those hypothalamic regions (hatched) where lesions block photoperiodically-induced gonadal growth: 1, in preoptic area; 2, in median eminence; 3, in posterior infundibular region. Black dot shows approximate position of suprachiasmatic nuclei (SCN), cf. Fig. 6.6. (Adapted from Davies & Follett, 1975.)

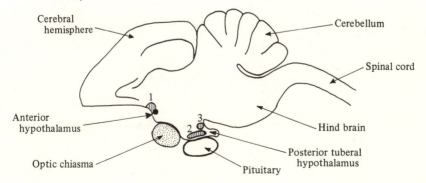

6.2.4   *Mammal photo-neuroendocrine mechanisms*

In rodents, both the eyes and pineal have major functions in photoperiodism (Fig. 6.6). This has been demonstrated most convincingly in the golden hamster (Reiter, 1978). A hypothalamic receptor is not involved, and blinding of sexually mature animals on long days causes immediate gonadal regression (even with light bright enough to penetrate into the brain), just as if they had been transferred to short days. Pinealectomy (i.e. removal) prevents this regression. It also leads to rapid testicular growth if carried out on sexually immature hamsters living on short days; in fact pinealectomised hamsters are no longer photoperiodic, and remain in breeding regardless of day-length. This has led to the conclusion that under short days a pineal hormone somehow manages to suppress reproduction either directly or indirectly, whereas in long days, either the secretory pattern of this hormone is altered or there is a change in the target tissues and, whichever holds true,

Fig. 6.6. Diagrammatic representation of the innervation of the pineal gland in the rodent; the view is from above and is not to scale; see also Figs. 6.5 and 11.4. (Adapted from Moore, 1978.)

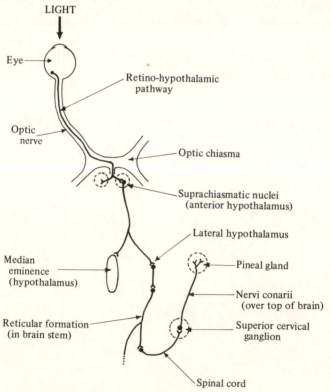

the hamster grows its gonads. As a result of this system, particular emphasis is laid on the shortening days of autumn which cause gonadal regression via the pineal (cf. quail). Growth in spring comes about spontaneously as, somehow, the 'anti-gonadotrophic' effects of the pineal are overcome or become ineffective. In addition, once the hamsters break hibernation they are exposed to long days and this inhibits the pineal.

The results of some surgical experiments that have attempted to unravel the photo-neuroendocrine pathways are shown in Fig. 6.7. The pineal 'anti-gonadotrophin' may be melatonin, and certainly implants of this indole cause testicular regression in hamsters. However, the pineal produces other indoles and peptides as well and these may also be involved. How the

Fig. 6.7. Summary of the surgical procedures carried out in golden hamsters that lead to the conclusion that a pineal 'anti-gonadotrophin' is heavily involved in seasonal breeding of mammals. The bold crosses represent the site of the lesion, the thickness of the arrows showing the degree of 'anti-gonadotrophic' activity released from the pineal. SCG, superior cervical ganglia; SCN, suprachiasmatic nuclei. (From Reiter, 1978.)

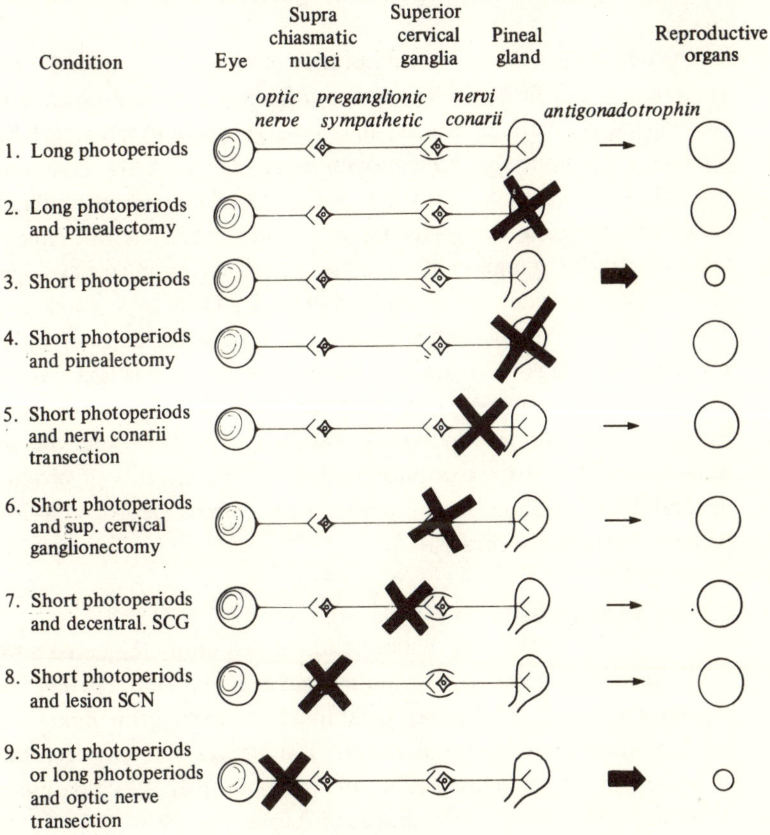

Condition	Eye	Supra chiasmatic nuclei	Superior cervical ganglia	Pineal gland	Reproductive organs
		optic nerve	*preganglionic sympathetic*	*nervi conarii*	*antigonadotrophin*
1. Long photoperiods					
2. Long photoperiods and pinealectomy					
3. Short photoperiods					
4. Short photoperiods and pinealectomy					
5. Short photoperiods and nervi conarii transection					
6. Short photoperiods and sup. cervical ganglionectomy					
7. Short photoperiods and decentral. SCG					
8. Short photoperiods and lesion SCN					
9. Short photoperiods or long photoperiods and optic nerve transection					

'anti-gonadotrophic' action of the pineal is mediated remains unknown. The pattern of melatonin release may be different under short and long days, and this may be sufficient for it to act centrally to suppress gonadotrophin secretion. Alternatively, its site of action may be in a different state under short days, so rendering it sensitive to the anti-gonadotrophic properties of melatonin.

As to the clock itself, knowledge is more advanced in rodents than in birds. Destruction of the suprachiasmatic nuclei (SCN) that lie in the anterior hypothalamus upsets many circadian functions (§11.4.2). In the hamster it also leads to the loss of the photoperiodic response, the gonads promptly growing if the animals are living in short days. There are various possibilities as to why this should occur. Perhaps the lesions upset the rhythmic output of the pineal, so making it less effective, or they may alter the photoperiodic clock, so rendering it incapable of responding to the pineal's message.

To summarise: hamsters use some component in their eyes to detect light; information probably flows from the eye to the SCN by a retino-hypothalamic tract; the light's duration is presumably measured in the SCN by a circadian clock.

The next stages are unknown but they must involve the sending of signals via a neural link through the brain, out from the spinal cord to the superior cervical ganglion and thence via an adrenergic nerve to the pineal. The pineal secretes a hormone that seems to suppress LH and FSH secretion through an action on the clock. To what extent this arrangement applies to other seasonally breeding mammals has yet to be established, but removal of the superior cervical ganglion in Soay sheep leads to testicular development and an inability to switch off reproduction under long days (Lincoln & Short, 1980). As pineal removal affects seasonal processes other than reproduction, for example pelage (fur) change and fat deposition, it is now suspected that melatonin acts more as a transducer of seasonal information to the brain, rather than being merely 'anti-gonadotrophic'. However, the somewhat different system existing in birds underlines the hazards of propounding a generalised physiological mechanism for the photo-neuroendocrine control of gonadotrophin secretion.

6.3   Photoperiodism in insects

Probably the most widespread, and certainly the best-known use of photoperiodism in insects is to control seasonal diapause, but day-length also regulates many other processes, including body form, growth rate, migration, fat deposition and winter coloration. The whole topic has been the subject of numerous reviews (Lees, 1955, 1973; Danilevskii, 1965; Saunders, 1976; de Wilde, 1978; Beck, 1980; and see Chapter 5).

6.3.1 *Diapause*

Diapause is a type of dormancy (see the Glossary) widely used by insects to avoid harsh conditions. It involves a shutdown of the neuroendocrine system and usually lasts for many weeks. In temperate regions, day-length and temperature are key influences in its regulation. While no single type of response exists for all species, it is often the case (Tauber & Tauber, 1976) that shortening days induce diapause, and that this is aided by relatively warm temperatures. Diapause is then maintained by short days, but, as autumn proceeds, changes occur; the photoperiodic response becomes less intense, whilst the cold actually begins to promote development. Diapause usually ends, therefore, after the winter solstice, without the intervention of a specific stimulus but after a minimal period in dormancy of some weeks. There are some insects, however (e.g. the oak silkworm, *Antheraea pernyi*), where diapause is terminated by long days. Diapause can occur at any stage in the life cycle: many species have a larval diapause (for example the corn borer, *Ostrinia nubilalis*); butterflies and moths commonly have a pupal diapause; beetles an adult (reproductive) diapause; and some species (for example the silkworm, *Bombyx mori*) diapause as eggs. In these different situations the photoperiodic effect is mediated by various endocrine routes, three of which are shown in Fig. 6.8.

In species with pupal diapause, the short days suppress the secretion of prothoracotropic hormone (PTTH) from the corpora cardiaca, thus decreasing ecdysone release and so stopping growth and development (Fig. 6.8A). This may also be true for some cases of larval diapause, but at least in the caterpillars of some moths, short days cause a reduction in juvenile hormone secretion which leads to a moult into a diapausing caterpillar; long days cause a still greater fall in juvenile hormone and the caterpillar then pupates. For pupal diapause, experiments with *Antheraea pernyi* (Williams, 1969) suggest that the photoreceptors lie in the brain, not the eyes or ocelli, and that the photoperiodic clock may be located in the protocerebrum. The clock acts on the neurosecretory cells in the pars intercerebralis which synthesise PTTH, and which terminate in the corpora cardiaca.

A somewhat different situation holds in insects like the Colorado beetle, *Leptinotarsa decemlineata*, which show adult diapause for 7–8 months each year (de Wilde, 1978). In the autumn, reproduction and feeding cease, there is a drop in the metabolic rate and the animals often burrow. Light is again detected by a brain photoreceptor but the site of the photoperiodic clock is not known. Under short days some of the medial neurosecretory cells in the pars intercerebralis become inactive. The axons of these cells terminate in the corpora allata and control juvenile hormone secretion. Thus in winter, juvenile hormone secretion is lowered and this stops yolk synthesis and oogenesis; long days re-activate the system and cause egg-laying (Fig. 6.8 B).

An even more intriguing control system exists in those insects where day-length acts on the mother and she produces diapausing or non-diapausing offspring. The best known example is the silkworm, *Bombyx mori* (Fig. 6.8 C). If female silkworms are exposed to long days when they are eggs or young larvae, then as adults they secrete a neurosecretory diapause hormone from the suboesophageal ganglion. This enters the eggs and causes them to diapause at a very early stage in development. Refinements to this arrangement exist in various insects of which the most studied is the parasitic wasp, *Nasonia vitripennis* (Saunders, 1976). In this species, diapause occurs in the fourth instar, just before the pupal ecdysis, but whether or not it takes place depends upon the photoperiod to which the *mother* was exposed. Changing the day-lengths under which the larvae are developing has no influence on their type of development (diapause or non-diapause); it was pre-programmed into them while they were still embryos within the mother's ovary.

Fig. 6.8. Schemes showing the control of diapause in three types of insect. (A) Larval–pupal diapause, as in the oak silkworm, *Antheraea pernyi*. (B) Adult reproductive diapause, as in the Colorado beetle, *Leptinotarsa decemlineata*. (C) Diapause in eggs, as induced in the silkworm, *Bombyx mori*. Active glands shown in black, inactive glands marked with a star. Short and long refer to the experimental day-lengths used, as indicated by the circles above (nights stippled). (Adapted from Saunders, 1976.)

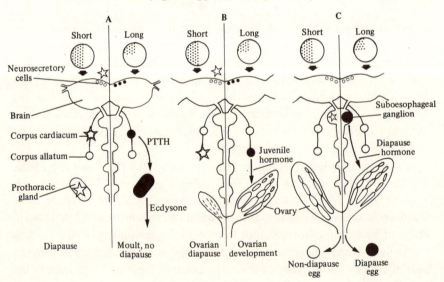

6.3.2 *Aphid polymorphism*

Aphids have elaborated a breeding system giving them the evolutionary advantages of both sexual and asexual (parthenogenetic) reproduction. In the vetch aphid, *Megoura viciae*, the switch from one form to another is controlled by photoperiod and has been extensively analysed by Lees (e.g. 1973). Eggs overwinter in diapause and then develop into adults that reproduce sexually and are oviparous. Once the day-lengths exceed 14.5 h, however, the females switch to parthenogenesis and produce asexual females by viviparity. These mature and continue reproducing parthenogenetically until the photoperiod falls to below 14.5 h when they revert to sexual reproduction and lay eggs. One consequence of man's activities in developing greenhouses, and thereby obliterating the annual cycle, has been the appearance of wholly asexual strains of aphids.

As in *Nasonia* (above), the photoperiodic control is exercised maternally. The embryos developing in parthenogenetic females pass through a stage when they can be switched into one of two pathways, either towards development as another parthenogenetic female or towards development as an egg-laying female. This is determined by the photoperiod being experienced by the mother. A recent series of experiments by Steel (1976) has established more about the pathways involved. The vital neuroendocrine control is exercised by ten neurosecretory neurones lying medially in the protocerebrum. The axons of these cells do not terminate in the corpora cardiaca or allata (cf. Fig. 6.8) but can be traced down the ventral nerve cord and into the thoracic ganglionic mass. They probably terminate in the ovary, where it is thought they deliver their neurosecretory product locally near the embryos. Under long days the cells are active and promote the development of parthenogenetic females. They are switched off under short days and the embryos then develop into oviparous females. The photoperiodic clock *and* its photoreceptor lie in the brain slightly lateral to the neurosecretory cell bodies. No special cytological features have been observed in these areas, however, a situation reminiscent of the non-retinal photoreceptor in birds (§6.2.3).

6.4   Conclusions

In this survey it has been possible to deal with only a few examples of animal photoperiodic physiology, and even these have been oversimplified. They do reflect, however, the balance of present-day research, with its emphasis on reproduction, diapause and polymorphism. It is to be hoped that the future will see other processes being studied, and it would be especially valuable to analyse a number of photoperiodic phenomena within one species in order to distinguish between clock-controlled events and those physiological processes coupled to the clock. Photoperiodism is widespread because it can so accurately synchronise particular parts of the life cycle to the time of the year, and one suspects that its adaptive value stretches beyond seasonal breeding and diapause to pervade many aspects of an organism's physiology.

The extent to which research on photoperiodism is supported by Government funds emphasises that it is important not only to academic biology, but also to agriculture. Long photoperiods prevent a decline in egg production by chickens in winter, and allow turkeys to be bred throughout the year. Even though such treatments are standard practice, further improvement should be possible. The development of refractoriness in turkeys on long days is one reason for their poor egg production of about a hundred (as compared with 270 in egg-laying strains of chickens), and this might be overcome with more sophisticated photoperiodic arrangements. The horse-racing industry assigns an arbitrary birth date of 1 January to all foals born in that year. This avoids some problems, but does encourage the breeding of mares early in the year when the ovary is not at peak performance, the main oestrous period being April–June. As a result, the photostimulation of mares to hasten oestrus is being applied at some thoroughbred studs. Other examples where manipulation of day-length could be valuable include the induction of oestrus in sheep after spring lambing, and the smoothing out of fry production in trout farms by ensuring mature females at all times of the year. For insect pests on glasshouse crops, diapause can be manipulated by light-regime changes. A final important application comes from cattle (Tucker & Oxender, 1980): cows exposed to long days through the winter months yield 6–8% more milk than do controls on natural day-lengths. Similarly, such long days may also accelerate the growth rates of heifers by 10–15% at relatively constant levels of feed utilisation. The effects may be due to enhanced prolactin secretion, but whatever their cause they warrant extensive farm trials.

6.5   Further reading and key references

Books and review articles are indicated by asterisks

*Beck, S. D. (1980). *Insect Photoperiodism*. 2nd edn. New York: Academic Press.

*Danilevskii, A. S. (1965). *Photoperiodism and Seasonal Development of Insects*, 1st English edition. Edinburgh and London: Oliver & Boyd.

Davies, D. T. & Follett, B. K. (1975). The neuroendocrine control of gonadotrophin release in the Japanese quail. *Proceedings of the Royal Society of London* B, **191**, 285–315.

*Farner, D. S. & Follett, B. K. (1979). Reproductive periodicity in birds. In *Hormones and Evolution*, **2**, ed. E. J. W. Barrington, pp. 829–72. London: Academic Press.

*Follett, B. K. (1978). Photoperiodism and seasonal breeding in birds and mammals. In *Control of Ovulation*, ed. D. B. Crighton, N. B. Haynes, G. R. Foxcroft & G. E. Lamming, pp. 267–94. London: Butterworths.

*Follett, B. K. & Follett, D. E. (Eds.) (1981). *Biological Clocks in Seasonal Reproductive Cycles*, 288 pp. Bristol: John Wright.

*Follett, B. K. & Robinson, J. E. (1980). Photoperiod and gonadotrophin secretion in birds. In *Progress in Reproductive Biology*, **5**, ed. R. J. Reiter & B. K. Follett, pp. 39–61. Basel: S. Karger AG.

Follett, B. K., Davies, D. T. & Gledhill, B. (1977). Photoperiodic control of reproduction in Japanese quail: changes in gonadotrophin secretion on the first day of induction and their pharmacological blockade. *Journal of Endocrinology*, **74**, 449–60.

Follett, B. K., Mattocks, P. W. & Farner, D. S. (1974). Circadian function in the photoperiodic induction of gonadotrophin secretion in the white-crowned sparrow. *Proceedings of the National Academy of Sciences, U.S.A.*, **71**, 1666–9.

*Lees, A. D. (1955). *The Physiology of Diapause in Arthropods*. Cambridge: Cambridge University Press.

*Lees, A. D. (1973). Photoperiodic time-measurement in the aphid *Megoura viciae*. *Journal of Insect Physiology*, **19**, 2279–316.

Lincoln, G. A. & Short, R. V. (1980). Seasonal breeding: nature's contraceptive. *Recent Progress in Hormone Research*, **36**, 1–52.

Menaker, M., Roberts, R., Elliott, J. A. & Underwood, H. (1970). Extra-retinal light perception in the sparrow. III. The eyes do not participate in photoperiodic photoreception. *Proceedings of the National Academy of Sciences, U.S.A.*, **67**, 320–5.

*Moore, R. Y. (1978). The innervation of the mammalian pineal gland. In *Progress in Reproductive Biology*, **4**, ed. R. J. Reiter, pp. 1–29. Basel: S. Karger AG.

*Murton, R. K. & Westwood, N. J. (1977). *Avian Breeding Cycles*. Oxford: Clarendon Press.

Oliver, J. & Baylé, J.-D. (1976). The involvement of the preoptic-suprachiasmatic region in the photosexual reflex of the quail: effects of selective lesions and photic stimulation. *Journale de Physiologie, Paris*, **72**, 627–37.

*Reiter, R. J. (1978). Interaction of photoperiod, pineal and seasonal reproduction as exemplified by findings in the hamster. In *Progress in Reproductive Biology*, **4**, ed. R. J. Reiter, pp. 169–90. Basel: S. Karger AG.

*Saunders, D. S. (1976). *Insect Clocks*. 279 pp. Oxford: Pergamon Press.

Steel, C. G. H. (1976). Neurosecretory control of polymorphism in aphids. In *Phase and Caste Determination in Insects*, ed. M. Lüscher, pp. 117–30. Oxford: Pergamon Press.

*Tauber, M. J. & Tauber, C. A. (1976). Insect seasonality: diapause maintenance, termination and postdiapause development. *Annual Review of Entomology*, **21**, 81–107.

Tucker, H. A. & Oxender, W. D. (1980). Seasonal aspects of reproduction, growth and hormones in cattle and horses. In *Progress in Reproductive Biology*, **5**, ed. R. J. Reiter & B. K. Follett, pp. 155–80. Basel: S. Karger AG.

*de Wilde, J. (1978). Seasonal states and endocrine levels in insects. In *Environmental Endocrinology*, ed. I. Assenmacher & D. S. Farner, pp. 10–19. Berlin: Springer-Verlag.

Williams, C. M. (1969). Photoperiodism and the endocrine aspects of insect diapause. *Symposia of the Society for Experimental Biology*, **23**, 285–300.

Wingfield, J. C. & Farner, D. S. (1980). Control of seasonal reproduction in temperate-zone birds. In *Progress in Reproductive Biology*, **5**, ed. R. J. Reiter & B. K. Follett, pp. 61–101. Basel: S. Karger AG.

DAPHNE VINCE-PRUE

7 Phytochrome and photoperiodic physiology in plants

7.1 Introduction

Photoperiodic responses in plants and animals exhibit a number of common features in their formal properties, which may indicate control by the same kind of underlying clock (§5.2). On the other hand, it is clear that in the two kingdoms quite different photoreceptor pigments are involved in the perception of the light signals which act as zeitgebers in photoperiodic time measurement. The subsequent effector pathways must also be different, but in plants a great deal more is known about the photoreceptive pigment itself than about the biochemical changes that follow its activation, whereas for many animal responses the reverse is true (§6.1). Consequently, this chapter is largely devoted to a consideration of phytochrome, the red/far-red photoreversible pigment which, in higher plants, is probably the only photoperiodic photoreceptor.

A great many adaptive responses of plants are under the control of day-length, the one environmental factor which from year to year gives totally reliable information about the passage of the seasons (§5.1). For example, day-length signals may synchronise the energy demands of reproduction with the season of greatest light receipt or, as with autumnal short days for trees of high latitudes, induce bud dormancy and low-temperature hardiness to enable the plant to survive the following winter. In other species, the formation of resting structures may be induced by long-day conditions which accompany or precede a period of water stress. Even in tropical latitudes, many plants are responsive to day-length and may utilise this signal to synchronise flowering or other activities with seasonal events such as dry or rainy periods.

The switch from vegetative growth to flowering is under day-length control in many plants. In most of these, floral induction requires repeated exposures to appropriate day-length cycles but there are a few plants (e.g. *Xanthium strumarium*, *Pharbitis nil* cv. Violet, *Lolium temulentum* cv. Ceres) where a single photoperiod cycle of the correct length can effect the transition to reproduction. As it is relatively easy to give complex experimental treatments during a single 24-h cycle, such plants have been intensively studied and many current ideas about the photoperiodic mechanism are based on studies of floral induction in them, and in some other plants (e.g. *Perilla* spp.), which require only a few inductive photoperiodic cycles. However, other processes, such as tuber formation and dormancy, are also photoperiodically regulated by mechanisms that apparently operate in a manner similar to that which controls floral induction, even though the ultimate effector pathways are different.

In all cases, the consequence of exposing plants to particular photoperiods is the generation of a hormonal stimulus which evokes responses in target cells remote from the site of photoperiodic induction. The stimulus appears to travel largely in the phloem and has been shown to arrive at the target sites a few hours after the end of a particular day-length cycle (Fig. 7.1). Thus, photoperiodic induction in plants leads rapidly to the synthesis or release of a hormonal stimulus from the photoreceptive sites in the leaves or cotyledons.

The subject has been regularly reviewed, for example by Evans (1969, 1971), Vince-Prue (1975) and Zeevaart (1976).

7.2   The properties and functions of phytochrome

Understanding the role of phytochrome in photoperiodism is complicated by the fact that this photoreceptor pigment also controls a multitude of direct responses to light, that is responses that do not have a timing component and are collectively referred to as photomorphogenesis (see Smith, 1975). For example, the transition of an etiolated seedling raised in darkness to a normal green plant following exposure to light involves many phytochrome-mediated changes which are independent of photoperiodism. Phytochrome has been detected *in situ* in, or extracted from, all parts of higher plants, including coleoptiles, roots, leaves, buds, inflorescences and developing fruits, and it is thought to play a major functional role in the control of all adaptive responses of plants to their light environment.

In contrast to this location of phytochrome throughout the plant, photoperiodic perception is largely confined to young leaves, where exposure to light–dark cycles of appropriate duration leads to the production of a stimulus which is translocated to target cells in stem apices (e.g. transition to reproduction, flower development and bud dormancy); stolon tips (tuber formation); roots (root tubers); other leaves (leaf expansion); or stem sub-apical meristems (elongation). In some plants other receptor sites can function in photoperiodic induction (e.g. regenerating buds or stem tissue in internode segments of *Plumbago indica*) but it is not known what features of the organ and/or cell enable phytochrome to elicit photoperiodic responses.

Phytochrome is a chromophoric protein with a molecular weight of about

120 000 Daltons, the chromophore being a non-cyclic tetrapyrrole similar to the phycocyanin pigments of blue-green algae (Kendrick & Spruit, 1977; Pratt, 1978). The pigment exists in two forms, namely P_r (absorbing mainly red light) and P_{fr} (absorbing mainly far-red light), and these two isomers are interconvertible by irradiation (Fig. 7.2). Many physiological responses to light are triggered by brief exposure to red light (forming P_{fr}) but are not observed when the red light is immediately followed by far-red light, which phototransforms the pigment back to the apparently inactive P_r form:

$$\text{Initial synthesis of phytochrome in darkness} \rightarrow P_r \underset{\substack{\text{in far-red}\\\text{light}}}{\overset{\substack{\text{in red}\\\text{light}}}{\rightleftharpoons}} P_{fr} \rightarrow \text{Observed physiological response}$$

Fig. 7.1. Induction of flowering and translocation of the floral stimulus in the short-day plant *Pharbitis nil*, in which the seedling cotyledons are both the site of photoperiodic detection and the source of flower-inducing hormone. Seedlings were exposed to a single dark period varying from 12 to 24 h (abscissa); on transfer to light they were either left intact (solid circles, the 'production' curve) or their cotyledons were immediately removed (open circles, the 'translocation' curve). When cotyledon removal no longer significantly affected flowering (i.e. after 17–18 h of darkness), it is assumed that the floral stimulus had already arrived at the apex: this therefore occurred 4–5 h after darkness had lasted for the critical night-length of 12.5 h. (From Zeevaart, 1962.)

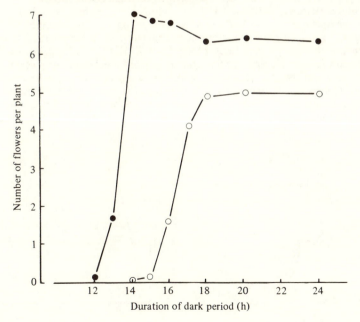

The detection and measurement of phytochrome are usually based on its photoreversible properties. *In vivo* it is estimated by measuring the difference between apparent absorbance at two pre-selected wavelengths, usually 660 nm and 730 nm (which generates the larger signal) or 730 nm and 815 nm (which shows less interference by chlorophyll). The relative amount of phytochrome present is then calculated from the difference before and after irradiation of the sample with 'actinic' red or far-red light, which photo-transform the pigment from one isomer to the other. P_{fr} and P_r can be estimated separately by appropriate irradiation sequences.

This assay for phytochrome is limited by chlorophyll interference (Pratt, 1978) so that *in vivo* measurements cannot be made in green leaves, even though they are the usual sites of photoperiodic perception. However, phytochrome is detectable in some photoperiodically sensitive light-grown tissues that do not have chlorophyll, such as photobleached cotyledons and seedlings grown on herbicide. Research on these may therefore provide a better understanding of the behaviour of phytochrome under different photoperiodic regimes and the consequence of this for photoperiodic induction.

The absorption spectra of P_r and P_{fr} overlap appreciably in the red part of the spectrum (Fig. 7.2A); hence in red light there is a continuous

Fig. 7.2. The absorption spectra of phytochrome and action spectra for three photoperiodic responses. (**A**) The absorption spectra of the P_r and P_{fr} forms of phytochrome (solid lines) and the proportion of phytochrome that is present as P_{fr} at photo-equilibrium as a function of the wavelength shown on the abscissa (dashed line). (After Pratt, 1978.) (**B**) Solid lines, action spectra for the inhibition of flowering by a night-break, and for reversal of this effect in the short-day plant, *Xanthium strumarium* (tested with a brief night-break of less than 0.5 h (see §5.3, and cf. Fig. 6.3). (After Hendricks & Siegelman, 1967.) Broken line, action spectrum for promotion of flowering in the long-day plant, *Hyoscyamus niger*, with a night-break of 8 h. (After Schneider, Borthwick & Hendricks, 1967.)

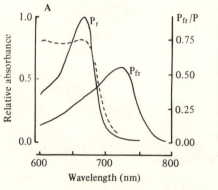 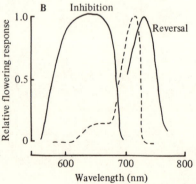

interconversion between P_r and P_{fr} with a dynamic eqilibrium of about 75% P_{fr} and 25% P_r (Pratt, 1978). The wavelengths of sunlight are strongly absorbed by both P_{fr} and P_r so that under natural daylight conditions phytochrome is continuously cycling between the two forms at a rate which is dependent on the irradiance.

Although a brief exposure to red light saturates the photoconversion of P_r to P_{fr}, several light-dependent responses in plants require, or are increased by, continuous irradiation with red *or* far-red light, and are irradiance-dependent. It is commonly thought that such responses are nevertheless mediated by phytochrome, and that they may depend in some way on the continual cycling of the pigment between the two forms, since the interconversion rate will increase with irradiance. Thus phytochrome may operate to control physiological responses in two ways: (1) by a high irradiance reaction where the responses are irradiance-dependent and require the quasi-continuous input of light energy, and (2) by a red/far-red reversible reaction where the responses are dependent on P_{fr} and can continue in darkness if P_{fr} remains in the tissue (Jose & Vince-Prue, 1978).

In addition to its photochemical transformations, phytochrome undergoes a number of non-photochemical reactions (Kendrick & Frankland, 1976; Marmé, 1977; Pratt, 1978) some of which may be important in photoperiodic induction. These are summarised in Fig. 7.3.

Phytochrome is initially synthesised in the much more stable, but probably inactive P_r form; the P_{fr} form is relatively unstable and is converted to a non-photoreversible form by a process called *destruction* (Fig. 7.3), which involves degradation of the protein moiety. As soon as it is formed, some of the P_{fr} rapidly associates with a particulate cell fraction, which appears to consist largely of membrane (see §7.5); following photoconversion to P_r, it disassociates from this only slowly. Destruction may take place entirely from the particulate-bound form (Fig. 7.3). A consequence of the destruction

Fig. 7.3. Schematic representation of the major pathways of phytochrome interconversions.

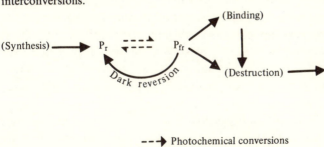

(Synthesis) ⟶ P_r ⇄ P_{fr}

(Binding)

Dark reversion

(Destruction) ⟶

- - ➤ Photochemical conversions

⟶ Thermal (dark) conversions

reaction is that exposure to light causes the total phytochrome content of the tissue to decrease below that present in darkness.

In many plants phytochrome also undergoes a dark process called *reversion*; this is a non-photochemical transformation of P_{fr} to P_r which maintains the photoreversibility and integrity of the molecule (Fig. 7.3). There is evidence that this reaction may take place only from the soluble, unbound form of P_{fr}. Although many models of photoperiodic induction have implicated the dark reversion of the phytochrome molecule to P_r as the basis for time measurement or its initiation, no evidence of this process has ever been obtained in monocotyledons, where all dark loss of P_{fr} appears to occur by destruction, even though the plants are nevertheless photoperiodic.

Most studies of phytochrome have been made on dark-grown etiolated tissues, but there is no reason to suppose that the conclusions drawn from such work do not also apply to green leaves. Nevertheless, few measurements have been made in photoperiodically sensitive tissues and, since the rates and patterns of non-photochemical transformations of phytochrome are known to vary in different organelles and subcellular fractions of the cell (Marmé, 1977), we still lack precise information about the properties of the pool of phytochrome which acts in photoperiodic induction.

7.3   Phytochrome and photoperiodic induction

The classification of plants according to their photoperiodic responses has usually been made on the basis of flowering. These responses seem to be of three basic types: short-day plants (SDP) which only flower, or flower earlier, when days are *shorter* than a critical value; long-day plants (LDP) which only flower, or flower earlier, when days are *longer* than a critical value; and day-neutral plants where day-length has no effect on time of flowering. In a natural 24-h cycle, short days are associated with long nights, and *vice versa*. Time measurement could thus be effected in light or darkness, or in both. From the results of varying the durations of light and darkness independently, early workers were led to conclude that photoperiodic time measurement occurs primarily in darkness and it is the night-length rather than the day-length which is critical for flowering. Thus in many plants, the onset of darkness appears to initiate a process which, after a sufficiently long period of uninterrupted darkness (> the critical night-length) results in a long-night (= short-day) response. Moreover, the effect of a long night can be prevented when a short exposure to light, called a night-break, is given at a particular time (Figs. 5.3A, 5.4A).

The time of maximum sensitivity varies between species and varieties but is extremely constant for any one. In many, the optimum night-break response occurs after 8–10 h of darkness, irrespective of the overall duration of the night, unless the preceding day is very short (§7.3.1). The time of maximum sensitivity to a night-break often varies less with temperature than does the critical night-length; for example, in *Pharbitis nil*, lowering the temperature from 20 °C to 17 °C lengthens the critical night when a single inductive dark period is given but does not change the time of maximum sensitivity to a night-break.

The discovery that flowering could be controlled in certain plants by a brief night-break illumination enabled critical studies of the photoperiodic pigment to be made. The action spectra for the night-break effect on flowering in *Xanthium*, and its reversal (Fig. 7.2**B**), resemble the absorption spectra of P_r and P_{fr} respectively. Moreover, red/far-red reversibility of the night-break effect has been demonstrated for many day-length-dependent processes, confirming that phytochrome is the light-sensitive controlling pigment. Examples include the inhibition of flowering in other short-day plants, promotion of flowering in long-day plants, control of dormancy, prevention of cold acclimatisation and the inhibition of tuber formation (see Vince-Prue, 1975, and in Smith, 1976).

On the basis of the results of these and other physiological experiments, and a knowledge of the properties of phytochrome in etiolated tissues, a general working hypothesis for phytochrome action in photoperiodism has been developed. It runs as follows. During daylight, the phytochrome concentration in the leaf reaches a constant value which depends on the rate of synthesis of P_r and the rate of loss, mainly from P_{fr}. Phytochrome constantly cycles between the two forms, and a photostationary equilibrium is maintained in the leaf with P_{fr} predominant. On transfer to darkness, P_{fr} falls (by reversion and/or destruction); at the same time P_r accumulates from new synthesis and in some plants by reversion from P_{fr}. When P_{fr} is below a certain threshold, the dark processes of induction can proceed; these continue for as long as P_{fr} remains below the threshold value but are interrupted or prevented when P_{fr} is re-established by dawn, or by a light-break. The formation of P_{fr} prevents floral induction in short-day plants but is required for it in long-day plants. Implicit in this overall concept is the assumption that day is sensed by the formation and/or presence of P_{fr} while darkness is sensed by its absence (but see §7.3.2).

Although, as outlined above, phytochrome appears to have a demonstrable switching function in floral induction at certain times, its role in photoperiodic *time* measurement is much less clear. If time measurement is effected by a circadian clock in an 'external coincidence' mechanism of the Bünning type (§5.5), P_{fr} phytochrome could interact with an inducible light-sensitive phase (ϕ_i) of a rhythm generated by dawn or dusk. Phytochrome is, however, also known to cause phase shifts in some overt rhythms (e.g. Wilkins & Harris, in Smith, 1976) and thus could have a dual role, acting both to entrain the rhythm to a particular phase relationship with the light cycle and, at some particular phase (i.e. ϕ_i), as a signal to induce or prevent induction. On the other hand, if an 'internal coincidence' mechanism operates, that is, light acts to synchronise two endogenous rhythms (§ 5.5), phytochrome would only affect the phases of the circadian oscillation.

Phytochrome could, of course, equally well interact with an hour-glass component of time measurement (§ 5.4), or even, by its reversion or destruction, generate such a component. For example, an hour-glass type of interval-timer based on P_{fr} disappearance in darkness has been postulated for *Chenopodium rubrum*. Nevertheless, the external coincidence explanation appears to give the best description of many plant photoperiodic responses, even though it leaves unanswered problems of the kind outlined below (and see also § 7.2 penultimate paragraph).

7.3.1   *Problems associated with the need for light*

The rhythm of sensitivity to light for the control of floral induction usually requires several hours of light to re-set the clock to a particular phase point. For example, in *Xanthium strumarium* the time of maximum sensitivity to a night-break occurs consistently about 8 h after the end of the preceding light period when this is more than about 5 h long; for shorter light periods, however, the time of maximum sensitivity still seems to be controlled by the phasing set in the previous cycle (Papenfuss & Salisbury, 1967). Crude action spectra for re-setting the photoperiodic clock show a broad band of effectiveness in the red, with little action by the far-red. Many overt rhythms in higher plants also seem to be re-set most effectively by red light (e.g. Wilkins & Harris, in Smith, 1976). This responsiveness to red light implies that phytochrome is probably the active pigment, but its mode of operation is less certain.

In both *Chenopodium rubrum* (King & Cumming, 1972) and *Lemna perpusilla* (Hillman, in Evans, 1969), the need for continuous light can be partially satisfied by giving 5–15 min of red light approximately every hour. The effectiveness of such intermittent exposures may imply that P_{fr} is the effector and that it must be maintained in the leaf tissue for several hours. Repeated exposures would be needed to maintain P_{fr} if dark loss is rapid (but see § 7.3.2). However, in neither case has reversal by far-red light been demonstrated, as would be expected if light is required *only* to maintain P_{fr}. Thus other photoreactions, perhaps involving phytochrome cycling (§ 7.2), may be concerned in the process of clock re-setting which allows dark time measurement to begin at a particular phase point.

7.3.2   Problems associated with dusk perception

Following clock re-setting in light, dark timing begins when plants are transferred to darkness. It is often assumed that this transition to darkness is sensed in the leaves by the reduction in P_{fr} which occurs when they are no longer illuminated (§7.2). Where it has been possible to make direct spectrophotometric measurements, that is, in plants without chlorophyll, P_{fr} does decrease in the early hours of the night, but there seems to be no simple relationship between the rate and pattern of this P_{fr} loss and the initiation of dark time measurement (King, Vince-Prue & Quail, 1978). Attempts have also been made to estimate phytochrome changes by a physiological method that can be used with green plants. These experiments indicate that P_{fr} may not always fall immediately following transfer to darkness; for example, high P_{fr}/P ratios may persist for 30 h in *Chenopodium rubrum*, for up to 6 h in *Pharbitis nil* (Fig. 7.4, squares) and for *ca* 10 h in the long-day plant, *Lemna gibba*. On the other hand, the same type of approach indicates that in the long-day plant *Lolium temulentum*, and in non-green seedlings of *Pharbitis nil* (Fig. 7.4, circles and triangles), P_{fr}/P ratios begin to fall immediately following transfer to darkness.

The apparent variation in the rate and pattern of P_{fr} loss in darkness makes it difficult to accept the view that the dusk signal is sensed in any simple way by a reduction in P_{fr}, and it is necessary to consider alternative possibilities. Operation of phytochrome in a reaction involving cycling has been suggested as one possibility by Jose & Vince-Prue (1978); during the day, a reaction depending on phytochrome cycling could arrest dark timing, and cessation of cycling at the end of the day could allow dark timing to begin. This assumes that P_{fr} is lost during the early hours of darkness, and that its absence when a photo-inducible phase (ϕ_i) is reached allows induction to occur in short-day plants, but does not allow it in long-day plants. On the other hand, it has been proposed that a lowering of P_{fr} could effect the dusk signal under natural conditions, since the marked increase in the relative amount of far-red light that frequently occurs at sunset would lower P_{fr} photochemically with precise timing. However, such spectral shifts are not essential in artificial conditions and they also vary in extent with geographical location and weather conditions (see also Fig. 2.3); thus, it is not yet clear how important they are for the initiation of dark time measurement.

7.3.3   Problems associated with night-break experiments

The disappearance of P_{fr} in darkness is generally thought to occur before the light-sensitive ϕ_i phase is reached and, when a red night-break is given, newly formed P_{fr} (from P_r that has either been newly synthesised or generated by reversion from P_{fr}) must therefore act during ϕ_i to promote floral induction in long-day plants or prevent it in short-day plants. Action by P_{fr} in this way is implied by the results of the many experiments in which the action of a red night-break is prevented by subsequent far-red light. This shows that P_{fr} is the effector, as removing it prevents the effect.

Some experimental evidence does not, however, accord with this concept. For instance, in some night-break experiments, both red and far-red light are inhibitory to the induction of a long-night response at certain times and red/far-red reversibility is not observed (Fig. 7.5); moreover, flowering may be inhibited by far-red light given at the beginning of darkness or for many hours afterwards (Fig. 7.5). A possible explanation could be that P_{fr} is completely stable in darkness (but cf. Fig. 7.4) and must be present at ϕ_i for induction to occur. If this is so then the effect of red light cannot depend on P_{fr} formation but must occur through some other red-sensitive photoreaction.

Fig. 7.4. Phytochrome changes during an inductive dark period in the short-day plant *Pharbitis nil*. The P_{fr}/P ratios were estimated from the plant's flowering responses to different combinations of red and far-red light; the combination having no effect (the null point) is assumed not to change the P_{fr}/P ratio, which is then calculated from the percentage of red relative to red-plus-far-red light in the null combination. Triangles, plants previously exposed (i.e. up to 0 h on abscissa) to 24 h far-red plus 10 min red light (at 27 °C); circles, plants previously exposed to 24 h white light (at 18 °C); squares, same at 27 °C. Only the plants pre-treated with white light at 27 °C contained chlorophyll. Despite the marked differences in their phytochrome changes during darkness, the plants did not vary by more than 1 h in their critical night-lengths nor did they differ in the time at which they were most sensitive to a night-break. (After Evans & King, 1969; King *et al.*, 1978.)

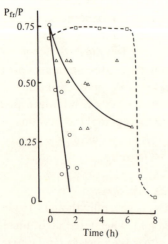

However, there are alternative explanations for the apparently anomalous data of Fig. 7.5 if P_{fr} is assumed always to be the effector molecule. For example, the P_{fr} which is newly formed by the red night-break could act differently from any P_{fr} still present in the tissue at that time, or else the direction of the response to P_{fr} might change. Promotion of flowering by red light early in the night is photoreversible by far-red, indicating that P_{fr} *is* needed for induction at this time; later in the night red light is inhibitory, and if at these times of maximum inhibition of flowering the sensitivity were also high, even the small amount of P_{fr} established by far-red light (Fig. 7.2 A) could be sufficient to effect a night-break response.

It is clear that, despite the many types of experimental approach used, our understanding of the way in which the phytochrome system operates in photoperiodism is far from complete. The working hypothesis that light is

Fig. 7.5. Changes in response to a single saturating pulse of red or far-red light during an inductive dark period. Each test plant was given a single exposure at different times (indicated on abscissa) in a dark period of 48 h for *Pharbitis nil* (A) (see Takimoto, in Evans, 1969), or 72 h for *Chenopodium rubrum* (B) (after Cumming, Hendricks & Borthwick, 1965). Far-red light inhibits flowering from the beginning of the night, and at certain times both red and far-red light inhibit flowering.

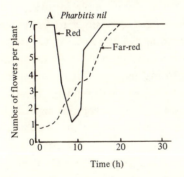

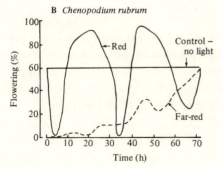

signalled by the presence of P_{fr}, whereas darkness is signalled by its rapid loss, with induction and non-induction being dependent on the presence or absence of P_{fr} during a photo-inducible phase of a rhythm generated by the light-off signal, explains many observations but leaves many questions unanswered.

7.4   Induction under prolonged exposures to light

Many long-day plants flower poorly or not at all in response to short days plus night-breaks, treatments which completely prevent flowering in short-day plants. Such long-day plants show maximum flowering only when exposed to long night-breaks of several hours duration, or to long photoperiods during which light is given more or less continuously (Vince-Prue, 1975; and in Smith, 1976). The difference between the two types of day-length response has been recognised for many years. In the one case it appears to be largely dependent on exposure to a sufficiently long night, with light acting at a particular time to prevent the effect of darkness. In the other, prolonged exposures to light are necessary to effect the response.

The need for long daily exposures to light is most commonly found in long-day plants and has sometimes been called the 'long-day' response, in contrast to the 'long-night' response which appears to be particularly important for the induction of flowering in short-day plants. However, the *inhibition* of flowering in some short-day plants, for example, strawberry, has been shown similarly to depend on prolonged exposures to light, while flowering in some long-day plants, for example *Fuchsia hybrida*, is primarily dependent on the inhibitory effect of exposure to a long night. Consequently, the term 'long-day' response is rather confusing and *light-dominant* is a better description of those photoperiodic responses which depend on prolonged exposures to light. Examples of such light-dominant responses are found in the control of flowering in many long-day plants (e.g. *Lolium temulentum*), in some short-day plants (e.g. strawberry and *Portulaca oleracea*) and in the regulation of bud dormancy in some trees (e.g. *Picea abies*) (see the chapter by Vince-Prue, in Smith, 1976).

The need for exposure to light far in excess of that needed to photoconvert phytochrome to the active P_{fr} form, raises the question of whether phytochrome is the photoreceptor under these conditions and, if so, why such long exposures are necessary. Although a contribution from photosynthesis cannot be ruled out, light-dominant photoperiodic responses show a number of characteristic features resembling those seen in the high-irradiance photomorphogenetic responses of seedlings, which are thought to be under phytochrome control (§7.2). Perhaps the most important of these concern light-quality effects. When short night-breaks control the response, the action spectra for promotion and inhibition resemble the absorption spectra for P_r and P_{fr} (Fig. 7.2A, **B**). When long night-breaks are given, the spectral characteristics are changed and the peak of effectiveness occurs at about 710 nm (Fig. 7.2**B**) with no photoreversibility. Similarly, when broad-band red and far-red light sources are used, long exposures with mixtures of red and far-red light are much more effective than red light alone. Mixtures of red and far-red light, and radiation at 710 nm would both be highly effective in causing cycling of phytochrome between the two forms, and such interconversions may be implicated under these conditions.

Further evidence that phytochrome cycling may be important comes from experiments with the long-day *Lolium temulentum*, in which plants were exposed for several hours to 10-min cycles in which 1-min red and 1-min far-red pulses were given in different sequences. There was no red/far-red reversibility, since cycles of 1-min red immediately followed by 1-min far-red and then 8-min darkness were just as effective as when the sequence of red and far-red was reversed; however, cycles containing both red and far-red in any sequence were always more effective than cycles of red pulses alone. Thus, phytochrome seems to be involved (because red and far-red wavelengths were effective) but the reaction does not appear to depend on maintaining P_{fr} above a certain level.

Other characteristics of the high-irradiance photomorphogenetic reaction of phytochrome are that the response is a function of the irradiance and requires the quasi-continuous input of light energy (Smith, 1975). Light-dominant photoperiodic responses show similar irradiance-dependency (as, for example, in *Brassica campestris* and *Lolium temulentum*), and for maximum effect the prolonged exposures to light must be given continuously, or at least as brief exposures repeated at frequent intervals. In the long-day plant, *Hyoscyamus niger*, for example, even cycles of 6 s of light every minute are less effective than continuous light.

Many lines of evidence indicate that the light-dominant responses in plant photoperiodism may be mediated through the phytochrome system, but that P_{fr} is not the effector molecule. On the other hand, a particular feature of these responses is that, during a long day, the spectral sensitivity to red and far-red changes. During the first *ca* 8 h of the day, red promotes flowering but, for the next *ca* 8 h, red light is inhibitory; and later still in the long photophase, red light again promotes flowering (Evans, 1971; Vince-Prue, 1975). For *Lolium*, there is good evidence that the changing sensitivity to red depends on a change in the response to P_{fr}, which is inhibitory to flowering at certain times of day but is required at others (see Vince-Prue, 1975).

Both light-dominant and long-night responses, therefore, seem to exhibit changes in sensitivity to P_{fr} during a 24-h cycle, but the times when P_{fr} is required or inhibitory are out of phase in the two response patterns. These changes in response to red light have been interpreted as rhythms in the optimum P_{fr}/P ratio as shown schematically in Fig. 7.6. However, in addition to showing shifts in the optimum ratio of red:red+far-red light during the long photophase, light-dominant photoperiodic responses also require prolonged exposures to light. Control of flowering may therefore depend on a reaction of phytochrome which involves cycling, with modulation by a response to P_{fr} which undergoes a rhythmic change in sensitivity (Jose & Vince-Prue, 1978). An alternative proposal is that the sensitivity to a phytochrome cycling reaction undergoes a rhythmic change during the photoperiod.

7.5   The action of phytochrome via circadian rhythms and membranes

Oscillatory changes in cell membranes may be closely associated with the clock mechanism (Sweeney, 1978; §11.5.6). The initial site of phytochrome action in photomorphogenesis may also be at membranes (Marmé, 1977). Although phytochrome is a water-soluble protein located in the cytosol, a small fraction of the total phytochrome (about 5–7%) appears to be always associated with membranes, even in totally dark-grown plants. Moreover, the

Fig. 7.6. Postulated rhythms of sensitivity to the P_{fr} form of phytochrome during a 24-h cycle. The ratio of P_{fr}/P which is optimal for floral induction is assumed to change during the course of the 24 h and the rhythms for light-dominant (or long-day) and long-night responses are out of phase. (After Vince-Prue, 1975.)

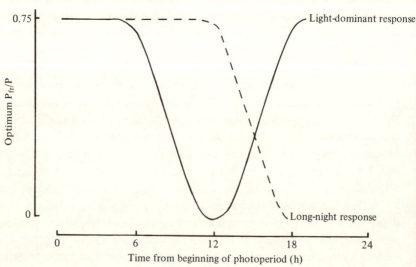

P_{fr} form of phytochrome is capable of binding *in vivo* to subcellular structures; association takes place in a few seconds and is rapid enough to account for the fastest observed responses to light. Phytochrome has been shown to affect the permeability of membranes and the transport of substances across them. It also modulates the activity of some membrane-bound enzymes.

Thus, while the evidence is by no means conclusive, phytochrome may operate at membrane sites, and a working hypothesis for its action in photoperiodism is that circadian changes in membranes allow phytochrome to bind at some phases of the rhythm and not at others. Some properties of phytochrome are known to change in a circadian manner; for example, there are rhythms in pelletability, that is, in the amount of phytochrome that is associated with particulate material (Jabben & Schäfer, 1976; see §7.2), and in the wavelength of maximum absorbance by P_{fr} *in vivo*, which varies between 727 and 737 nm (Horwitz & Epel, 1978). The amount of light needed for photoconversion *in vivo* may also vary rhythmically. Such changes could be related to changes in the properties of the membrane itself, or perhaps in other cell constituents that affect the phytochrome/membrane association.

The strongest circumstantial evidence that phytochrome–membrane interactions are involved in photoperiodic induction comes from studies on overt circadian rhythms. Satter & Galston (1971) have shown that the mechanism which operates leaflet movement in certain legumes is the same whether they close under the immediate photocontrol of phytochrome or by a circadian oscillation. Leaflet movements are effected by a K^+/Cl^- shuttle (Satter, Schrempf, Chaudri & Galston, 1977) with an alternation in the membrane between 12 h of pumping and 12 h of leakiness. A rhythm of transmembrane potential was demonstrated in the motor cells of the pulvinus, and phyto-chrome phototransformation also caused a change in transmembrane potential (cf. §10.6).

There is, however, little direct evidence for the proposal that photoperiodic responses are under the control of phytochrome/membrane interactions, or that induction occurs at membrane sites. One case that does provide such evidence is the duckweed, *Lemna*. Daily transfer to distilled water inhibits flowering in both the short-day *Lemna perpusilla* and the long-day *Lemna gibba*. In *L. perpusilla*, however, distilled-water treatment is most inhibitory at the time of greatest sensitivity to a night-break light pulse, whereas in *L. gibba*, the greatest inhibition occurs when plants are treated after the photo-inductive phase, i.e. during what would normally be the night after an inductive day (Oota & Nakashima, 1978). In both cases, the membrane apparently leaks ions at certain times and this is somehow associated with the flowering response. Lithium ions, which slow the circadian rhythm of petal movement in *Kalanchöe*, also affect flowering in both species of *Lemna* but do so differentially, being inhibitory for *L. gibba* and inductive for *L. perpusilla*.

The involvement of membranes is also indicated by the fact that ionophores, such as valinomycin and gramicidin, can substitute for the red light pulse which gives a light-on signal for an inductive skeleton day in the long-day *L. gibba*. These ionophores are not, however, able to substitute for the light signal which terminates such a skeleton day, although other substances which may also interact with membranes (e.g. DL propranolol, which blocks β-adrenergic receptor sites in animal systems) may do so. No chemical treatment is, however, able to substitute for both light exposures and so induce flowering in darkness (Oota & Nakashima, 1978).

Irrespective of whether or not the light signals operate at membrane sites, the consequences of exposing leaves to photoperiodic cycles is the release or synthesis of hormones which are transported to the responding cells, where they effect a variety of responses (Fig. 7.1). Photoperiodic floral initiation is often attributed to the action of a unique *florigen* which is formed (or released) only in appropriate day-length cycles. Results from grafting experiments indicate that 'florigen' is the same, or physiologically equivalent, in plants of different photoperiodic classes (Vince-Prue, 1975; Zeevaart, 1976). Thus, there appears to be only one hormone, although the conditions for its formation are different in different plants. This hormone has never been isolated, however. In other photoperiodic responses, known categories of growth hormones appear to be involved (e.g. possibly gibberellins and abscisic acid in control of bud dormancy, and gibberellins and cytokinins in tuber formation), but the way in which day-length effects changes in the content and metabolism of such hormones is unknown, and it is often far from clear which hormonal changes are actually involved in eliciting particular developmental responses.

7.6   Further reading and key references

Books and review articles are indicated by asterisks

Cumming, B. G., Hendricks, S. B. & Borthwick, H. A. (1965). Rhythmic flowering responses and phytochrome changes in a selection of *Chenopodium rubrum*. *Canadian Journal of Botany*, **43**, 825–53.

*Evans, L. T. (Ed.) (1969). *The Induction of Flowering*. Melbourne: McMillan.

*Evans, L. T. (1971). Flower induction and the florigen concept. *Annual Review of Plant Physiology*, **22**, 365–94.

Evans, L. T. & King, R. W. (1969). Role of phytochrome in photoperiodic induction of *Pharbitis nil*. *Zeitschrift für Pflanzenphysiologie*, **60**, 277–88.

*Hendricks, S. B. & Seigelman, H. W. (1967). Phytochrome and photoperiodism in plants. In *Comparative Biochemistry*, **25**, ed. M. Florkin & E. H. Stotz. Amsterdam: Elsevier.

Horwitz, B. A. & Epel, B. L. (1978). Circadian changes in activity of the far-red form of phytochrome: physiological and *in vivo* spectrophotometric studies. *Plant Science Letters*, **13**, 9–14.

Jabben, M. & Schäfer, E. (1976). Rhythmic oscillations of phytochrome and its pelletability in *Cucurbita pepo* L. *Nature*, **259**, 114–15.

*Jose, A. M. & Vince-Prue, D. (1978). Phytochrome action: a reappraisal. *Photochemistry and Photobiology*, **27**, 209–16.

*Kendrick, R. E. & Frankland, B. (1976). *Phytochrome and Plant Growth*. Studies in Biology, No. 68. London: Edward Arnold.

Kendrick, R. E. & Spruit, C. J. P. (1977). Phototransformations of phytochrome. *Photochemistry and Photobiology*, **26**, 201–14.

King, R. W. & Cumming, B. G. (1972). Rhythms as photoperiodic timers in the control of flowering in *Chenopodium rubrum* L. *Planta*, **103**, 281–301.

King, R. W., Vince-Prue, D. & Quail, P. H. (1978). Light requirement, phytochrome and photoperiodic induction of flowering of *Pharbitis nil* Chois. III. A comparison of spectrophotometric and physiological assay of phytochrome transformation during induction. *Planta*, **141**, 15–22.

*Marmé, D. (1977). Phytochrome: membranes as possible sites of primary action. *Annual Review of Plant Physiology*, **28**, 173–98.

*Oota, Y. & Nakashima, N. (1978). Photoperiodic flowering in *Lemna gibba* G3: time measurement. *Botanical Magazine*, Tokyo, Special Issue, **1**, 177–98.

Papenfuss, H. D. & Salisbury, F. B. (1967). Properties of clock re-setting in flowering of *Xanthium*. *Plant Physiology*, **42**, 1562–8.

*Pratt, L. H. (1978). Molecular properties of phytochrome. *Photochemistry and Photobiology*, **27**, 81–105.

*Satter, R. L. & Galston, A. W. (1971). Potassium flux: a common feature of *Albizzia* leaflet movement controlled by phytochrome or endogenous rhythm. *Science*, **174**, 518–19.

Satter, R. L., Schrempf, A., Chaudri, J. & Galston, A. W. (1977). Phytochrome and circadian clocks in *Samanea*. Rhythmic re-distribution of potassium and chloride within the pulvinus during long dark periods. *Plant Physiology*, **59**, 231–5.

Schneider, M. J., Borthwick, H. A. & Hendricks, S. B. (1967). Effects of radiation on flowering of *Hyoscyamus niger*. *American Journal of Botany*, **54**, 1241–9.

*Smith, H. (1975). *Phytochrome and Photomorphogenesis*. London: McGraw-Hill.

*Smith, H. (Ed.) (1976). *Light and Plant Development*. London: Butterworths.

*Sweeney, B. M. (1978). Circadian rhythms. *Photochemistry and Photobiology*, **27**, 841–7.

*Vince-Prue, D. (1975). *Photoperiodism in Plants*. London: McGraw-Hill.

*Zeevaart, J. A. D. (1962). Physiology of flowering. *Science*, **137**, 723–31.

*Zeevaart, J. A. D. (1976). Physiology of flower formation. *Annual Review of Plant Physiology*, **27**, 321–48.

PART III

Circadian physiology and clock mechanisms

JOHN BRADY

8 Circadian rhythms in animal physiology

8.1 Introduction

Almost all animals are readily classifiable as diurnal, nocturnal, or crepuscular, broadly dividing their daily lives into two characteristic states, one mainly active and 'awake', the other mainly inactive and 'asleep'. The active phase is generally associated with raised locomotor activity, feeding, metabolic rate, body temperature, digestion, excretion, etc., the inactive phase with the depression of most of these functions (see Figs. 9.1 and 9.4). These functions, moreover, usually retain their rhythmicity and keep approximately the same phase relationship when free-running in constant conditions (Fig. 9.3).

Circadian timekeeping thus has profound consequences, not only ecologically, which is its adaptive function, but also behaviourally and physiologically. Broadly, it operates at three organisational levels: cell, tissue and whole animal. This division, however, though convenient for the descriptive purposes of this chapter, can clearly not be followed too literally; tissues depend on cells, whole animals on tissues, and behaviour can only be seen in whole animals but arises from the interactions of cells within the nervous system.

8.2 Cellular rhythms

The fact that rhythms occur in Protista (§10.4) shows that circadian clocks can work in single cells. Most of the research has been done on autotrophs, in which light/dark-controlled rhythms associated with photosynthesis are perhaps to be expected, but rhythms of cell division have been demonstrated in *Tetrahymena* and rhythms of mating in *Paramecium* (Barnett, 1966; and in Aschoff, 1965). The *Paramecium* rhythm is particularly interesting because, although under suitable conditions the cells divide more frequently than daily, the mating rhythm nevertheless continues unaffected at its *ca* 24-h periodicity, thus showing that, vital though nuclear division may be to the life of the cell, it does not necessarily interrupt the functioning of the clock. In *Gonyaulax*, on the other hand, the cell division cycle is synchronous with the other circadian rhythms (Fig. 10.4).

Each protistan cell evidently contains its own clock. Perhaps more surprisingly, the same is also true for the cells of metazoa. Rhythms have been demonstrated in organ culture (e.g. Fig. 11.1), but they have also, more rarely, been demonstrated in cell culture. In such cell suspensions or monolayers, cell divisions characteristically occur with a *ca* 24-h periodicity (e.g. in mouse L-strain cells and in chick-muscle fibroblasts (see the chapter by Bruce, in Aschoff, 1965)). Since cell division and the cell cycle can be independent of circadian rhythmicity, however, it is more interesting to see which other physiological functions of metazoan cells are sustained as circadian rhythms in culture. A particularly beautiful example has been demonstrated by Deguchi in chicken pineal cells (Fig. 11.6B). Here is a case where the rhythmic output is of an enzyme (*N*-acetyl transferase, NAT) that is vital, via its role in melatonin secretion, in maintaining circadian periodicity in the whole animal (§11.4.2). It occurs, moreover, in a suspension of largely – though not completely – dissociated cells, which strongly suggests that each cell contains its own clock for the cyclic production of NAT, and hence that the pineal's rhythmic secretion of melatonin is due to the coordinated efforts of all its cells' individual clocks.

8.3   Tissue rhythms

Physiological rhythms, though due to the activities of particular tissues, are commonly measured in whole animals. Often this is because the rhythms are recognisable as such only in the intact animal, as the emergent properties of the activities of several tissues. Oxygen consumption, blood-sugar level, development, and behaviour are obvious examples (see §8.4). Other physiological rhythms, however, even though mainly due to the activities of single tissues or organs, may still be measured in whole animals as an experimental convenience. Some important examples are considered below.

8.3.1   *Endocrine rhythms*

Perhaps the most physiologically important rhythms in animals are those involved in the secretion of hormones, whose role in coordinating the body's circadian organisation is crucial. Measurement of circadian change in endocrine activity has been of four kinds: (a) animals sampled from a synchronous population are killed, then their glands are removed, and the gland contents are assayed in some way (e.g. histologically, as in Fig. 8.1); (b) the endocrine titre is inferred from the level excreted in the urine (e.g. 17-OHCS and adrenaline in Fig. 9.4); (c) blood samples are taken at regular intervals and assayed (as in Fig. 6.4); (d) the whole gland is isolated in organ culture and its secretions measured in the bathing fluid (e.g. Fig. 11.6A).

In the event, almost every hormone that has been looked at has proved to vary rhythmically across the 24 h. Often many hormones change their titre in near synchrony. To determine cause and effect relationships is thus not easy. Consider Fig. 8.1: how does one decide which of the peaks and troughs causes the others? Mere temporal coincidence can be no guide, without other knowledge of the endocrine interactions. However, in *Drosophila*, for example,

Fig. 8.1. Cellular rhythms in endocrine and other tissues in last instar fruit fly larvae (*Drosophila melanogaster*); measured as nuclear 'volume' (in fact as the departure from the mean growth curve in the developing larvae of the products of the longest and shortest diameters of the nuclei, measured in sections); night-time data points repeated for clarity; abscissa shows the LD 12:12 regime used (black indicates darkness). Note that endocrine cells (top three curves) as well as non-endocrine cells change their nuclear volume (presumed to represent synthetic activity) rhythmically and synchronously. (Compiled from Rensing, 1966, 1969.)

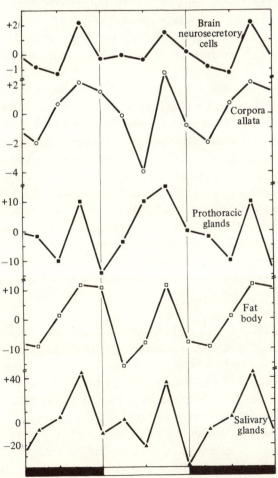

there is suggestive evidence that pulses of ecdysone (i.e. insect moulting hormone, secreted from the prothoracic glands) phase shift the salivary gland-cell rhythm. The latter may thus in nature be driven by the prothoracic gland rhythm.

In vertebrates, far more is known both about endocrines generally, and their circadian relationships in particular (see e.g. Fig. 6.2). For example, when the adrenal glands of hamsters are isolated in organ culture, they retain a clear rhythm of steroid output which can be phase-shifted by pulses of adrenocorticotropic hormone (ACTH) (Andrews, 1971). The circadian organisation of this and many other endocrine rhythms lies in the hypothalamus, with its key position in the control of the body's homeostasis, especially as regards temperature, metabolic rate and ion balance. Through its control over the pituitary's production of ACTH it almost certainly entrains the endogenous rhythmicity of the adrenal cortex, and hence the rhythmic secretion of several corticosteroid hormones with far-reaching effects. The hypothalamus derives this circadian pre-eminence from the fact that it contains the suprachiasmatic nuclei which, in mammals at least, are the single most important driving oscillator, or master clock (§11.4.2).

Although there are therefore clear driver/driven or driver/entraining hormonal circadian relationships, presumably in all animals, it should not be thought that these cycles occur only in the smooth-wave forms implied by Figs. 6.4, 8.1, 9.4, 11.6, etc. What has recently emerged from studies involving almost continuous sampling of blood plasma via chronically-implanted catheters (especially in man and sheep) is that hormone secretion is typically episodic, that is, it occurs in relatively brief, discrete spurts that vary in frequency and intensity across the 24 h (Weitzman & Hellman, 1974; Goodman & Karsch, 1981). For man it is now clear that at least four hypothalamic–pituitary hormone systems (ACTH–cortisol, growth hormone, prolactin, and luteinising hormone (LH)) all function this way. They often do so, moreover, in relation to the similarly episodic nature of sleep (§8.5).

8.3.2   Excretory rhythms

The adrenal corticosteroid rhythms were first detected by their daily variation in the urine, the changing make-up of which has provided a convenient and painless insight into the rhythmic physiology of laboratory mammals, especially man (Fig. 9.4). Such urinary rhythms arise in two ways: (a) from changes in the kidney's excretory activity (both in glomerular filtration rate and in tubular recovery); and (b) from changes in the level of metabolites, hormones, etc., circulating in the blood plasma. 'Masking', non-circadian physiological influences on urine production and composition are thus manifold, and include irrelevant inputs from drinking, eating, posture, excitement, and so on. The following brief comments are accordingly rather simplified generalisations, the precise nature of the circadian control of excretory rhythms still being far from clear (see Mills, 1973).

In man, sodium, potassium, chloride and hydrogen ions all remain at fairly constant levels in the blood plasma throughout the day, but appear rhythmically in the urine, apparently because the kidney excretes them more actively during the daytime (Fig. 8.2; and see Conroy & Mills (1970, p. 47)). This is probably due to a combination of rhythmicity inherent in the kidney cells plus a rhythm of tubular activity driven hormonally, especially from the pituitary (anti-diuretic hormone) and adrenal glands (cortisol) (Mills, 1973, p. 29). The control evidently primarily concerns the excretion of cations, since the removal of chloride is coupled to the removal of sodium, and the amount

Fig. 8.2. Urinary rhythms in a human subject isolated in an underground 'bunker' without time-cues from the external environment (as in Fig. 9.2); the first five days of a 24-day experiment. The K^+ rhythm, not shown, followed the Na^+ rhythm closely; rectal temperature rhythm (top curve) shown for comparison. Vertical marks on abscissae indicate true midnights; black and white bar, the subject's self-selected, free-running sleep/wakefulness cycle. (After Aschoff, Gerecke & Wever, 1967.)

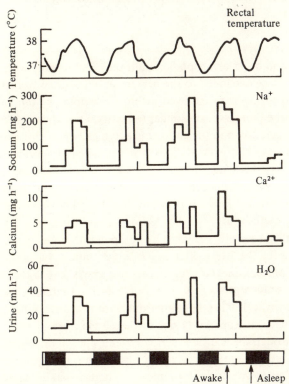

of water passed into the filtrate is proportional to the total amount of cations excreted. However, other ions (for example calcium and magnesium, the concentrations of which are much affected by meals, and phosphate), and metabolites (for example, corticosteroid hormones, urea and uric acid), pass through the kidney roughly in proportion to their concentration in the plasma, so their rhythmic appearance in the urine is mainly a consequence of physiological activities elsewhere.

A striking feature of the kidney's rhythmicity is the marked and convenient decline in urine production during sleep (Fig. 8.2). This decline is not, as might be thought, a consequence of the cessation of drinking, since it also occurs in subjects taking continual small drinks across the 24 h. It is, rather, an adaptive feature of the body's excretory timekeeping, being due mainly to the circadian control of sodium and potassium excretion.

Virtually all of this research has been done on only a few mammals, much of it on man, but there is evidence for similar rhythms in invertebrates (Wall, 1970; Lettau, Foster, Harker & Treherne, 1977); and since so much is known of the biophysics and hormonal physiology of urine production by insect Malpighian tubules – a very simple kidney – they would seem to be a useful model for future work on rhythms in relation to cell membranes and hormone action.

8.3.3   *Arthropod cuticle rhythms*

When insects and other arthropods moult, they first emerge with a pale, soft, thin cuticle. Once expanded to the new instar's definitive size and shape, the paleness and softness are removed within a few hours by tanning and sclerotisation, but the thinness takes longer to rectify. Over the next few days further layers are laid down in the endocuticle, typically in a circadian pattern. During the night, chitin crystallites are deposited in organised lamellae; during the day, the same amount of chitin is deposited but in non-lamellate form. As a consequence, sections of cuticle viewed under crossed polaroid filters reveal alternate bi-refringent (lamellate) and dark (non-lamellate) daily growth layers (Neville, 1975).

This rhythm is in reality a secretory rhythm by the epidermal cells, and has interesting implications for the study of circadian organisation. In locusts, the rhythm persists in constant darkness for at least two weeks, and is almost perfectly temperature-compensated, with a Q_{10} of 1.04 for frequency (see §2.2.4). In constant light at 100 lux it damps out within a day. What is intriguing is that this effect is apparently not mediated via normal photo-receptors and thence through the neuroendocrine system, since, if an insect is kept in constant light but has one leg covered in black paint, the epidermis in this leg continues to lay down cuticle rhythmically, whereas that in the rest of the animal does not (Neville, 1975).

It seems that the epidermal cells themselves are both directly sensitive to light and endogenously rhythmic, a conclusion further supported by Lukat's demonstration (1978) that cuticle deposition remains rhythmic in cockroaches made overtly (i.e. behaviourally) arrhythmic by the removal of their optic lobes (see §11.4.1). Apparently, central nervous arrhythmicity does not necessarily cause total physiological arrhythmicity, and cells in intact animals can retain their own timekeeping ability when deprived of central control (see §8.6).

8.4   Whole animal rhythms

As we have seen, physiological rhythmicity arises in tissues as a result of their constituent cells' timekeeping ability. In the same vein, whole animal rhythmicity arises from the timekeeping of the tissues. Four major examples of tissue (and hence cellular) rhythmicity, which in practice are identifiable only in whole animals, are metabolic rate, chemical sensitivity, development and behaviour. These are considered below.

8.4.1   *Metabolic rhythms*

Metabolic rate is usually measured as oxygen consumption, or sometimes as carbon-dioxide production. Changes in these across the day obviously arise from all the energy-demanding processes that vary in the animal, such as locomotor activity, digestion, excretion and growth. Oxygen-consumption rhythms therefore emerge as the integrated outcome of all such activities. In plants they tend to be simple and smooth-wave because of the simple life-style of plants. In animals, by contrast, they are often complex; and even though much of the pattern is due to the rhythm of behavioural activity, it is usually overlaid by other effects.

Fig. 8.3 shows one such case, in an insect. The tsetse fly takes infrequent, but vast blood-meals (often over twice its body weight), and the oxygen demand for digestion is initially very high, at least four or five times the basal rate. As the meal is dealt with over the next few days, however, this demand steadily declines. The outcome is that for the first 36 h the digestive demand for oxygen is so great that it completely obscures any diel pattern in consumption due to locomotor activity. Thereafter, although the pattern of consumption due to activity now shows through, the overall daily demand still falls, even though the activity level is rising (Fig. 8.3, figures).

Such oxygen consumption rhythms have most commonly been measured in man (Mills, 1973, p. 36) and other large animals (even though small animals such as insects seem more convenient to hold in respirometers). In mammals and birds, metabolic rate and motor activity are loosely coupled to the rhythm of body temperature. This link is not necessarily causal, however, as the phase relationships may drift when the rhythms free run in constant conditions.

Moreover, in man both the oxygen consumption and the body-temperature rhythms, independently survive in their usual forms when sleep times are changed.

8.4.2 *Sensitivity rhythms*

Circadian physiology is also expressed as daily changes in the susceptibility of whole animals to treatment with all sorts of chemical agents (see §9.8), including anaesthetics, allergens, antibiotics, drugs, hormones, toxins, insecticides and X-rays. For example, at the end of their behaviourally active phase, *Pectinophora* moths are about twice as susceptible to cholinesterase-inhibiting insecticides, and about half as susceptible to X-irradiation, as they are throughout the rest of the day (Fig. 8.4). Likewise, mice show a $\pm 60\%$ daily variation in their sensitivity to ouabain (a specific inhibitor of Na^+/K^+-linked active transport), and humans show dramatic changes in their reactions to anaesthesia (Fig. 9.9).

Many such sensitivity rhythms have been measured, mainly for applied purposes – for example to determine optimum drug regimes, or to standardise insecticide testing, etc. The results, though serving these ends, rarely reveal much of value to the understanding of circadian physiology,

Fig. 8.3. (**A**) Metabolic and (**B**) locomotor activity rhythms in fed tsetse flies (*Glossina morsitans*). (**A**) Hourly oxygen consumption of a single mature male in a recording respirometer; figures at top, mean hourly consumption for each 24 h. (After Taylor, 1977.) (**B**) Mean number of spontaneous flights per hour by each of 23 similar males in individual actographs; figures beneath, mean total number of flights per fly per 24 h. (From Brady, in Loher, 1982.) Note that digestive demand for oxygen is so great initially that it obscures any pattern in demand due to flight, and even after this does show through, the mean level continues to fall although activity level is increasing (cf. figures at top and foot).

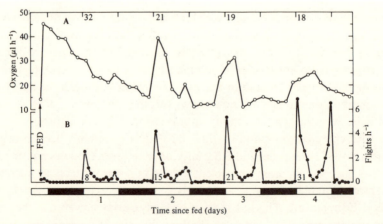

however. The pharmacological effects of the experimental treatments are simply far too widespread. (This stricture does not, of course, affect the arguments about metabolic inhibitor effects on clock mechanisms (§11.5.3).)

8.4.3 *Developmental ('gated') rhythms*

There is a whole class of physiological events that occur once only in each individual's lifetime, but which are nevertheless timed by a circadian rhythm – e.g. birth (in mammals), egg-hatch, and, *par excellence*, moulting in arthropods. This kind of phenomenon cannot be detected as a rhythm in an individual; it becomes apparent only in mixed-age populations. What happens in the individual is that it typically completes the morphogenetic aspects of its development at random with respect to time of day – in poikilotherms, at a speed largely determined by ambient temperature. The individual does not then immediately emerge (or moult, or hatch, etc.), however, but waits until the appropriate species-specific time of day (or, in free-running conditions, until the appropriate circadian phase). Thus, although individuals become ready to emerge at all times, they only do so through a narrow span of time each day, when a so-called circadian *gate* is open. If they

Fig. 8.4. Diel cycle of sensitivity in an insect (female pink bollworm moths, *Pectinophora gossypiella*); points from first 8 h repeated for clarity. (A) Mean survival in days after X-irradiation of 25 krad at the different times of day indicated on the abscissa. (B) Susceptibility to azinphosmethyl (an organophosphate insecticide) expressed as LD_{50}s to treatment at different times of day. Cross-hatching, distribution of maximum locomotor activity. (After Brady, 1974.)

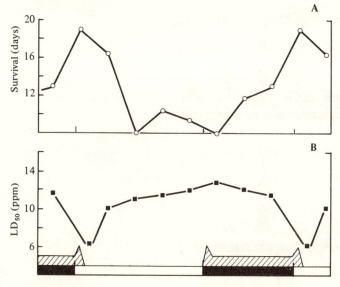

are not quite ready to emerge through Monday's gate, for example, they must wait for Tuesday's, and so on.

By far the most extensive research has been performed on the adult emergence (eclosion) rhythm of fruit flies, especially *Drosophila melanogaster* and *pseudoobscura*, whose eclosion gates are open for about 6 h following each dawn. Many years of work on these species by C. S. Pittendrigh and his colleagues have provided much of our basic understanding of circadian phenomenology.

As with any gated rhythm, the *Drosophila* eclosion rhythm is detectable

Fig. 8.5. Adult emergence (eclosion) rhythm in *Drosophila pseudoobscura*. (**A**) Distribution of eclosions from a large, mixed-age population held in constant darkness (DD). (**B**) Eclosions from an identical population that was given a single 4-h light exposure just as the adults first started emerging; note that this converted the random eclosions in **A** into a clear circadian rhythm. Black abscissa bar shows light regime for **B**, with marks at 24-h intervals from the first eclosion peak. (**A** and **B** compiled from Pittendrigh, 1954.) (**C**) The eclosion of adults from a batch of larvae collected over a single hour as they pupated 9 days earlier in constant light (LL), at which point the pupae were placed in DD. (**D**) The eclosion pattern of adults from a batch treated identically to that in **C**, but collected over a 24-h period; dashed line shows eclosion distribution of flies from a similar 24-h batch kept in LL. Note that transfer from LL to DD converted the random eclosions in LL into three 'gated' peaks on days 8, 9 and 10 after pupation. (See Fig. 2.6 for phase–response curve.) (**C** and **D** compiled from Pittendrigh, 1966.)

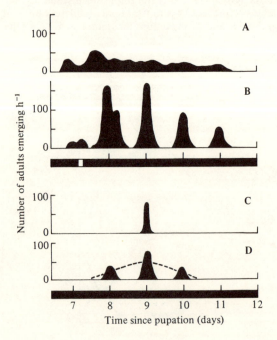

only in mixed-age populations. Flies reared for generations in constant darkness emerge arrhythmically (Fig. 8.5A), but a single brief exposure to light (1 min is enough, and it can be given as early as during the first larval instar) synchronises such a population into later emerging in a clear circadian rhythm (Fig. 8.5B). A population of larvae pupates continuously, at all times of day, even in light-pulse synchronised populations, and if the larvae are collected as they pupate over one hour and are then kept in constant darkness and temperature (20 °C), they do not emerge in a rhythm, but as a single peak nine days later. If, however, larvae are collected in similar hourly batches over one 24-h period, they do not emerge in 24 separate batches nine days later, but as three discrete peaks on the mornings of days eight, nine and ten, representing the opening of the circadian gate on those days (Fig. 8.5, cf. C and D). Each fly only emerges once, but its doing so is nevertheless timed by a circadian clock.

Gated rhythms of this type are often thought of as being developmental, but it should be borne in mind that the actual gated act is in fact behavioural, not morphogenetic. When the gate opens, some form of stereotyped 'breaking-out' programme is switched on in the CNS, under the control, for insects at least, of a brief, timed release of an eclosion hormone (Truman, 1979; see § 11.4.1). Presumably vertebrate egg-hatch and birth are similarly controlled, even though their circadian gating may be rather less precise than that of insects.

8.4.4. *Behavioural rhythms*

By far the most obvious circadian, and also tidal rhythms in animals are those involving behaviour. In practice, the spontaneous locomotor activities of running, swimming and flight have been the most commonly studied aspects because of the ease with which they can be recorded (e.g. Figs. 2.5, 3.2). However, in general, spontaneous activity is only one overt expression of a more deep-seated cycle of CNS excitability. When other behaviours are measured, they often follow the same circadian pattern. In the tsetse fly, the animal most closely studied from this point of view, six or seven different behaviours follow roughly the same, co-phasic pattern across the day (Fig. 8.6). Although the only other extensive relevant work has been on man, in whom a similar situation prevails (Fig. 9.1), lesser evidence from other species, including birds and insects, suggests that the phenomenon is common.

Three apparently general features of behavioural rhythmicity are revealed by Fig. 8.6. First, and most obviously, many different behaviours (though certainly not all) change in parallel across the day. Second, these changes arise not only in spontaneous behaviours, but are also apparent in *evoked*

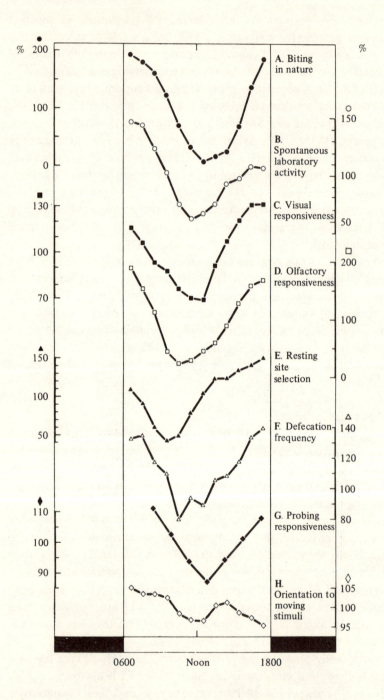

responses; the thresholds of responses to exogenous stimuli therefore change with the endogenous excitation of 'spontaneous' behaviour. Third, the changes involve behaviours operating through widely different sensori-motor systems; for example, curves **B**, **C** and **D** all involve take-off and flight, but **G** concerns only the leg, neck and proboscis muscles and receptors (see Brady, 1975; and in Aschoff, 1981).

There are, in principle, three ways in which rhythmic behavioural change can arise: (1) peripherally, by changes in the sensitivity of the sense organs across the day; (2) centrally, by changes in threshold levels at integrative centres within the CNS; and (3) by a combination of these two. The first arrangement certainly can occur, at least in photoreceptors, in which circadian changes in photosensitivity are well known (Fig. 2.7). Eyes, however, have to cope with a highly predictable diel change in light intensity (of at least six log units for most animals (see Fig. 2.3)), and circadian visual sensitivity changes are therefore perhaps to be expected. How far they actually influence behavioural responsiveness is uncertain (cf. §2.3.2, final paragraph).

Evidence for peripheral rhythmicity in other sensory modalities, for which stimulus intensity changes are relatively unpredictable, is largely lacking, and in three cases where the matter has been critically examined, it is apparently central control that causes the change in responsiveness. These cases are: the visual response of tsetse flies to moving objects (Fig. 8.6C), the olfactory responses of male moths to female sex pheromone, and the gustatory response of blowflies to sugar-water (see Brady, in Loher, 1982).

In the case of the blowfly, there is a clear, free-running circadian rhythm in the behavioural responsiveness (whether measured as the proportion of flies responding, or as the sugar concentration threshold in individual flies), but there is no circadian change in the level of spiking in the relevant tarsal sugar receptors involved (Fig. 8.7). This is the most rigorous examination so far of the relation between peripheral and central inputs in circadian behavioural control, and it clearly reveals that in this animal the rhythm in food

---

Fig. 8.6. The diel behavioural spectrum of tsetse flies (*Glossina morsitans*) in LD 12:12; all ordinate units are percentages of their respective mean response levels. (**A**) The number of flies coming to bite a bait ox in the field (Zimbabwe). (**B**) Number of flies flying spontaneously in actographs (as in Fig. 8.3**B**). (**C**) Number of flies taking off when visually stimulated by a large, slowly moving vertical black stripe (5° wide, moving $14°$ s^{-1} horizontally). (**D**) Number of flies taking off to stimulation with human body odour. (**E**) Proportion of flies electing to settle on well-lit surfaces. (**F**) Defecation frequency. (**G**) Number of fixed, suspended flies probing a warmed artificial feeding surface. (**H**) Number of flying flies attracted towards the moving stripe used in **C**. (From Brady, 1975.)

responsiveness is due exclusively to circadian changes in the *central* processing of the sensory input, with the latter being constant for a given stimulus intensity at all times of day.

Two other general points about behavioural rhythms should be made. First, there are two qualitatively different kinds of behaviour that are rhythmic: (a) the gated, once-in-a-lifetime programmes performed uniquely at birth, hatching and arthropod moulting (§8.4.3), and (b) all the more typical, daily-repeated, on-going behaviour of the type that is measurable in *individual* animals (e.g. Figs 2.5, 3.2, 8.6 and 9.1). It seems inevitable that the form of circadian control of these two types of behaviour must be different. For gated rhythms, control is probably in the form of a 'single-shot' hormonal release of each unique and largely fixed behaviour pattern (§11.4.1). For on-going behaviour, continuous control must be exerted right round the clock, since if the individual is suitably stimulated (by the arrival of predator, mate, food, etc.) it can and will perform the behaviour at *any* time; all that changes with circadian phase is the probability that it will do so (e.g. as in Fig. 8.6**C**, **D**, or Fig. 8.7).

Fig. 8.7. Circadian changes in (**A**) behavioural responsiveness of blowflies (*Protophormia terraenovae*) compared with (**B**) total lack of change in the chemoreceptors upon which the behaviour depends. (**A**) Solid squares and upper left ordinate, percentage of flies extending their proboscis in response to stimulation of their tarsi with 1.0 M sucrose (this rhythm free runs in LL for at least 2 cycles); open squares and right ordinate, sucrose concentration necessary to elicit proboscis extension in 50% of flies (= sucrose threshold). (**B**) Circles and lower left ordinate, spikes generated by one tarsal hair in the first 0.5 s of stimulation with 0.3 M sucrose. Bars, ±s.e.; abscissa, LD 12:12 with only part of night shown. (After Hall, 1980.)

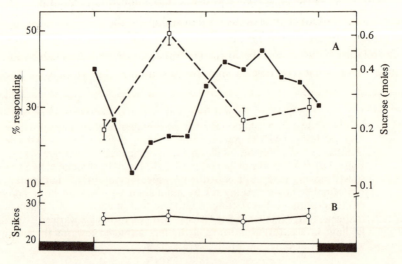

The other general point is that non-circadian physiological inputs may markedly change the level of behaviour in a rhythm. Temperature, for example, much affects the amount of locomotor activity in poikilotherms, and sexual drive or hunger may do the same in many species (e.g. as in Fig. 8.3 **B**). Less well known, and quite unexplained, are the changes that such inputs can cause in circadian *pattern*. Although temperature (§2.2.4), sex and hunger, etc., apparently have no influence on circadian *period*, the changes they effect in the level of behaviour may alter its distribution across the 24 h. In the tsetse fly, for example, when food deprivation raises mean activity level over a series of days, it also radically changes the balance between morning and evening activity (Fig. 8.3 **B**). Similar work on mosquitoes shows that insemination, oviposition and feeding all cause comparable differential pattern changes (Jones & Gubbins, 1978). This seems to imply a rather complex link between behaviour and its circadian control, and is an aspect of circadian organisation that has been little studied.

In summary, the circadian control of behaviour thus involves the following features.

(1) The performance of normal, on-going, daily-repeated behaviour is controlled continuously, right round the clock. The circadian pattern of this control, however, represents only a probabilistic average, since it does not prevent animals from making instantaneous, *ad hoc* responses when need arises.

(2) Once-in-a-lifetime behaviour of the birth and moulting type, which occurs exclusively during the opening of a daily gate, is 'push-button' controlled so that once initiated it cannot be stopped, altered or repeated.

(3) The evidence suggests that the primary circadian control of daily-modulated behaviour is neural at least in mammals, in which it is driven by the suprachiasmatic nuclei, and in insects, in which it is driven by the optic lobes or brain, though in birds pineal hormones are important (see §11.4). Gated, once-in-a-lifetime behaviours, on the other hand, are probably switched on by a daily shot of a releasing hormone (§11.4.1).

(4) Circadian changes in behaviour occur around mean levels that change from day to day under the influence of non-circadian inputs such as temperature, starvation and sexual drive; and these may differentially alter the distribution of the behaviour within the circadian cycle.

(5) Rhythms in responsiveness are probably due mainly to changes in central nervous thresholds, rather than to changes in receptor sensitivity, though this may also occur, at least in photoreceptors.

(6) In each species, circadian changes in many, widely differing behaviours occur synchronously across the 24 h, though other responses, especially those that conflict, are out of phase with this pattern. This synchronous rhythmicity

seems to imply a degree of cross-linking in the behavioural organisation that may amount to a circadian change in general, i.e. non-specific, central excitability.

8.5   Sleep

Sleep, as opposed to mere akinesis, is objectively definable only in vertebrates, in which it involves marked and characteristic changes in the pattern of brain waves. Though coinciding with the absence of consciousness, it is much more than just the absence of wakefulness; it is a state, or rather a series of states, of specific brain-centred neural activity.

This brain activity is normally measured indirectly by electro-encephalogram (EEG), which involves attaching a conducting pad to the animal's scalp, an indifferent electrode somewhere more distant from the brain (e.g. the ear), and then monitoring the potential difference between the two sites on a pen-recorder running at ca 2 cm s^{-1}. The potential difference is in practice very small (at most $ca \pm 50\ \mu$V; cf. typical nerve resting potentials -70 mV) but is detectable at all times. It is due to the integrated net electrical activity of the few million cortical cells immediately underlying the scalp electrode. Not many species have been studied, but in man, monkeys, sheep,

Fig. 8.8. Typical electro-encephalogram (EEG) patterns during sleep in man. (A) EEG traces when awake, sleeping (stages 1 to 4), and dreaming (REM = rapid eye movement); wave-forms slightly idealised. (B) The changing levels of sleep during a single 'typical' night; hatching shows REM episodes (i.e. periods of dreaming). (Compiled from Kleitman, 1960.)

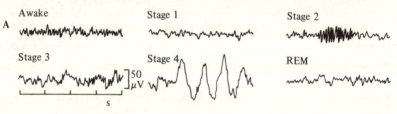

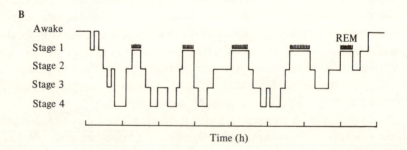

Time (h)

cats and rodents roughly the same EEG changes correlate with the same behavioural changes. The phenomena, in mammals at least, are therefore presumed to be general.

In the awake, but relaxed animal, the EEG is characterised by low amplitude (*ca* ± 20 μV), high frequency (*ca* 10 Hz), so-called *alpha* waves (Fig. 8.8A). When the animal is sharply stimulated, this switches instantly to the alert, rapid *beta* waves (*ca* ± 5 μV, 40 Hz). When the animal drifts into sleep, on the other hand, the EEG activity begins to synchronise so that its amplitude increases and frequency decreases – at first as what is called stage 1 sleep. There then ensue episodes of 'spindling' (so-called from their appearance), where 2-s bursts of high-frequency, high-amplitude waves intervene on the otherwise lengthening alpha rhythm (Fig. 8.8A, 2). As this stage 2 sleep passes into stage 3, the spindles give way to the large, slow (*ca* 2 Hz) *delta* waves, and finally to stage 4, with the largest and slowest (i.e. most synchronised) waves of all (Fig. 8.8A, 4).

As the animal falls asleep it generally passes successively through these four stages, becoming increasingly harder to arouse as it does so, but the sequence may also regress and skip about (Fig. 8.8B). Superimposed on these switching episodes, there are sudden phases when, although the animal is at its most difficult to arouse, its EEG switches back to something close to a stage 1 alpha rhythm. These paradoxical phases are evidently associated with dreaming (at least in man, whom one can awaken and ask). They also coincide with rapid movements of the eyes, as indicated by the dashes in Fig. 8.8B; hence the name used to describe this sleep stage, *rapid-eye-movement* sleep (or REM sleep, this name being synonymous with 'paradoxical,' 'active', or 'dreaming' sleep).

Because sleep is the behavioural obverse of being awake (see §2.4.1), and the sleep–wakefulness cycle is usually the most obvious manifestation of daily rhythmicity, it might be thought that the control of sleep would be an integral part of the circadian timekeeping of behaviour. That turns out not to be so, however. In mammals, sleep is apparently induced by the release, especially within the forebrain, of serotonin (5-hydroxytryptamine) by neurones from the raphe nuclei in the brain stem. This is antagonised, both in waking and in REM sleep, by the secretion of catecholamines such as noradrenaline. Destruction of the raphe nuclei in rats leads to greatly increased activity during the daytime, and in cats to almost permanent arousal, but does not disrupt the circadian periodicity of their running activity (Block & Zucker, 1976). Conversely, destruction of their suprachiasmatic nuclei (SCN) (§11.4.2), to which the raphe neurones also deliver serotonin, makes rats behaviourally arrhythmic as regards running, drinking and sleep, but does not much change their total amount of sleep per 24 h (Stephan & Nunez, 1977). Destruction of other hypothalamic areas is without effect.

Hence it seems that circadian rhythmicity is maintained by the SCN, and that sleep is mainly a driven rhythm that involves the serotoninergic suppression of forebrain activity. The whole problem of neural circadian control of sleep–wakefulness cycles, in vertebrates and in invertebrates, is examined in depth by Rusak & Zucker (1979) (see also §11.4.2).

8.6   Circadian organisation of animal physiology

Cockroaches and crickets, silkmoths, sparrows, and rodents are all made overtly arrhythmic by having small pieces of their brains removed (i.e. their optic lobes, medial brain tissue, pineal body, and suprachiasmatic nuclei, respectively (§11.4)). This has been taken to imply that each of these bits of tissue is a 'master clock', the driving oscillator that runs the animal's timekeeping machinery. It must be abundantly clear from the rest of this chapter, however, that this puts matters much too simply.

The cells of complex metazoa are not only rhythmic when in the intact animal (Fig. 8.1), but can be shown to remain rhythmic when suspended in culture (Fig. 11.6). Likewise, organs such as glands are not only rhythmic in their secretory output while they form part of the living body (Fig. 9.4), but can continue thus when isolated in culture (§8.3.1). Even more informative is Lukat's work on cockroach cuticle (§8.3.3), which shows that the cells of an animal retain their own rhythm undiminished although the animal itself is made overtly arrhythmic by having its brain lesioned so that it shows no sign of behavioural rhythmicity. Clearly, central nervous arrhythmicity does not signify total physiological arrhythmicity; just as they do in culture, cells in intact animals retain their own timekeeping ability when deprived of central control.

It thus appears that each metazoan cell possesses its own circadian clock, presumably as inherited from its protistan ancestry. However, when incorporated into a tissue, cells not only cooperate to perform that tissue's normal specialist function, but do so in a temporally coordinated manner so that all the cell clocks run in unison (as in the pineal, §8.2). Presumably this unison occurs through a combination of intercellular physico-chemical mutual entrainment and the cells' responses to rhythmic changes in hormone levels. Certainly in any one animal, many different tissues show approximately synchronous cellular rhythmicity (Fig. 8.1).

An animal is therefore a complex system of clocks – in cells, tissues and especially brain. Indeed, even in the brain there may be several clocks: not only are the known optic lobe and suprachiasmatic nuclei clocks bilaterally replicated, but also there is the multiplicity implied by circadian behavioural pattern changes of the kind discussed in §8.4.4 (paragraph 7) and §11.4.3 (under rhythm splitting).

This plethora of clocks functions in the whole animal, however, as a unified, intimately coupled timekeeping system (§11.4.3). The significance of the brain clocks in this system is likely to be not that they are 'master clocks', in the sense of having evolved specifically to drive or entrain the rest of the system, but that they do so largely adventitiously, simply because they regulate the timing of behaviour. It is hard to think of physiological functions that do not either subserve behaviour in some way or are not heavily influenced by its effects. Hence, in any active animal, behavioural rhythmicity must inevitably drive, or at least entrain, much of the body's physiological rhythmicity.

Fig. 8.9. The hierarchical arrangement of clocks in an animal. The linked spheres represent direct neural connections, the black arrows hormonal or other coupling mechanisms (see §8.6, and cf. Fig. 11.5). (After Brady, 1979.)

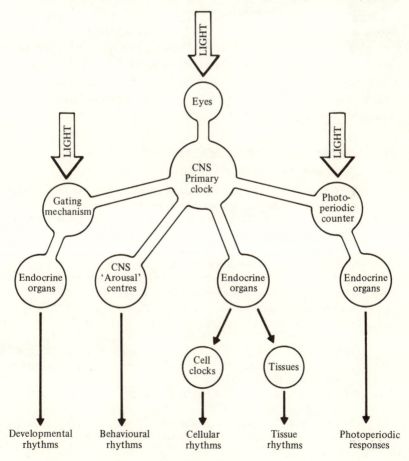

Perhaps the best way of visualising the body's overall circadian organisation is as a hierarchical system of the kind outlined, highly simplified, in Fig. 8.9.

This envisages the central circadian (or circatidal) control of behaviour by the suprachiasmatic nuclei, pineal, optic lobes, etc., as being effectively primary in all higher animals, with this 'primary' clock being entrained by light cycles perceived by the eyes (§2.3.1), and acting to drive or entrain second-order clocks, principally in endocrine organs. These rhythmic endocrine secretions then drive or entrain the lower-order clocks in other tissues and in individual cells. The outcome is all the overt measurable rhythms in cells, tissues and behaviour that we have considered in this chapter. In addition, however, since there is evidence that both developmental gating (§8.4.3) and photoperiodic timekeeping (especially when it involves an hourglass timer (§5.2, 5.4, 6.2.3)) are independently controlled by CNS centres which are directly sensitive to light, these are shown as separate 'primary' clocks.

The whole system is thus thought of as a complex matrix of coupled clocks (see also §11.4.3), but with a bias of effective influence running down the levels implied in Fig. 8.9. The same kind of timekeeping organisation presumably operates in circatidal rhythms (Chapter 3) on the 12.4-h time scale. Not shown in Fig. 8.9, but presumed to be associated with the circadian photoperiodic system, must be subsystems controlling circalunar and circannual timekeeping.

8.7   Further reading and key references
Books and review articles are indicated by asterisks

Andrews, R. V. (1971). Circadian rhythms in adrenal organ cultures. *Gegenbaurs Morphologisches Jahrbuch*, **117**, 89–98.

*Aschoff, J. (Ed.) (1965). *Circadian Clocks*, 479 pp. Amsterdam: North Holland.

*Aschoff, J. (Ed.) (1981). *Biological Rhythms – Handbook of Behavioural Neurobiology*, **4**. New York: Plenum.

Aschoff, J., Gerecke, U. & Wever, R. (1967). Desynchronization of human circadian rhythms. *Japanese Journal of Physiology*, **17**, 450–7.

Barnett, A. (1966). A circadian rhythm of mating type reversals in *Paramecium multimicronucleatum*, syngen 2, and its genetic control. *Journal of Cellular Physiology*, **67**, 239–70.

Block, M. & Zucker, I. (1976). Circadian rhythms of rat locomotor activity after lesions of the midbrain raphe nuclei. *Journal of Comparative Physiology*, **109**, 235–47.

*Brady, J. (1974). The physiology of insect circadian rhythms. *Advances in Insect Physiology*, **10**, 1–115.

Brady, J. (1975). Circadian changes in central excitability – the origin of behavioural rhythms in tsetse flies and other animals? *Journal of Entomology (A)*, **50**, 79–95.

*Brady, J. (1979). *Biological Clocks.* Studies in Biology No. 104, 60 pp. London: Arnold.

*Conroy, R. T. W. L. & Mills, J. N. (1970). *Human Circadian Rhythms,* 236 pp. London: Churchill.

Goodman, R. L. & Karsch, F. J. (1981). The hypothalamic pulse generator: a key determinant of reproductive cycles in sheep. In *Biological Clocks in Seasonal Reproductive Cycles,* ed. B. K. and D. E. Follett, pp. 223–36. Bristol: John Wright.

Hall, M. J. (1980). Circadian rhythm of proboscis extension responsiveness in the blowfly: central control of threshold changes. *Physiological Entomology,* **5,** 223–33.

Jones, M. D. R. & Gubbins, S. J. (1978). Changes in the circadian flight activity of the mosquito *Anopheles gambiae* in relation to insemination, feeding and oviposition. *Physiological Entomology,* **3,** 213–20.

*Kleitman, N. (1960). Patterns of dreaming. *Scientific American,* November, p. 82.

Lettau, J., Foster, W. A., Harker, J. E. & Treherne, J. E. (1977). Diel changes in potassium activity in the haemolymph of the cockroach *Leucophaea maderae. Journal of Experimental Biology,* **71,** 171–86.

*Loher, W. (Ed.) (1982). *Behavioral Expressions of Biological Rhythms.* New York: Garland Press.

Lukat, R. (1978). Circadian growth layers in the cuticle of behaviourally arrhythmic cockroaches (*Blaberus fuscus,* Ins., Blattoidea). *Experientia,* **34,** 477.

*Mills, J. N. (1973). Transmission processes between clock and manifestations. In *Biological Aspects of Circadian Rhythms,* ed. J. N. Mills, pp. 27–84. London and New York: Plenum.

*Neville, A. C. (1975). *Biology of Arthropod Cuticle,* 448 pp. Berlin: Springer.

Pittendrigh, C. S. (1954). On temperature independence in the clock system controlling emergence time in *Drosophila. Proceedings of the National Academy of Sciences, U.S.A.,* **40,** 1018–29.

Pittendrigh, C. S. (1966). The circadian oscillation in *Drosophila pseudo-obscura* pupae: a model for the photoperiodic clock. *Zeitschrift für Pflanzenphysiologie,* **54,** 275–307.

Rensing, L. (1966). Zur circadianen Rhythmik des Hormonsystems von *Drosophila. Zeitschrift für Zellforschung,* **74,** 539–58.

Rensing, L. (1969). Circadiane Rhythmik von *Drosophila*-Speicheldrüsen *in vivo, in vitro* und nach Ecdysonzugabe. *Journal of Insect Physiology,* **15,** 2285–303.

*Rusak, B. & Zucker, I. (1979). Neural regulation of circadian rhythms. *Physiological Reviews,* **59,** 449–526.

Stephan, F. K. & Nunez, A. A. (1977). Elimination of circadian rhythms in drinking, activity, sleep, and temperature by isolation of the suprachiasmatic nuclei. *Behavioral Biology,* **20,** 1–16.

Taylor, P. (1977). A continuously recording respirometer, used to measure oxygen consumption and estimate locomotor activity in tsetse flies, *Glossina morsitans. Physiological Entomology,* **2,** 241–5.

Truman, J. (1979). Interaction between abdominal ganglia during the performance of hormonally triggered behavioural programmes in moths. *Journal of Experimental Biology*, **82**, 239–53.

*Weitzman, E. D. & Hellman, L. (1974). Temporal organization of the 24-hour pattern of the hypothalamic-pituitary axis. In *Biorhythms and Human Reproduction*, ed. M. Ferin *et al.*, pp. 371–95. New York & London: Wiley.

JÜRGEN ASCHOFF

9 Circadian rhythms in man

9.1 Introduction

Like many animals, man has adjusted to the 24-h period of the natural environment so as to be prepared for efficient activity during the daytime and to rest at night. As the basis of this programme, almost all of his structures and functions undergo regular 24-h changes (Conroy & Mills, 1970). Under normal conditions, these diverse rhythms maintain distinct phase relationships with one another, implying a high degree of temporal order. Taken together, the 24-h rhythms represent a 'circadian organisation' (§8.6), that is, a system capable of self-sustaining oscillations in the absence of any periodic input from the environment. As with many other organisms, under constant conditions and in complete isolation, human subjects develop a free-running circadian rhythm, the period of which differs from 24 h (see the Glossary). It has also been shown that the human circadian system consists of a multiplicity of oscillators which are normally coupled to each other, but which may change their phase relationship, depending on conditions, and may even become uncoupled and then free run at different frequencies.

This chapter examines man's physiological timekeeping by first introducing the reader to the concept of internal temporal order and the relationship between this and man's sleep–wake cycle; it then surveys what is known about his free-running rhythms, and their entrainment by external periodic signals, including 'jet-lag' and shift work; finally, it looks briefly at medical aspects.

9.2 Internal temporal order

To illustrate the variety of rhythms that can be demonstrated in man, Fig. 9.1 depicts the changing hourly levels of five psycho-physiological variables: sleep–wakefulness, body temperature, two psycho-motor abilities, and self-assessed alertness, as measured in 12 subjects exposed to a light–dark schedule (first three days only). Four other physiological rhythms, measured as the levels of compounds excreted in the urine, are shown in Figs. 9.2 and 9.4, namely: cortisol, 17-hydroxycorticosteroids, potassium and adrenaline.

In fact almost any human physiological function, when measured across the day in this way, proves to vary rhythmically (see Conroy & Mills, 1970).

While the subjects studied in Fig. 9.1 were in a light–dark cycle and sleeping during the dark phase, it was not possible to say whether their sleep–wake cycle was causing the rhythmicity in the other four functions (see 'masking'

Fig. 9.1. Circadian rhythms in: rectal temperature, two psycho-motor performance measurements (multiple choice reaction time and speed of adding two digits), and self-rated alertness, during a 7-day period which included two days of sleep deprivation. Values are the means (of percentage deviation from each individual's 8-day mean level) from 12 subjects. Hatched areas, sleep in darkness, subjects awakened twice for tests; double-hatched area, sleep without tests. (Adapted from C. Ringer, medical thesis, Munich, 1972.)

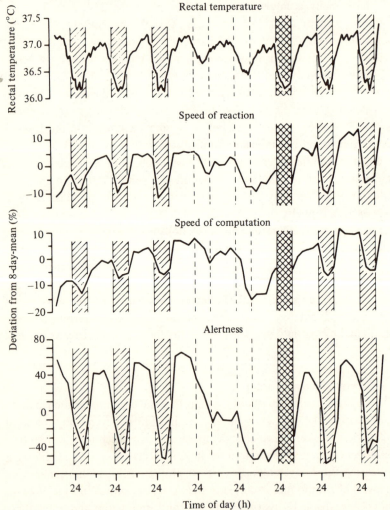

effects in §9.7). However, as can be seen on days 4 and 5, the rhythms persisted when the subjects were deprived of sleep for 48 h. Although there was a decrease in amplitude, indicating that sleep does have some effect on these rhythms, the clear continuation of the rhythmic patterns (especially in temperature) during sleep deprivation points to a sleep-independent component which is coupled to an endogenous oscillator, that is, a circadian clock. In order to investigate the properties of this clock, experiments have to be performed with subjects kept in isolation units where environmental factors can be controlled.

9.3   Free-running rhythms

When isolated in sound-proof chambers, human subjects usually show free-running rhythms with periods somewhat longer than 24 h. The results shown in Fig. 9.2 are from an experiment in which the subject knew the time of day for the first seven days; hence his rhythms of wakefulness and sleep, rectal temperature and urinary cortisol excretion were entrained to 24 h. From day 8 on, after all time-cues were removed, all three variables continued to be rhythmic, but their common period was close to 26 h, after some initial instability. This deviation of the free-running rhythm from 24 h is more conspicuous in Fig. 9.3, which summarises data on the sleep–wake cycle and rectal temperature from three isolated subjects. The left diagram shows a typical record from constant conditions (including constant light). The two other diagrams demonstrate that the rhythms were not affected either when bright illumination was replaced by continuous darkness or when a leisurely way of life was switched to one involving several work sessions on a bicycle ergometer each day. Sometimes, these changes in conditions show slight effects on the period of the free-running rhythms, but the predominant impression one gets is that the system is highly stable. The inter-individual

Fig. 9.2. Circadian rhythms of: wakefulness (α) and sleep (ρ), rectal temperature, and urinary cortisol excretion in a subject living alone in an isolation unit; first seven days in contact with the experimenter, thereafter without contact. (From R. Lund, medical thesis, Munich, 1974.)

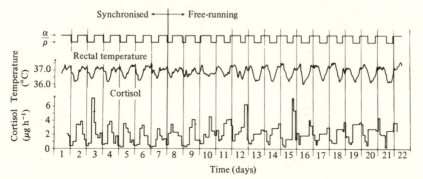

variability is also remarkably small: for 147 subjects, the overall mean period of the free-running rectal temperature rhythm was 25.0 h, with a standard deviation of only 0.50 h (Wever, 1979).

The internal temporal order of the free-running circadian system in man differs from that of his system when entrained (synchronised) to 24 h. Under entrained conditions, the maximum of rectal temperature occurs in the late afternoon, and the minimum during the second half of sleep time (Fig. 9.1). When free-running, these two extremes are advanced by several hours relative to the behavioural sleep–wake cycle (cf. Figs. 9.1 and 9.2 or 9.3). As a consequence, temperature mainly decreases during wakefulness and increases during sleep. These changes in the internal phase relationship, which are illustrated for a variety of functions in Fig. 9.4, contradict the hypothesis of a simple cause-and-effect relationship between the activity rhythm and other rhythmic functions within the organism. They imply rather that the various rhythms are coupled to different circadian oscillator pacemakers (see also §11.4.3) which change their mutual phase relationships according to conditions.

9.4   Entrainment by zeitgebers

Under normal conditions, circadian rhythms are usually entrained to 24 h by means of periodic factors in the environment, the so-called zeitgebers (see the Glossary). A light–dark cycle is the most powerful zeitgeber for most animals, but human subjects, exposed to light–dark cycles provided by the main ceiling lights of an isolation unit, are not easily entrained as long

Fig. 9.3. Circadian rhythm in three subjects each of whom lived alone in an isolation unit. Left, constant light conditions throughout the experiment. Middle, change from constant illumination to continuous darkness (DD). Right, first half without, second half with, seven work sessions a day on a bicycle ergometer. Black and white bars, wakefulness and sleep, respectively. Triangles, rectal temperature maxima (above bars) and minima (below bars). τ, mean period of the circadian rhythm (see the Glossary). (From Aschoff, 1978*b*).

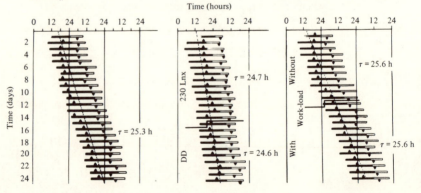

as they can make use of a small reading lamp at will. Under those conditions, their rhythms often continue to free run, crossing through the 24-h zeitgeber cycle with a circadian period longer then 24 h (Fig. 9.5 A). Entrainment does, however, occur when an additional time structure is provided, for example by gong signals given at regular intervals. These signals tell the subject to

Fig. 9.4. Circadian rhythms of rectal temperature and of three urine constituents (17-hydroxycorticosteroids (17-OHCS), potassium and adrenaline) in a subject who lived alone for 31 days in an isolation unit. Above, mean values from 14 days of contact with, and entrained to, the external environment. Below, mean values from the last seven days free-running in constant conditions without time-cues (mean period (τ) = 26.0 h). Hatched areas, asleep. To ease comparison, the abscissa is expressed in angular degrees of the rhythm (one full circadian period = 360°) instead of hours. (Adapted from Kriebel, in Scheving *et al.*, 1974.)

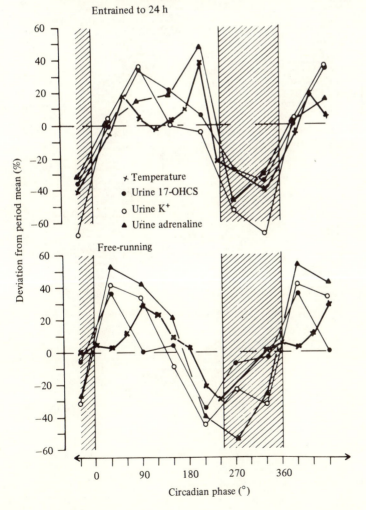

Fig. 9.5. Circadian rhythms of wakefulness and sleep (black and white bars) and of rectal temperature (triangles above and below bars for maxima and minima, respectively) in three subjects each of whom lived alone in an isolation unit under the influence of a light–dark cycle (hatched area, darkness). For **A** and **B**, reading lamp available in addition to the main lights; for **C**, no reading lamp. Further conditions: **A** without, but **B** and **C** with, regular gong signals (see the text). T, period of the light–dark cycle; τ, mean circadian period (see the Glossary). (From Aschoff, 1978a).

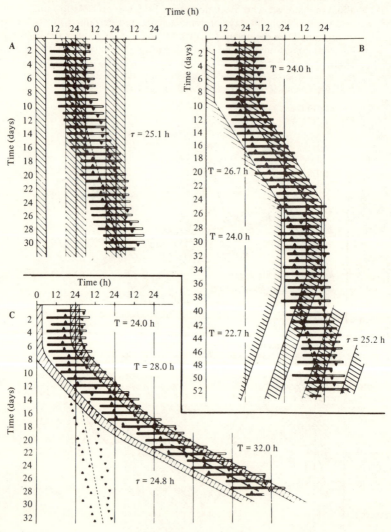

collect his urine, and are perceived by the subjects, according to their accounts, as a more direct social contact with the experimenter than that provided by the light cycle.

By means of such an 'enriched' zeitgeber, subjects can be entrained to periods other than 24 h. Fig. 9.5**B** presents the results of an experiment in which the subject was exposed successively to a 24-h, 26.7-h and 22.7-h light-plus-gongs day. As can be seen from the onsets of black bars (wakefulness), the subject was a late riser in the 24-h day, but became (to his surprise) an early riser in the 26.7-h day. This change in the phase relationship between rhythm and zeitgeber follows from a general rule in oscillation theory, according to which the phase relationship between two coupled oscillators depends on the ratio of the two frequencies (Aschoff, 1979). In the 22.7-h day, entrainment was lost and the rhythm free ran with a period close to 25 h.

A series of similar experiments, performed to determine how fast or how slowly human circadian rhythm can be driven by such entrainment, has revealed that the limits are reached when the zeitgeber approaches 23- or 27-h cycles (i.e. short or long artificial days), even with gong signals. Within this range of entrainment, however, the various physiological rhythms change their phase relationship in a systematic manner not only to the zeitgeber but also among themselves, again suggesting that they are driven by different pacemakers (Wever, 1979). Further support for this view comes from the observation that the circadian system can be split into components that run with different frequencies. This is shown in Fig. 9.5**C** by the record of a man kept in comparable conditions of isolation but without a reading lamp. Since he was thus virtually forced to adjust his behavioural activities to the light–dark cycle, it was possible to entrain his sleep–wake rhythm to periods of 28- and even 32-h 'days'. However, these long periods were evidently beyond the limits of entrainment for his body-temperature rhythm, since that (as indicated by the triangles in Fig. 9.5**C**) remained entrained only in the 24-h day, and free ran with a mean period of 24.8 h in the 28-h day as well as in the 32-h day. This phenomenon has been called forced *internal desynchronisation* (Wever, 1979).

9.5   Spontaneous internal desynchronisation

While internal desynchronisation can always be enforced in this way by means of a strong zeitgeber of unnatural period, it also sometimes occurs spontaneously in free-running rhythms, as shown in Fig. 9.6. This can happen either at a substantial lengthening or at a shortening of the activity rhythm. In both the cases shown, the rhythm of rectal temperature continued to free run with a period close to 25 h. The subject. in which desynchronisation occurred by a lengthening of the activity rhythm had had to begin with a relatively long period to his circadian system, and his temperature rhythm was slightly shortened after desynchronisation. By contrast, the subject in which the activity cycle suddenly shortened had originally had a relatively short period, and his temperature rhythm was slightly lengthened after

Fig. 9.6. Circadian free-running rhythms of wakefulness and sleep (black and white bars) and of rectal temperature (triangles above and below bars for maxima and minima, respectively) in two subjects each of whom lived alone in constant light in an isolation unit. In each record, part **a** shows internal synchronisation, part **b** spontaneous internal desynchronisation. τ, mean circadian period. (From Aschoff & Wever, 1976.)

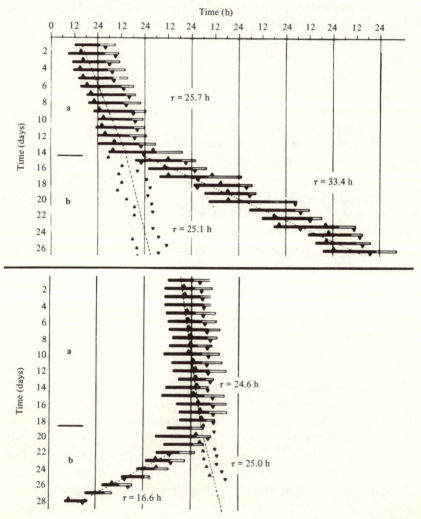

desynchronisation. These findings, corroborated by the results from 26 other experiments (Aschoff & Wever, 1976), suggest that in humans the circadian system consists of two oscillators (or sets of oscillators) with different characteristics and varying importance for the overt, measured rhythms. The oscillator that mainly controls the behavioural sleep–wakefulness rhythm is highly variable in frequency, whereas that which controls the temperature rhythm is relatively stable. When coupled to each other, the oscillators apparently have to compromise on a common period which, due to the difference in variability, is much closer to that of the temperature rhythm than that of the activity rhythm.

The reasons for internal desynchronisation are not yet understood. In a sample of 159 subjects each of whom was individually studied in constant conditions, spontaneous desynchronisation was observed in 24%, and the proportion was greater among subjects older than 40 yr (70%) as compared with the younger group (22%) (Wever, 1979). There was also a significantly higher incidence of internal desynchronisation in subjects who had relatively high scores in tests for neuroticism (Lund, 1974).

During internal desynchronisation, the rhythms of autonomic functions (i.e. temperature and excretion) usually had periods close to 25 h in subjects whose rhythms were free-running in constant conditions. However, desynchronisation was also observed in the presence of a light–dark cycle which did not entrain the activity rhythm. In several such instances (though not in Fig. 9.5A), the rhythm of rectal temperature, instead of free-running, locked on to the zeitgeber, suggesting that whereas light may be a powerful zeitgeber for some parts of man's circadian system, different zeitgebers may vary in their effectiveness to entrain the different components of the system.

9.6   Transmeridian flight and 'jet-lag'

Modern air travel gives everyone the opportunity to experience re-entrainment at first hand and to see how circadian systems can be upset. After a flight across several time zones, one's rhythms first continue to run more or less in accordance with local time at the place of departure, so that they are all out of phase with the new local time. Due to its inertia (i.e. the stability of the underlying oscillators), one's system takes several days to regain its normal phase relationship to the new environment. This is illustrated in Fig. 9.7 by the slow shift of a performance rhythm. Twelve subjects were tested for their ability to keep a pre-programmed course in a flight simulator. On the control day before the (real) flight (day -1), minimal errors were made in the early afternoon, and maximal errors at about 03.00 h. Immediately after the flight, either no rhythm was detectable (day 1) or a distorted rhythm with a small amplitude, still many hours out of phase (day 3). During these days of re-entrainment, the mean daily level of errors increased (cross-hatching in Fig. 9.7). A clear rhythm reappeared on day 5, but the normal phase setting was not regained until day 8.

The conclusions from many such flight experiments can be summarised as follows:

(a) Different physiological and behavioural rhythms re-entrain at different rates; hence, the organism is temporally 'out of order' after a transmeridian flight (i.e. somehow internally desynchronised, §9.5).

(b) Performance decrements and a loss in the sense of well-being observed after flights are partly caused by sleep deficits, but may also be due to the disorder of the circadian system.

(c) Re-entrainment often takes longer after an eastbound than after a westbound flight. This is in accordance with the fact that the human circadian system tends to free run with periods longer than 24 h, and hence may undergo phase delays more easily than phase advances (see §2.3.3).

(d) Re-entrainment is enhanced in subjects who are allowed to go outdoors after a flight, as compared with those who have to stay in their hotel rooms (Klein *et al.*, in Mackie, 1977), underlining the importance of social zeitgebers for man.

During re-entrainment, it sometimes happens that not all rhythms move in a direction that corresponds with that of the flight. In an experiment in which eight subjects were flown across nine time zones, all subjects phase-

Fig. 9.7. Circadian rhythm in a simulated airline pilot performance test (percent of errors in holding a set course) before and after an eastbound flight across eight time zones (i.e. a phase advance of 8 h). Mean values from 12 subjects tested every other hour. Arrows, expected times for minimum and maximum after completion of the 8-h shift. Dashed horizontal line, 24-h mean; hatching indicates increase in this mean error level over day -1. (Adapted from Klein *et al.*, 1970.)

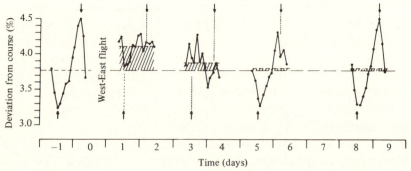

delayed both their behavioural and their body-temperature rhythms after the westbound flight (i.e. a 9-h delay). After the eastbound flight (a 9-h phase advance), however, only four of the subjects advanced their temperature rhythm by 9 h, in accordance with the advance shifting of their sleep–wake cycle, the other four re-entrained by phase-delaying their temperature rhythm by 15 h, notwithstanding that their sleep–wake cycle had phase-advanced by the 9 h. In other words, two components of the circadian system (behaviour and temperature) moved in opposite directions. Such re-entrainment by partition has also been observed in subjects exposed to shifts of zeitgebers in isolation units; and it is apparently more common after eastbound flights (advance shifts) than after westbound flights (delay shifts) (Aschoff, in Johnson, Tepas, Colquhoun & Colligan, 1981).

9.7 Shift work

Flying across time zones means that after arrival the passenger finds himself in a situation where *all* zeitgebers act together to shift his rhythms. This is in strong contrast to the situation of a night-worker who lives in an environment in which some zeitgebers may be phase shifted, for example an artificial light–dark cycle, while others remain unshifted, for example the life of his family. Consequently, the night-worker is in a situation which does not allow a complete re-entrainment of his circadian system, but instead distorts it.

To indicate some of the problems involved, Fig. 9.8 presents data collected from four subjects who worked initially on an 8-h day-shift and thereafter for 21 days on a night-shift. The curve of rectal temperature was normal during the control days and also during the first day of night-shift. In the following days, however, the temperatures measured during sleep were progressively depressed, and the minimum slowly drifted from early to late in the sleep time. This change in the timing of the minimum contrasts with the behaviour of the maximum which, on the twenty-first day of night-shift, still occurred at the same time of day as during day-shift.

In interpreting such data, one has to differentiate between a true phase shift of a rhythm and what is called a *masking effect*. The term 'masking' has been introduced to describe what may happen when either a zeitgeber or the sleep–wake cycle itself has effects on the overt state of some rhythmic physiological function but has no immediate bearing on the phase control of the rhythm. Examples are the decreases of body temperature *whenever* a subject falls asleep, and the increases *whenever* he becomes active. The curves shown in Fig. 9.8 probably represent an interaction between masking and partly shifted components of the circadian system. It is also noteworthy that even by the second recovery day the curve of rectal temperature again approximated to that measured during the control days. This fast re-adjustment supports the view that, during the night-work, the circadian system as a whole (i.e. the assemblage of pacemakers) was only partly shifted.

Fig. 9.8. Circadian rhythms of rectal temperature obtained in a semi-natural condition of shift work in the laboratory. Four days of day-shift followed by 21 days of night-shift and two recovery days without work. Mean values from four subjects. Hatched areas, sleep in darkness. Dotted lines, temperature curves from initial control days. (Adapted from Knauth & Rutenfranz, 1976.)

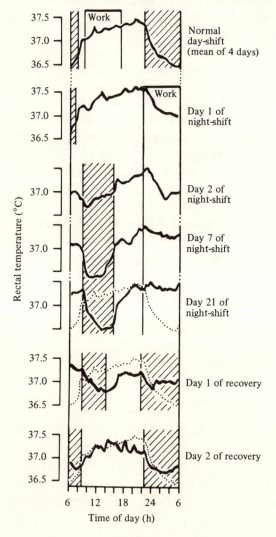

9.8 Medical aspects

Three features of the circadian system seem to be of potential importance for the physician: (a) the drastic changes from hour to hour that occur in many of the variables measured for diagnostic purposes; (b) the high degree of temporal order that characterises a healthy organism; and (c) the dependence on circadian phase of the organism's responsiveness to drugs.

With regard to the first (a), care has to be taken that measurements are made at the same circadian phase (which does not necessarily mean at the same time of day) in order to get information on 'normal' values (e.g. on the plasma level of a hormone (Fig. 6.4)) and on deviations from that norm during a disease. As for the second factor (b), the existence of standard circadian physiological patterns, now available for a number of variables, allows one to test whether certain diseases are characterised by distinct

Fig. 9.9. Circadian rhythms in **(A)** the threshold for tooth pain (compiled from Reinberg & Reinberg, 1977), and **(B)** in the duration of local anaesthesia in the jaw (compiled from Pöllmann & Hildebrandt, 1977).

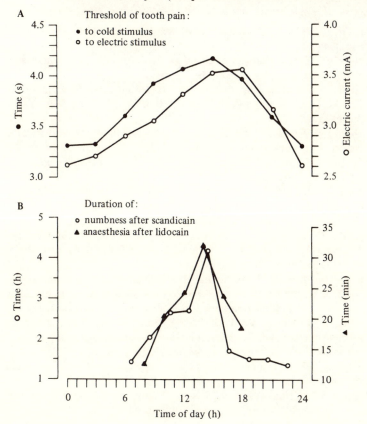

abnormalities in temporal order. In this context, disorder (including internal desynchronisation) must be considered not only as a symptom but also as a possible cause of a diseased condition, especially in psychiatry.

Concerning the third feature (c), the response of an organism to any stimulus usually depends on circadian phase (see Fig. 8.4). In medicine, such rhythms of responsiveness are of relevance with regard to the action of drugs. As was first shown by Haus & Halberg in 1959, a given dose of ethanol kills about 60% of mice when they are injected at the beginning of their activity time, but only 20% at the beginning of their rest time. For man, phase-dependent differences both in the effectiveness of drugs and in responses to other stimuli are also well documented. As examples, Fig. 9.9 shows the 24-h variation in the thresholds for a pain reaction (**A**) and the duration of local anaesthesia (**B**). An increasing number of studies on rhythms of sensitivity to drugs have opened a whole new area of 'chrono-pharmacology'; indeed the use of 'chrono-therapy' may soon become general. (See also §8.4.2.)

9.9   Further reading and key references
Books and review articles are indicated by asterisks

Aschoff, J. (1978a). Zirkadiane Rhythmen des Menschen. *Arzneimittel-Forschung*, **28**, 1850–957.

Aschoff, J. (1978b). Features of circadian rhythms relevant for the design of shift schedules. *Ergonomics*, **39**, 739–54.

Aschoff, J. (1979). Circadian rhythms: general features and endocrinological aspects. In *Endocrine Rhythms*, ed. D. Krieger, pp. 1–61. New York: Raven Press.

Aschoff, J. & Wever, R. (1976). Human circadian rhythms: a multi-oscillator system. *Federation Proceedings*, **35**, 2326–32.

*Conroy, R. T. W. L. & Mills, J. N. (1970). *Human Circadian Rhythms*. London: J. & A. Churchill.

Haus, E. & Halberg, F. (1959). 24-hour rhythm in susceptibility of C mice to a toxic dose of ethanol. *Journal of Applied Physiology*, **14**, 878–80.

*Johnson, L. C., Tepas, D. I., Colquhoun, W. P. & Colligan, M. J. (Eds) (1981). *The 24-Hour Workday. A Symposium on Variations in Work–Sleep Schedules*. Washington, DC: National Institute for Occupational Safety and Health.

Klein, K. E., Brüner, H., Holtmann, H., Rehme, H., Stolze, J., Steinhoff, W. D. & Wegmann, H. M. (1970). Circadian rhythms of pilots' efficiency and effects of multiple time zone travel. *Aerospace Medicine*, **41**, 125–32.

Knauth, P. & Rutenfranz, J. (1976). Experimental shift work studies of permanent night and rapidly rotating shift systems. *International Archives of Occupational and Environmental Health*, **37**, 125–37.

Lund, R. (1974). Personality factors and desynchronization of circadian rhythms. *Psychosomatic Medicine*, **36**, 224–8.

*Mackie, R. R. (Ed.) (1977). *Vigilance: Theory, Operational Performance and Physiological Correlates*. New York: Plenum Press.

Pöllmann, L. & Hildebrandt, G. (1977). Über die suggestive Steuerbarkeit der Schmerzschwelle an gesunden Zähnen. *Deutsche zahnärztliche Zeitschrift*, **32**, 343–45.

Reinberg, A. & Reinberg, M. A. (1977). Circadian changes of the duration of action of local anaesthetic agents. *Naunyn-Schmiedebergs Archiv für Pharmakologie*, **297**, 149–52.

*Scheving, L. E., Halberg, F. & Pauly, J. E. (Eds) (1974). *Chronobiology*. Stuttgart: Georg Thieme.

*Wever, R. (1979). *The Circadian System of Man*. Berlin–Heidelberg–New York: Springer-Verlag.

MANFRED KLUGE

10 Biochemical rhythms in plants

10.1 Introduction

It is obvious to the attentive observer that in plants, just as in animals, many manifestations of life do not proceed in a constant flow but run with changing intensities, and with minima and maxima that are separated by regular intervals. In other words, plants show annual, lunar and daily rhythms which, when tested in constant conditions in the laboratory, prove to persist – often for many cycles (Chapter 2 and 3). Evidently such rhythms are endogenously determined, but in natural conditions respond to the regular change of external stimuli by synchronising (i.e. entraining (see the Glossary)) to the periodicity of the environment. This endogenous rhythmicity is reflected in the ability of organisms to measure time, a property which enables them to prepare in advance for predictable changes in environmental conditions. For example, it is essential for certain plants to predict the onset of winter, so that they can harden their cells before the arrival of low temperatures and thus survive a sudden, unexpected frost (§7.1).

The phenomenon of the time measurement in organisms is one of the most exciting problems of experimental biology, and has attracted much recent research. In particular, there have been many attempts to understand the molecular mechanism of the underlying biological clock. Because life ultimately consists of integrated and controlled biochemical processes, the rhythmicity shown by some biochemical systems is of particular interest in this regard (Queiroz, 1974; Hastings & Schweiger, 1976; Hillman, 1976; Schweiger & Schweiger, 1977).

It is the aim of this chapter to introduce some of the biochemically-determined rhythmic phenomena in plants, with examples which one hopes are typical. For fuller reviews of the biology of plant timekeeping the reader is referred to Chapters 2, 5 and 7, and to Sweeney (1969), Wilkins (1969, 1973) and Bünning (1973).

10.2   Energy metabolism

10.2.1   *Rhythmic glycolysis in fermenting yeast*

After perturbing the metabolic steady state in suspensions of yeast cells by transferring them to anaerobic conditions or by adding substrate, oscillations are set up in the reduction of pyridine nucleotides and in the pool sizes of the metabolites used in glycolysis (Fig. 10.1); the oscillations have periods of some minutes. The system can be extracted from the cells and will then continue to oscillate in cell-free preparations. It can therefore be studied *in vitro*, though the cell-free preparation oscillates slightly faster than the *in vivo* system. Because of this experimental accessibility, the oscillatory behaviour of glycolysis is now the best understood high frequency biochemical rhythm in plants, and there is the exciting possibility that the principles behind the mechanisms involved may serve as a general model for other biochemical rhythms (e.g. circadian), and not only in plants.

The rhythmic behaviour of glycolysis depends on the characteristics of the control system established and how this regulates the intensity with which matter flows through the glycolytic pathway. At strategically important points in this pathway, the metabolic steps are catalysed by allosteric enzymes that can be activated or inhibited by effectors. Among the most powerful effectors are certain metabolites of the pathway itself, and the ATP/ADP/AMP system. Hence, glycolysis is regulated by both feedback and feed-forward loops; and it is a general characteristic of negative feedback systems that they are capable of oscillation.

Fig. 10.1. Rhythmical alteration of NAD-reduction performed by yeast cells after adding trehalose as substrate to the cell suspension. (Adapted from Pye & Chance, 1966.)

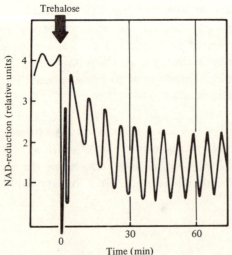

In order to make the principles of feedback and feed-forward control clearer, let us consider some crucial steps of glycolysis. Phosphofructokinase converts fructose-6-phosphate (F-6-P) to fructose diphosphate (FDP), and the enzyme is allosterically activated by its own product, FDP. An acceleration of FDP production due to the activation of phosphofructokinase will, however, diminish the concentration of the initial substrate, F-6-P; thus further FDP production is inhibited (Fig. 10.2). This system is clearly a regulatory circuit with negative feedback. At proper concentrations and metabolite flow rates, the levels of F-6-P and FDP will rhythmically change, each with inverse phase but equal period (Fig. 10.3).

The phosphofructokinase system is the most important, but not the only control point of glycolysis. The conversion of glyceraldehyde-3-phosphate to 3-phosphoglyceraldehyde, and of phosphoenolypyruvate (PEP) to pyruvate, are further sites where feedback loops cause metabolism to oscillate. Hence the whole glycolytic pathway may be considered as a regulatory system consisting of oscillating feedback circuits (see the chapter by Hess, in Hastings & Schweiger, 1976), and what is finally measured as an oscillation in pyridine nucleotide reduction represents the sum of many overlapping and coupled oscillations with various phase relationships to each other.

The most effective regulation of glycolysis is achieved by ATP, which is one of the main products, both of anaerobic (glycolytic) and aerobic (respiratory) metabolism. It is therefore advantageous for a metabolising cell that the ATP/ADP/AMP system is centrally involved in the regulation of the whole glycolysis system. ATP inhibits phosphofructokinase (negative feedback), and both ADP and AMP activate it (positive feedback). If the ATP level in the cell is low because of either anaerobiosis or high rates of energy consuming processes which convert ATP to ADP or AMP, a high flow of matter through the glycolytic and subsequent respiratory pathway will result, because phosphofructokinase then operates at high activity. If, however, the ATP level increases because the ATP-consuming processes become rate limiting, the phosphofructokinase is inhibited, and further wasteful breakdown of carbohydrate is prevented (Fig. 10.2).

Fig. 10.2. Diagram of the regulatory properties of the initial step of glycolysis (phosphofructokinase reaction) as linked to ATP production by glycolysis and respiration and to ATP consumption. Dotted lines, negative and positive feedback loops.

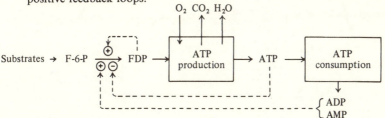

Since ATP plays an integral part in the control of an oscillating metabolic system which produces it, it is not surprising that the rate of ATP output, and therefore the cellular ATP level, also oscillates, and so do the levels of ADP and AMP (Fig. 10.3). Furthermore, this rhythmicity of the adenylate system may be transferred to other processes which depend on the availability of ATP (see §10.2.2 below).

The question often asked is 'what is the biological value of such rhythms?', but that is looking at the problem the wrong way round. The control system is there to prevent wasteful breakdown of valuable resources, and the occurrence of rhythmicity is simply the inherent consequence of the complex feedback peculiarities of the system. On the other hand, when such an oscillation is part of a circadian (or other) clock, the biochemical rhythm *per se* will clearly be of adaptive value, and very similar principles of operation to those outlined above for glycolysis may well be involved.

Fig. 10.3. Rhythmic alterations of relative pool sizes of glycolytic metabolites found in rhythmically fermenting yeast cells. Time scale arbitrary, but in the order of minutes.

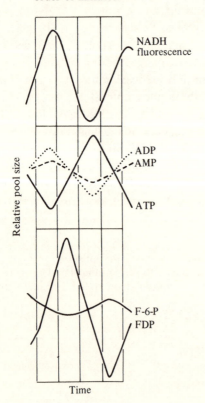

It is therefore of great theoretical importance that with a simple cell-free system consisting of three allosteric enzymes (phosphofructokinase, pyruvate kinase and adenylate kinase), metabolic oscillations with a 24-h (i.e. circadian) period have been achieved (Hess, in Hastings & Schweiger, 1976). The essential condition for this circadian period is that the input rates of the substrates are properly adjusted to the allosteric constants and turnover numbers of the enzymes. It is certainly conceivable that in a living cell such proper relationships between flow of matter, concentrations of substrates and co-factors, and the allosteric properties of the enzymes involved, are adjusted by cellular compartmentation and controlled transport across membranes (see Njus *et al.*, Wagner, and Sweeney, all in Hastings & Schweiger, 1976). This is considered in more detail below.

10.2.2 *Endogenous rhythms in the energy metabolism of* Chenopodium

The fundamental importance of energy metabolism in all living systems has led to a search for clock mechanisms that may be based on this energy metabolism of cells. Among the systems studied in this context, the higher plant *Chenopodium rubrum* is the most comprehensively investigated (see Hastings & Schweiger, 1976; Hillman, 1976; Wagner, 1977). Wagner lists nine different biochemical events showing simultaneous rhythms in this species, including betacyanin metabolism, energy charge, NADPH/NADH ratio and pool sizes of pyridine nucleotides, net photosynthesis, and dark respiration. There are also rhythms in the capacity (i.e. extractable activity) of several enzymes, in particular the adenylate kinases and various dehydrogenases (e.g. NADH/NADPH-dependent triose phosphate dehydrogenase, glucose-6-phosphate dehydrogenase, gluconate-6-phosphate dehydrogenase).

The period of the biochemical rhythms in *Chenopodium* is circadian, and that of the oscillation in enzyme capacities is in the range of 12–15 h (adenylate kinase has a period of 30 h). As in glycolysis rhythms, substrate availability and feedback control are assumed to be important constituents of the rhythmicity. The high frequency oscillations produced by feedback systems (see Fig. 10.1) are believed to be integrated and modulated by membranes and by the transport processes proceeding across these membranes. For example, the glycolytic NAD-triose phosphate dehydrogenase shows oscillations of capacity which are reciprocal to that of NADP-triose phosphate dehydrogenase. The latter is involved in photosynthetic carbon reduction and is thus strictly chloroplastic.

Furthermore, the integration of subunits, and with it the activity and capacity of both enzymes, is known to be affected by ATP and reduced pyridine nucleotides (which may be derived from photosynthesis). It is therefore conceivable that the primary cause of the rhythm in enzyme capacity is periodicity in the pool sizes of compartmentalised co-factors caused by the shuttles across the membrane which separate the compartments (in the above case, across the chloroplast wall). It is also important to note that some of the enzymes oscillating in *Chenopodium* are under the control of phytochrome (§7.5), which is assumed to interact with membranes (Wagner, 1977).

The ATP/ADP/AMP system mediates energy transfer in the cell. The actual capability of this system to feed energy into endergonic processes is characterised by the adenylate *energy charge*, which is:

$$\tfrac{1}{2}([ADP]+2[ATP])/([AMP]+[ADP]+[ATP])$$

An energy charge value of 1 means that all nucleotides of the system are converted to ATP, a value of 0.5 indicates that all are in the state of ADP or exist as an equimolar mixture of ATP and ADP. The rates of both ATP-requiring and ATP-generating processes are strongly influenced by the state of energy charge, and Wagner and his co-workers found that in *Chenopodium* the energy charge shows circadian oscillations. It is therefore reasonable to postulate that reactions depending on the adenylate system should follow the rhythm of energy charge, and thus also behave rhythmically. Similar speculations may be extended to the rhythmic changes in the NADPH/NADP ratio, or pool sizes of reduced pyridine nucleotides, which have also been observed in *Chenopodium*. The implication of mitochondrial involvement in rhythms in mutants of the fungus, *Neurospora*, is also of interest in this context (§11.5.1).

10.3   Rhythmic bioluminescence in *Gonyaulax*

The dinoflagellate, *Gonyaulax polyedra*, is a luminescent unicellular alga which occurs temporarily in huge quantities along the western coasts of North America. It is known to possesss four kinds of circadian rhythm (two in bioluminescence, one in photosynthesis, and one in cell division (Fig. 10.4)), and has been extensively studied by Sweeney and her colleagues (Sweeney, 1969; see also §11.3, 11.5.5). This behaviour of *Gonyaulax* leads to two important conclusions which are of general relevance for the interpretation of rhythmicity in organisms: (a) the occurrence of circadian rhythms is not restricted to multicellular organisms, but certainly also occurs in single cells (§8.2, 10.4, 11.4.2); (b) a single cell may simultaneously show more than one circadian rhythm.

Bioluminescence is the emission of light by living cells. The process is known to occur in bacteria, fungi, algae, and also in animals. The light-emitting biochemical system generally consists of a non-protein component ('luciferin') and an enzyme ('luciferase'), and depends on oxygen, ATP and Mg^{++}. The light is produced in a redox reaction where the change of free energy is conserved by exciting the luciferin molecule. When the molecule returns to the ground state, which is poorer in energy than the excited state, light quanta are emitted. The whole process may be described by the overall equation:

$$ATP + luciferin + O_2 \xrightarrow{\text{luciferase}} oxo\text{-}adenyl\text{-}luciferin + PP_i + light$$

In *Gonyaulax* the luminescing system seems to consist of particulate and soluble elements; together with the luciferin and luciferase, a specific luciferin-binding protein is involved in the light emission.

There are two different manifestations of bioluminescence shown by *Gonyaulax*: continuous low intensity 'glowing' which peaks towards the end of the night, and high intensity 'flashing' upon disturbance, which peaks in the middle of the night (Fig. 10.4). Under continuous illumination of low intensity, a free-running circadian rhythm of glowing persists for weeks. In continuous darkness, however, this rhythm damps out after a few cycles. That photosynthesis is necessary for the maintenance of the rhythm is indicated by the fact that the rhythm is restored by interruption of the continuous darkness with light breaks, and that the restored intensity of luminescence depends upon both the intensity of the light used and its wavelength, which follows the action spectrum for photosynthesis.

Fig. 10.4. Four simultaneous circadian rhythms in the unicellular alga, *Gonyaulax polyedra*. Bioluminescence occurs in two rhythms that are not in phase with each other: as background glowing, and as bright flashing in response to sudden mechanical disturbance. Photosynthesis is measured as the rate of incorporation of $^{14}CO_2$. Cell division occurs almost exclusively at lights-on. Abscissa shows LD 12:12 cycle used. See also Fig. 2.6 bottom curve. (Adapted from Hastings, Astrachan & Sweeney, 1961.)

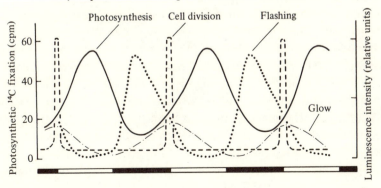

Since the light emission depends essentially on ATP, it is conceivable that the availability of ATP is the link between photosynthesis and bioluminescence. ATP should be readily available in the light, either directly from the photosynthetic light reaction, or indirectly from breakdown of photosynthetic products. In continuous darkness, however, the generation of ATP has to proceed at the expense of stored carbohydrates which are quickly exhausted; hence bioluminescence will disappear.

We have seen that the energy charge may rhythmically fluctuate in plants. So it may well be that the bioluminescence rhythms of *Gonyaulax* reflect such an energy charge rhythm. Other attempts to explain the rhythmicity are based on the finding that the *Gonyaulax* luciferase undergoes circadian oscillations of activity (Wilkins, 1973). It has also been suggested that membranes are involved (Sweeney, in Hastings & Schweiger, 1976). This latter idea is supported by the finding that membrane-active substances (e.g. alcohols, or the ionophore valinomycin which increases permeability to potassium ions) may shift the phase of the rhythm, and that rhythmical changes in the ultrastructure of membranes in *Gonyaulax* are reported (see §11.5.6). Inhibitors of RNA synthesis damp out the rhythm of luminescence, but whether RNA synthesis is an essential part of the basic oscillator itself, or is merely necessary for essential non-oscillatory supporting processes is unknown.

10.4   Rhythms of photosynthesis

Circadian rhythms of photosynthesis are apparently typical in plants, both unicellular and higher. If *Gonyaulax* is cultivated under continuous dim light just sufficient to maintain bioluminescence, photosynthesis proceeds at a constant, non-rhythmic rate. However, if samples are taken from the culture at appropriate intervals, and photosynthesis is measured under saturating light intensities (by monitoring either oxygen production or ^{14}C-carbon-dioxide incorporation), a circadian rhythmicity in the *capacity* for photosynthesis becomes evident (Fig. 10.4). This rhythm is, of course, measured in a large cell population, but it can be shown to be a property of each individual cell (Sweeney, 1969).

The control of photosynthetic rhythms has been investigated in detail in another unicellular alga, *Acetabularia*. This consists of a huge cell, 3–5 cm long and *ca* 1 mm in diameter. At one stage in development the nucleus is located in the rhizoid end of the cell, and is therefore easy to remove and transplant into another cell. The basic experiment is summarised in Fig. 10.5, from which it can be seen that the phase of the rhythm in each cell corresponds to the phase of the implanted nucleus.

It is tempting to conclude from this that the basic oscillator is located in the nucleus. However, enucleated *Acetabularia* cells also show a circadian rhythm in photosynthesis. Taken together, these two experiments suggest that the rhythm is intrinsic to the chloroplast, but can be modulated (entrained) by information released from the nucleus.

Although rhythmical changes have been found in the capacities of the enzymes involved in the photosynthetic dark reaction (e.g. NADP triose phosphate dehydrogenase (§10.2.2)), there is a stronger argument in favour of the light reaction being the element responsible for photosynthetic rhythmicity (Sweeney & Prézelin, 1978). In addition, changes in energy charge, chloroplast shape, chloroplast orientation, and in a hypothetical factor between the electron transport reaction and carbon-dioxide fixation, have all been proposed in the attempt to identify the oscillator.

10.5 Rhythmicity in crassulacean acid metabolism

Acid metabolism in the succulent Crassulaceae is a modification of the normal photosynthetic pathway of carbon fixation, and has evolved as an adaptation of water conservation in plants growing in arid environments. This crassulacean acid metabolism (known as CAM) is reviewed by Kluge & Ting (1978) and Osmond (1978). The pathway of metabolic carbon flow in CAM (Fig. 10.6) is initiated by the nocturnal fixation of carbon dioxide from the atmosphere. This step proceeds via β-carboxylation of phosphoenolpyruvate (PEP), catalysed by PEP-carboxylase. The product of this reaction, oxaloacetate, is reduced to malic acid which is transported into the vacuole of the cell where it accumulates during the night. During the day, malic acid is mobilised from the vacuole and decarboxylated by 'malic enzyme'. The carbon dioxide resulting from this decarboxylation is re-fixed

Fig. 10.5. Rhythmic photosynthesis control in *Acetabularia*. Two cultures were initially kept under LD 12:12 with opposite phases of light and darkness (shown at left). After a certain time of culture under these conditions, nuclei were reciprocally transplanted (solid arrows) and the rhythm of photosynthesis performed by the cells (curves at right) was monitored in constant light (previous dark phases shown by cross-hatched bars). (Adapted from Schweiger & Schweiger, 1977.)

LD 12:12------►LL

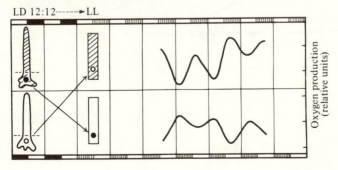

by photosynthesis and converted into carbohydrates. The three-carbon atom residue may either be further oxidised to carbon dioxide, or be converted to PEP at the expense of ATP. The value of this pathway is that the CAM plant harvests carbon dioxide from the atmosphere at night, stores it in the form of malic acid until the light period, and then keeps photosynthesis running behind closed stomata on the endogenous malic-acid-derived carbon dioxide.

There are two aspects to the rhythmicity in CAM; one is concerned with the metabolic control of the process; the other with the phenomenon of the carbon-dioxide exchange. The two are probably closely interrelated. We will look first at metabolic CAM regulation (see also Queiroz, 1974; Kluge, 1976, 1977; Kluge & Ting, 1978; Osmond, 1978).

As shown in Fig. 10.6, in the light, uncontrolled competition between PEP-carboxylase and photosynthetic carbon-dioxide fixation for the endogenous carbon dioxide has to be prevented, or else the carbon will not flow quantitatively from malic acid into the photosynthetic end-products. Hence,

Fig. 10.6. **(A)** Flow of carbon in crassulacean acid metabolism (CAM). **(B)** Regulatory properties of CAM. Black arrows, reactions dominating at night; open arrows, reactions dominating during the day; dotted arrows, regulatory properties. These processes interact in constant light to produce a circadian rhythm of carbon-dioxide fixation. PEP, phosphoenolpyruvate; OAA, oxaloacetic acid; MDH, malate dehydrogenase; ME, malic enzyme. (Adapted from Queiroz, 1979.)

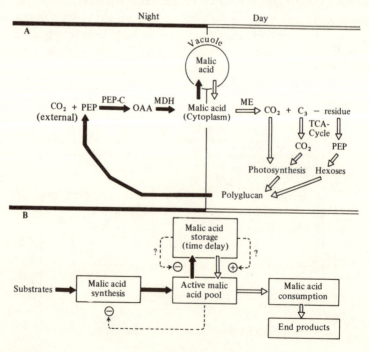

PEP-carboxylase must be inactive, or at least less active, during daylight, for at least as long as carbon dioxide is still being generated from malic acid. Queiroz and his colleagues postulate that carbon-dioxide fixation by PEP-carboxylase is low during the day and high during the night because of an endogenous circadian rhythm in the capacity of that enzyme (Queiroz, 1979).

Such rhythms have been described and extensively investigated in *Kalanchöe blossfeldiana* (Crassulaceae), in which there is also an endogenous rhythm of malic enzyme and aminotransferase capacity. The endogenous character of these enzyme rhythms is indicated by their persistence under continuous illumination, and the fact that they can be entrained by light cycles. Furthermore, it has been shown by Brulfert, Guerrier & Queiroz (1975), that the phytochrome system (Chapter 7) is involved in the rhythmic photocontrol of PEP-carboxylase. Queiroz suggests that this circadian rhythmicity in the capacity of the various CAM enzymes is due to the action of a basic driving oscillator.

There are two main points which need further clarification: (a) as is also still the case for other circadian rhythms, the nature of the driving oscillator is unknown (see Chapter 11); (b) the amplitude of the PEP-carboxylase rhythm is comparatively low (normally in the range of 30%), but even during the lowest point of the oscillation it has a capacity many times in excess of that necessary for the observed rate of carbon-dioxide fixation; effective regulation of carbon flow by the rhythm in enzyme capacity is thus difficult to understand.

Other hypotheses for CAM regulation are based on the finding that PEP-carboxylase is an allosteric enzyme strongly inhibited by malate (Kluge & Ting, 1978; Osmond, 1978). Hence, if the level of malate in the CAM-performing cell is high, as is true at the end of the night and during the first hours of the day, PEP-carboxylase can be expected to operate at only a low rate, because of feedback inhibition by malate (Fig. 10.6). If the malate is then consumed, PEP-carboxylase inhibition will be suspended, and the β-carboxylation pathway will be opened again.

Because PEP-carboxylase is considered to be located mainly in the cytoplasm, it is logical to suggest that only malic acid present in the cytoplasm will be directly involved in such control of the enzyme. However, the size of the cytoplasmic malic-acid pool is probably determined by the flux of malic acid across the tonoplast, the membrane of the storage compartment. The transport of malic acid between cytoplasm and vacuole therefore seems to be an important link in the regulation mechanism. It has been directly demonstrated by ^{14}C pulse-chase experiments that the sink-source behaviour of the vacuole varies periodically (Kluge, 1977). During the night, the cytoplasmic malic-acid pool is kept low because the vacuole acts as a strong sink for malic acid. At the end of the night, however, more malic acid is exported from the vacuole than is imported, so the metabolically active malic-acid pool in the cytoplasm will increase, and PEP-carboxylase will presumably be inhibited.

It has also been suggested that the nocturnal increase of malic acid content in the vacuole will increase osmotic water uptake by the vacuole, and thus increase turgor. This could alter the properties of the tonoplast and so trigger the change of the vacuole, from being a malic-acid sink to being a malic-acid source. This as yet tentative model would explain CAM regulation in terms of a relaxation oscillator (see Bünning, 1973, p. 117), with the filling of the vacuole being the tension phase, and its loss of malate the relaxation phase. The circadian periodicity is then seen as a function of the vacuole acting as a delay in the feedback control of PEP-carboxylase proposed above. Possibly the malate storage capacity of the vacuole has evolved to be of sufficient size for the delay to approach 24 h.

It should be emphasised that the two models of circadian CAM control – either by endogenous rhythmicity of enzyme capacity, or by feedback inhibition – are not necessarily mutually exclusive, and it has been suggested by Queiroz (1979) that in CAM plants PEP-carboxylase might be controlled by *both*.

As indicated earlier, the carbon-dioxide exchange also behaves rhythmically. In day–night cycles, CAM plants show a net uptake of carbon dioxide during the night and an extended depression of carbon-dioxide uptake during the day. In normal air, this rhythmicity persists for some further oscillations in continuous light (Fig. 10.7). Under continuous darkness, plants transferred into an air stream free of carbon dioxide, show a rhythmic output of carbon dioxide, which has been studied extensively in *Kalanchöe fedtschenkoi* by Wilkins (1973; see also Kluge & Ting, 1978). The carbon-dioxide output rhythm is in fact an expression of the rhythm of carbon-dioxide re-fixation, probably by PEP-carboxylase-mediated β-carboxylation. The carbon-dioxide rhythm is therefore consistent with the idea of endogenous PEP-carboxylase rhythmicity.

It is not yet clear, however, whether the rhythm of carbon-dioxide output is a normal property of CAM. The rhythm is measured by passing carbon-dioxide-free air over the plants for several days in continuous darkness, which must seriously affect the normal performance of CAM. Furthermore, not all CAM plants behave identically with respect to the rhythm. *Kalanchöe tubiflora*, for instance, shows the rhythm only in constant light, and not in constant darkness. In other species the rhythm may damp out rapidly after transfer to constant conditions. Finally, Lüttge & Ball (1978) have shown that the gas-exchange rhythm may persist without a corresponding malic-acid rhythm, even though the latter is an essential criterion of CAM performance.

10.6   Rhythmic movements of leaves – a biochemical problem?

The day–night rhythmic movements of leaves in certain plants, especially in species of Leguminosae, were the first scientifically documented examples of endogenous circadian rhythmicity (Figs. 2.1, 5.4A). It is beyond the scope of this chapter to analyse the biophysical basis of the movements (see §7.5), but one aspect is interesting in the context of biochemically determined rhythmicity in plants. Schildknecht (1978) has isolated a group of substances which he named 'leaf movement factors' from the leaves of *Mimosa pudica*, the 'sensitive plant', that shows the rhythm well. These substances are capable of initiating leaf movements when applied to *Mimosa*. One of them has been identified as a glycoside having 2,5-dihydroxybenzoic acid as the aglycone, and both glucose and apiose as sugar components.

Schildknecht has further reported that *Mimosa* shows differences in the tissue levels of the substances across the 24 h, and that the differences correspond with the leaf movement activity shown by the plant. It is thus possible that plant movement rhythms, which are due to ion transport and turgor pressure changes in the pulvini at the leaf and petiole hinges, are regulated by the rhythmic synthesis of leaf movement 'hormones'. However, this does not explain the mechanism of the driving clock; that is still unknown. Schildknecht's work merely shifts the level of investigation, and identifies a coupling mechanism (§11.3), rather than really answering the question of what the clock is.

10.7   Further reading and key references

Books and review articles are indicated by asterisks

Brulfert, J., Guerrier, D. & Queiroz, O. (1975). Photoperiodism and enzyme rhythms: kinetic characteristics of the photoperiodic induction of Crassulacean Acid Metabolism. *Planta* (*Berlin*), **125**, 33–44.

*Bünning, E. (1973). *The Physiological Clock*, 3rd edn. Berlin, Heidelberg, New York: Springer-Verlag.

Fig. 10.7. Endogenous rhythm of net carbon-dioxide uptake performed by the CAM plant *Kalanchöe tubiflora*. The plants were held under LD 12:12 and afterwards transferred to continuous light (at 20 °C; and 10 000 lux).

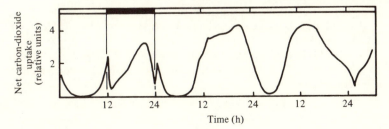

Hastings, J. W., Astrachan, L. & Sweeney, B. M. (1961). A persistent daily rhythm in photosynthesis. *Journal of General Physiology*, **45**, 69–76.

*Hastings, J. W. & Schweiger, H. G. (Eds) (1976). *The Molecular Basis of Circadian Rhythms*. Berlin: Report of the Dahlem workshop.

*Hillman, W. S. (1976). Biological rhythms and physiological timing. *Annual Review of Plant Physiology*, **27**, 159–79.

Kluge, M. (1976). Models of CAM regulation. In *CO$_2$ Metabolism and Plant Productivity*, ed. R. H. Burris & C. C. Black, pp. 205–16. Baltimore, London, Tokyo: University Park Press.

Kluge, M. (1977). Regulation of carbon dioxide fixation in plants. In *Integration of Activity in the Higher Plant. Symposia of the Society for Experimental Biology*, **31**, 155–75.

*Kluge, M. & Ting, I. (1978). Crassulacean Acid Metabolism. Analysis of an ecological adaptation. *Ecological Studies*, **30**. Berlin, Heidelberg, New York: Springer-Verlag.

Lüttge, U. & Ball, E. (1978). Free-running oscillations of transpiration and CO$_2$ exchange in CAM plants without a concomitant rhythm of malate levels. *Zeitschrift für Pflanzenphysiologie*, **90**, 69–77.

*Osmond, C. B. (1978). Crassulacean Acid Metabolism. A curiosity in context. *Annual Review of Plant Physiology*, **29**, 379–414.

Pye, K. & Chance, B. (1966). Sustained sinusoidal oscillations of reduced pyridine nucleotides in cell-free extracts of *Saccharomyces calsbergensis*. *Proceedings of the National Academy of Sciences, U.S.A.*, **55**, 888–94.

*Queiroz, O. (1974). Circadian rhythms and metabolic patterns. *Annual Review of Plant Physiology*, **24**, 115–34,

Queiroz, O. (1979). CAM: rhythms of enzyme capacity and activity as adaptive mechanisms. In *Photosynthesis II. Encyclopedia of Plant Physiology*, **6**, eds M. Gibbs & E. Latzko. Berlin, Heidelberg, New York: Springer-Verlag.

Schildknecht, H. (1978). *Über die Chemie der Sinnpflanze Mimosa pudica* L. Berlin, Heidelberg, New York: Springer-Verlag.

*Schweiger, H. G. & Schweiger, M. (1977). Circadian rhythms in unicellular organisms: an endeavor to explain the molecular mechanism. *International Review of Cytology*, **51**, 315–42.

*Sweeney, B. M. (1969). *Rhythmic Phenomena in Plants*. London, New York: Academic Press.

Sweeney, B. M. & Prézelin, B. B. (1978). Circadian rhythms. *Photochemistry and Photobiology*, **27**, 841–7.

*Wagner, E. (1977). Molecular basis of physiological rhythms. In *Integration of Activity in the Higher Plant. Symposia of the Society for Experimental Biology*, **31**, 33–72.

*Wilkins, M. B. (1969). Circadian rhythms in plants. In *Physiology of Plant Growth and Development*, ed. M. B. Wilkins, pp. 647–71. London: McGraw-Hill.

*Wilkins, M. B. (1973). Circadian rhythms in plants. In *Biological Aspects of Circadian Rhythms*, ed. J. N. Mills, pp. 235–79. London and New York: Plenum.

JON W. JACKLET

11 Circadian clock mechanisms

11.1 Introduction

Whenever one observes a circadian rhythm in constant conditions, running with precision but without the aid of external time-signals (as in Figs. 2.1, 3.2 and 5.6), one is presented with the question of what is it that times the precision of the rhythm. How does the clock work? What cellular and physiological mechanisms keep it oscillating cycle after cycle? To answer these questions it is necessary to know where the clock is and how it regulates the overt activity that one observes as the rhythm. This chapter examines present knowledge on the location of such clocks, their connection or 'coupling' to the overt physiological rhythms they control, and their possible cellular mechanisms. The evidence relates almost exclusively to circadian rhythms, but it can be assumed that the same principles will apply to circatidal clocks, and perhaps also to circalunar (Chapter 3) and even circannual clocks (Chapter 5). The reader is also referred to the several reviews written on clock mechanisms; in ascending order of sophistication these include Brady (1979), Edmunds (1976) and Hastings & Schweiger (1976) (see also Chapter 10 above).

11.2 The *Aplysia* eye clock – a model system

The circadian rhythm shown in Fig. 11.1 is of neuronal firing from the eye of *Aplysia*, the sea hare, an opisthobranch mollusc. It is recorded from the optic nerve of an isolated eye maintained in organ culture for a week in constant darkness. This compound action potential (CAP) output rhythm is convenient for experimental study because it can be continuously monitored by electrical recording, so that the waveform, amplitude and period of the rhythm are known at all times. In the intact animal, the electrical activity from the eye is conducted to the cerebral ganglion where it influences locomotor control and modulates the circadian rhythm of locomotor behaviour (Lickey & Wozniak, 1979). The eye may also be linked to other physiological systems by neurosecretion, since it releases several polypeptides.

The isolated eye, which is composed of about 5000 cells, including 4000 photoreceptors and the 1000 neurones that generate the compound action potentials, evidently contains a circadian clock (or clocks), since the electrical firing proceeds with a free-running period of about 26 h, distinctly different from the external 24-h solar day (see the Glossary and §2.2). It must also contain the photoreceptor mechanism for entrainment, since the rhythm can be phase shifted by light signals (Jacklet, 1974; Lickey, Block, Hudson & Smith, 1976). The actual clock mechanism, which may be inherent in each cell of the electrically interacting population of neurones, is believed to be a cellular entity that controls the frequency of firing through a coupling mechanism that links the clock to the cell's spike-generating membrane. If the clock or the coupling is disrupted (arrow in Fig. 11.1), the spiking continues at a steady rate, but its circadian rhythmicity is abolished. This effect is common to other systems; when the clock is removed or uncoupled, the overt activity continues but is arrhythmic.

11.3   Coupling concepts

Coupling mechanisms exist at several levels in a circadian system: (1) linking environmental time-signals (zeitgebers) to a clock; (2) linking a cellular clock to other activities in the cell; (3) linking a population of clock cells together as a coherent unit at a clock site; (4) linking such a clock site to driven organs or tissues; and (5) linking distant clock sites to each other.

The first two levels of coupling are found in unicellular organisms, but are not restricted to them. Many of these unicells exhibit clear circadian rhythms and have been particularly important for biochemical research on rhythms

Fig. 11.1. Circadian rhythm of compound action potential frequency (CAP h^{-1}) recorded from the optic nerve of an isolated eye of the sea hare, *Aplysia*, maintained in organ culture in constant darkness. The eye is shown schematically in the inset with a recording suction electrode attached to the cut end of the optic nerve. The time axis shows solar days contrasted to circadian days as measured (dotted lines) from the free-running period of the rhythm. At the arrow, propionate was added, which stopped or disconnected the clock leaving the CAP activity continuing but arrhythmically. (After Jacklet, 1974.)

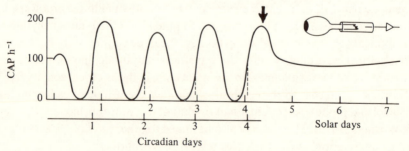

(see Chapter 10). For example, the alga, *Gonyaulax*, has four measurable circadian rhythms (Fig. 10.4) which are all apparently coupled to one clock because they proceed with the same period of oscillation and each rhythm maintains a constant phase relationship with the others. Little is known of the intracellular mechanism that links the clock to the four observable rhythms, but the system may be envisaged as shown in Fig. 11.2, with two kinds of couplings: (1) from the zeitgeber time-stimulus to the clock (to accomplish entrainment), and (2) from the endogenous clock entity to the various overt, measured rhythmic activities. Since the rhythms are usually assayed on populations of cells, the question arises as to whether each unicell has its own clock or whether the rhythm arises from dynamic interactions of the population. It appears, however, that each unicell has its own clock, since single *Gonyaulax* individuals express a rhythm (§10.3), just as do the much larger individual cells of *Acetabularia* (§10.4).

11.4 Clock sites and coupling in animals

In multicellular animals, the situation is more complex, and coupling exists at all of the five levels mentioned. Each cell or organ must have the potential to generate its own circadian rhythm (§8.2), but higher-order control exists so that the many rhythmic activities of an animal occur in an orderly manner (§8.6). Usually the higher control of temporal events can be traced to the nervous system, a system especially adapted for control and coordination. Specific sites in the nervous system generate circadian rhythms. They interact with one another and are coupled to the neuronal centres controlling overt behaviour such as locomotion, as well as being coupled to other, non-neural tissues and organs (Fig. 8.9). The means of coupling between the circadian clock site and the observed rhythms is generally considered to be either direct, via conventional neuronal pathways and

Fig. 11.2. Organisational scheme of a circadian system within a single cell. The zeitgeber entraining stimulus (Z) is transduced by a receptor (triangle) which couples the signal to the clock ($\sim$) and causes phase shifting. The clock is coupled to various cellular activity sites (A_1–A_n) causing the overt activities ($\sim_1$–$\sim_n$) to be rhythmic.

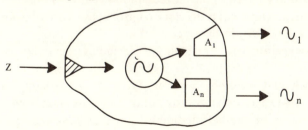

synaptic transmission, or humoral, involving the release of chemical substances that may be distributed throughout the organism by the vascular system.

Just where in the nervous system the clock resides, and the nature of its coupling to overt rhythms have been the subject of much investigation. The techniques used include: ablation (destruction) or lesion of the specific tissue; removal and then replacement of the tissue; isolation of the tissue within the organism; and isolation of the tissue outside the organism in organ or cell culture (Figs. 11.1, 11.6). In the ablation approach, the rhythm is monitored before and after the destruction of the suspected tissue. The absence of a rhythm after the ablation then indicates that the removed tissue may have contained the clock, or an important pathway for its expression; though since the rhythm is abolished, the evidence is essentially negative. Nevertheless the technique has been helpful.

11.4.1   *Insects – optic lobes and brain neurosecretion*

By using ablation on insects, the optic lobes of the brain have been identified as the probable site of the circadian clock controlling locomotory activity in cockroaches and crickets, and their compound eyes have been shown to be the photoreceptors that mediate their entrainment by light (Brady, 1974; Page, 1981). An intact neural pathway from the optic lobes to the thoracic ganglia is necessary for expression of the locomotor rhythm, so the coupling is believed to be neural, rather than by a specific blood-borne hormone as had once been thought (see Brady, 1969).

In crickets, the central area of the brain (the pars intercerebralis, which contains many neurosecretory cells) serves as a coupling site between the optic lobe clocks and the overt rhythms of locomotion, stridulation and spermatophore production. It appears that the control is exerted neurally, but a hormonal component is not yet ruled out (Sokolove & Loher, 1975).

In different insect orders, the clock sites and coupling mechanisms are not the same. In silkmoths, the flight activity rhythm is controlled by a central cerebral clock, rather than by the lateral optic lobes, and the clock is entrained via extra-ocular photoreceptors within the brain itself, rather than via the compound eyes. As in cockroaches and crickets, however, this clock is apparently neurally linked to the thoracic motor centres (Truman, 1974). In contrast to this arrangement is the clock control of eclosion behaviour (adult emergence (cf. Fig. 8.5)) in the same moths.

This clock is again in the central brain area, including the pars intercerebralis, and entrainment by light is mediated by brain photoreceptors. The coupling between clock and eclosion, however, is this time certainly hormonal (see Brady, 1974; Page, 1981): transplanting the whole brain from one pupa into the abdomen of another, de-brained pupa, induces subsequent adult eclosion at the appropriate time of day, although brain-less pupae otherwise emerge at random times. Furthermore, transplanting brains between species with different eclosion times, transfers the species-specific timing. Thus the brain not only contains the eclosion-releasing hormone, it also controls its circadian phase-setting, and thus must contain the clock. The actual motor 'tapes' for eclosion behaviour, on the other hand, are evidently sited in the abdominal nerve cord (Truman, 1979) and are simply switched on by the eclosion hormone. It should be noted in passing that eclosion is a once-in-a lifetime act for each individual; it may therefore be expected to be controlled differently from daily repeated on-going rhythmic behaviour of the locomotor activity or stridulation type (see §8.4.4).

11.4.2 *Vertebrates – pineal and suprachiasmatic nucleus*

The 'remove and replace' technique has produced positive results in other animals too. For example, the pineal gland of sparrows contains a circadian clock, and sparrows deprived of their pineal become arrhythmic when kept in constant darkness, lacking the free-running circadian activity cycle of normal birds. When a pineal gland is transplanted into the anterior chamber of the eye of a pineal-less bird, however, the recipient bird regains a circadian rhythm. Furthermore, as with Truman's silkmoth transplants, the *phase* of the induced rhythm is that of the donor bird, which had been kept on a different light schedule from the recipient (Fig. 11.3). There is evidently a clock in the pineal which is not perturbed significantly by transplantation, and which quickly recouples to the recipient bird's locomotor activity, presumably by the secretion of melatonin from the pineal (see §11.5.2).

The ablation technique has been used to identify the suprachiasmatic nuclei (SCN) of the mammalian brain as important circadian clocks controlling rhythms in locomotor activity, feeding, pineal secretion, etc. in rodents. The SCN consist of two small groups of nerve cells in the hypothalamus, lying just above the optic chiasma (Figs. 11.4, 6.6), and appear to be at or near the top of a hierarchy of oscillators that control rhythms in mammals (Rusak, 1979). When they are surgically semi-isolated but left *in situ*, they show a circadian rhythm of electrical activity that cannot be detected in neighbouring hypothalamic sites (Fig. 11.4; see Rusak & Zucker (1979); and see §8.5 for relation to sleep). This implies that the SCN are the site of a primary circadian clock, and that they are coupled to surrounding brain structures by neural connections (note the parallel with insect behavioural rhythms).

11.4.3 *Coupling between primary clocks*

Since the brains of higher animals are bilaterally symmetrical, each suspected clock site, that is the insect optic lobes and mammalian SCN (though not the bird pineal), is paired with a counterpart on the other side of the brain. It appears, however, that either half of the pair is by itself capable of driving the overt observed rhythm, since unilateral ablation in insects and rats does not create arrhythmicity. Nevertheless, some coupling between the two clocks does normally occur. In cockroaches, for example, removing one of the optic lobes almost invariably slows the free-running rhythm of locomotor activity, so the two lobes must interact.

A different line of evidence for a multiplicity of coupled driving oscillators (i.e. clocks) in animals comes from observations of the kind considered in §9.5. Not infrequently when men are held in isolation in constant light, their rhythms of behaviour (sleep–wake cycle) and body temperature (plus ion

Fig. 11.3. Activity records of donor and recipient sparrows in pineal transplantation experiments; each horizontal line represents 24 h of record, with thick blackening of the line indicating behavioural activity. (**A**) Sparrow entrained in a light–dark regime (shown by hatched and white bar). This bird's pineal was transplanted at the dot and arrow to the pineal-less recipient sparrow (**B**) that had previously been arrhythmic in constant darkness (hatched bar). (**C**) The recipient then became rhythmic while still in constant darkness. The phase of the rhythm of the recipient bird was identical with the expected phase of the donor, and the rhythm subsequently free ran. (After Zimmerman & Menaker, 1979.)

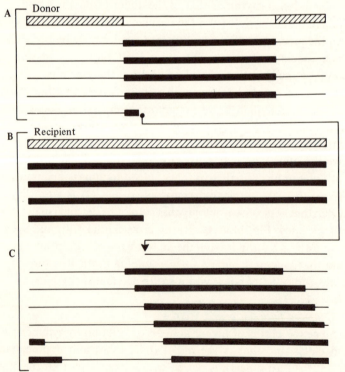

excretion) free run at different frequencies (Fig. 9.6). This internal desynchronisation indicates the existence of several circadian pacemakers, which are usually coupled together to run at a common period, but which when uncoupled reveal their different free-running characteristics.

Related to this phenomenon in man are the observations of so-called *rhythm splitting* in other vertebrates. This usually occurs in constant light, where the activity–rest cycle proceeds with a normal free-running periodicity for some time and then the active phase abruptly starts splitting into two peaks which get successively farther apart over a period of several days, until they stabilise at about 12 h out of phase with each other. This again is evidence for more than one pacemaker. To explain such phenomena Pittendrigh & Daan (1976) have proposed that circadian systems function with two kinds of oscillators ('evening' and 'morning'), with their spontaneous frequencies having opposite dependencies on light.

Something rather similar to splitting has been observed in the rhythm of neuronal activity in the eyes of *Aplysia* (Fig. 11.1). Each eye contains the complete organisation of a circadian clock, and if intact animals are entrained to light–dark cycles, the two ocular circadian clocks adopt identical phases.

Fig. 11.4. Frontal section through the hypothalamus of a rat showing (arrows) the two bilaterally symmetrical groups of nerve cell bodies, suprachiasmatic nuclei (SCN), at the tip of and lateral to the third ventricle (3) (see also Fig. 6.6). An 'island' of tissue containing the SCN can be isolated (dotted line) by the rotation of a special surgical knife; neuronal activity then retains a circadian rhythm within this isolated island but not outside it. OC, optic chiasma; OT, optic tract; AH, anterior hypothalamus; SO, supraoptic nuclei. (Adapted from Inouye & Kawamura, 1979.)

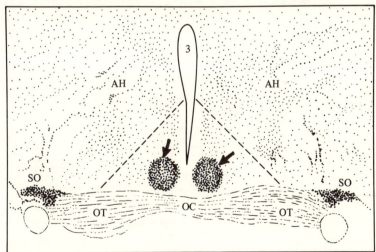

However, if the animal is placed in constant dim light for several days the ocular rhythms become out of phase with each other (Hudson & Lickey, 1980) and usually adopt a 180° (12-h) anti-phase relationship, as in the locomotor rhythm splitting observed in vertebrates. Again, the preference for the final 12-h difference must indicate the existence of weak coupling between the two separate clock sites.

Evidently, coupling between clocks and the various overt rhythms that they drive may be neural, humoral or both, and no simple generalisation emerges. Pairs of bilaterally symmetrical clocks, which are themselves populations of coupled cells in some instances, are typically weakly cross-coupled, but in addition, other clocks may also be coupled to the principal clocks. A schematic view of this organisation is shown in Fig. 11.5 (see also Fig. 8.9).

11.5   Cellular clock mechanisms

In order to study the biochemical basis of the clock, a common approach is to isolate the tissue that contains the clock and reduce it to the essential components. It should have a conveniently measurable rhythmic output for the assay of the clock's performance, and should ideally be assailable by the genetic approach. The closest approach to biochemical 'clockwork' has been in plants (Chapter 10), but two animal preparations have been revealing – the *Aplysia* eye (Fig. 11.1) and the bird pineal organ (Fig. 11.6).

Fig. 11.5. Organisation of a circadian system within an organism. Zeitgeber (Z) signals are sensed by paired receptors (hatched triangles) and coupled to the principal bilaterally symmetrical clock sites ($\sim_{BS}$) which are coupled at x to each other and other clock sites ($\sim_n$). Each clock is coupled to activities (A) to produce the overt observable rhythms (1, j, n) – cf. Fig. 8.9.

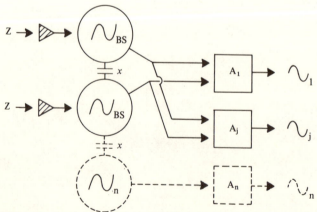

11.5.1 Clock genetics

A variety of organisms exhibit altered circadian periods as a result of induced mutagenesis. In *Drosophila*, Konopka (1979) produced three rhythm mutants by this means: arrhythmic (per^O) with no detectable rhythm, short (per^S) with a free-running rhythm of 19 h, and long (per^L) with a free-running period of 28 h; the wild-type free runs at *ca* 24 h. Interestingly, this circadian frequency mutation applied both to the adult emergence rhythm and to the locomotor activity rhythm. The mutation's locus is in a narrow band on the X-chromosome, probably linked with the genome of the head.

In *Neurospora*, a circadian rhythm is observed in the periodic (21.5-h) formation of conidia as cultures grow along cylindrical growth tubes. Mutagenesis has induced a number of mutants with altered periods (Feldman, Gardner & Denison, 1979). One group of seven are mutants of a single genetic locus, called frequency (*frq*): three have shorter periods than normal (down to 18 h), and four have longer periods (up to 29 h). Heterokaryons containing mutant and wild-type nuclei have circadian periods proportional in length to the percentage of mutant nuclei: a gene dose effect. While mutants at the *frq* locus are mutants of a single gene, mutations at five other genetic loci also alter period. Therefore, there is no unique locus that determines period length, and many gene products (proteins) are required for proper functioning of the circadian clock.

11.5.2 The avian pineal cell clock

The pineal gland of birds contains a circadian clock which controls the secretion of melatonin, a hormone that seems to couple the clock to locomotor activity (§11.4.2). Conveniently for the study of its clockwork, the chicken pineal can be isolated and kept for days in organ culture. The circadian rhythms in melatonin output and in the associated enzymes of the biochemical pathway then persist for days (Binkley, Riebman & Reilly, 1978). Melatonin is synthesised in the pineal as follows: the amino acid tryptophan circulating in the blood is converted to serotonin (5-hydroxytryptamine, 5-HT) in the pineal; serotonin is converted by the enzyme *N*-acetyl transferase (NAT) to *N*-acetylserotonin, which is acted on by hydroxyindole-O-methyl transferase (HIOMT) to produce melatonin. Melatonin is produced rhythmically by this pathway with highest production during the dark and lowest during the light, and the activity of the two enzymes, HIOMT and especially NAT (which seems the more important), changes rhythmically (Fig. 11.6A; see also §8.5 for role of 5-HT in sleep).

Still more interestingly, chicken pineal tissue has been dissociated, maintained in a cell culture, and the dissociated pineal cells shown to have rhythmic

NAT activity that will free run in constant darkness and even entrain to a reversed light cycle (Fig. 11.6 **B**). Since the cultured pinealocytes are not an organised tissue, these results strongly suggest that each cell contains its own circadian clock plus a photoreceptor for the clock's entrainment (cf. insect epidermis, §8.3.3). The clock is coupled to NAT in some unknown way, but the rise in NAT activity in darkness can be blocked by cycloheximide, showing that protein synthesis is essential, and RNA synthesis is required at some stages of the cycle.

Interestingly, the rat pineal also produces melatonin rhythmically, but the clock controlling much of the rat's circadian system is not in the pineal. The mammalian pineal rhythm is driven by the clock in the suprachiasmatic nucleus (§11.4), to which it is coupled neurally via connections in the sympathetic nervous system. The neurotransmitter of the sympathetic system, nor-adrenaline, is released when the sympathetic nervous system is activated, and combines with β-receptors in the pineal. Activation of the β-receptors promotes cyclic-AMP production which promotes the new synthesis of NAT.

Fig. 11.6. Rhythmic activities of the enzymes and products of the melatonin pathway in bird pineal glands. They are shown at the left (**A**) entrained to a light–dark (LD 12:12) cycle. In the dark, 5-hydroxytryptamine (5-HT) concentration decreases, N-acetyl transferase (NAT) activity increases, N-acetyl-5-hydroxytryptamine (NA-5HT) concentration increases, hydroxy-indole-O-methyl transferase (HIOMT) activity increases and finally the concentration of the product, melatonin, increases (for pathway, see §11.5.2). At light-on, the levels of all components except for 5-HT fall. (Compiled from Binkley *et al.* 1978.) The right-hand figures (**B**) show the rhythm in NAT activity from chicken pineal cells maintained in culture and (**a**) entrained to a light–dark cycle, (**b**) free-running in constant darkness, and (**c**) entrained to a reversed light–dark cycle. The pinealocytes were dissociated at the beginning of the record but not sampled for NAT until the time shown. (Adapted from Deguchi, 1979.)

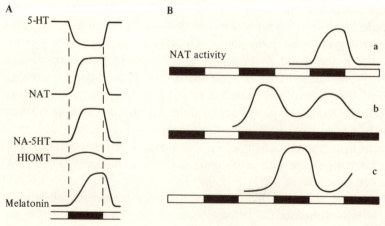

This forced rhythm of the rat pineal, driven by the SCN, is clearly quite different from the endogenously rhythmic organisation of the bird's pineal.

11.5.3 *Identifying treatments which affect the clock itself*

For any kind of biological clock that oscillates (see §1.3), it is accepted as a logical principle that treatments which systematically alter either the period or the phase of the overt measured rhythm are affecting the clock mechanism itself, rather than simply disturbing the coupling from it. This follows both from the interpretation of the results of phase shifting the clock with light pulses (i.e. phase–response curves (§2.3.2, 3.3.3)), and from theoretical considerations implicit in the idea that circadian (and tidal) clocks are limit-cycle oscillators and not conservative oscillators (such as a pendulum) (see §2.2.1). Two types of experiments are useful for sorting this out (see Tyson *et al.*, in Hastings & Schweiger, 1976): *pulse* experiments, in which a chemical (or other agent) is added for a few hours and then removed; and *step* experiments, in which the chemical is added and kept present.

Pulse experiments should advance or delay the phase of the rhythm in a manner that is dependent upon when in the cycle the pulse is given: after the phase shift the normal periodicity of the rhythm should then resume, but the phase shift should be permanent and measurable relative to the control rhythm in untreated individuals (see Fig. G.1B in the Glossary). In step experiments, the period of the rhythm is expected to be permanently changed (i.e. the rhythm should run faster or slower (cf. the *Drosophila* mutants, §11.5.1)) to an extent dependent upon the dose of the chemical or other agent under test. Chemicals which have these effects, without gross side effects, are thought to perturb the clock mechanism in a manner similar to natural zeitgebers such as light and temperature.

For pulse experiments, if the size and direction (advance or delay) of the phase shift are plotted as a function of the phase of the cycle when the pulse was given, the result is a phase–response curve (as in Figs. 2.6 or 3.4). This is a signature of how the test agent affects the clock and is therefore useful in interpreting results. Ideally, selectively perturbing the same element in the clock should give the same phase–response curve regardless of the perturbing agent, and agents that have the same mode of action, for example, the inhibition of protein synthesis, are expected to produce similar phase responses.

11.5.4 *Chemically dissecting the* Aplysia *eye clock*

The above approach should allow important elements in the clock mechanism to be identified, and has been employed using various chemicals on the *Aplysia* eye clock (Fig. 11.1). Among those agents which shift the eye's rhythm are protein synthesis inhibitors, some ions (manganese, lithium and potassium), the calcium ionophore A23187, metabolic inhibitors (dinitrophenol and sodium cyanide), an ion-pump inhibitor (strophanthidin), and one neurotransmitter (5-hydroxytryptamine). Many of these, however, have small effects, or have been only incompletely studied.

The phase–response curves for the agents that cause the largest shifts are shown in Fig. 11.7. The two most potent agents are a high potassium ion concentration and the protein synthesis inhibitor anisomycin, but their phase–response curves are different. Administration of anisomycin (curve **d**)

Fig. 11.7. (**A**) Phase–response curves for pulse perturbations of the *Aplysia* eye rhythm to: (**a**) high potassium pulses; (**b**) light pulses; (**c**) pulses of low temperature or of inhibitors of metabolism such as dinitrophenol or sodium cyanide; and (**d**) pulses of anisomycin, a protein synthesis inhibitor. Phase advances are upward and delays downward. Pulses lasted for 4 or 6 h, and were given once to each free-running DD-cultured eye at the time in its circadian cycle shown by the compound action potential (CAP) rhythm shown in **B**; this cycle is divided on the abscissa into 24 circadian 'hours' (i.e. 24 equal time divisions of a complete free-running cycle lasting some 26 real hours (see §2.3.2 paragraph 1)), with 'hours' 0–12 being the animal's normal day, and 'hours' 12–24 its normal night (cf. Fig. 2.6). (Compiled from Jacklet, 1978; and Eskin, 1979.)

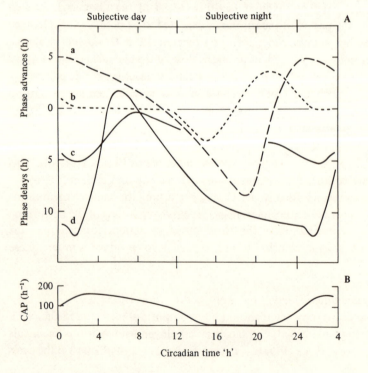

early in the subjective day at circadian time 0–3 h (see §2.3.2 first paragraph), produces large delays, whereas high potassium then causes large advances (curve **a**). Later on, however, at circadian time 20 h, both cause delays. All the tested agents have minimal effects when administered at circadian time 8 h. The effects of light (**b**) and metabolic inhibitors (**c**) are similar to those of high potassium and anisomycin respectively, but smaller; that is, they cause smaller phase shifts.

What can be concluded from this? If we assume that similar phase–response curves occur because the agents are acting on the same basic mechanism, then we may look for the common biochemical effect each of the agents should have, in the hope of identifying the mode of action and the mechanism affected. This logical process is not easy to achieve in practice, however. Phase responses following the pattern of curve **c**, for example, are produced both by inhibitors of metabolism (including sodium cyanide, dinitrophenol) and low temperature, and by the calcium ionophore, A23187. A23187 is thought to act by altering intracellular calcium regulation, but this specific effect could easily be mimicked by the more general effects of the metabolic inhibitors. Anisomycin, on the other hand, which has a greater but qualitatively similar effect, may inhibit production of a protein that is of importance in the clock by being involved in intracellular ion regulation.

As for a high concentration of potassium, its most obvious effect is to depolarise nerve cells, just as light depolarises photoreceptors in the eye of *Aplysia*. Since the phase–response curves for these two agents are roughly similar (curves **a** and **b**), one might expect other depolarising agents to have the same effects. And that indeed proves to be so: strophanthidin causes depolarisation and has a phase–response curve similar to the one for high potassium (Eskin, 1979). The difference between the high potassium curve (**a**) and the light curve (**b**), with the former causing the larger shifts, may be due to high potassium producing a greater and more prolonged depolarisation than light does. However, high potassium also inhibits protein synthesis, so it may have a dual effect. Another protein synthesis inhibitor, puromycin, which has a slight depolarising side-effect on the eye as well as causing specific inhibition of protein synthesis, gives rise to a phase–response curve nearly identical to that for anisomycin but with maximum delays of only six hours.

Since inhibitors may have side effects, as well as their more specific effect, it is important to show that these are minimal and that protein synthesis is actually inhibited at the concentrations which affect the clock being studied. For anisomycin, this has been demonstrated (Jacklet, 1980) by using derivatives of anisomycin which differ slightly from it chemically and which are inactive as inhibitors of protein synthesis. When tested on the *Aplysia* eye preparation, such compounds showed no detectable effect on the CAP rhythm, implying that the inhibitor's action on the clock is not via its side effects. Tests of this kind should always be performed when highly active inhibitors are being used, but are not always possible.

11.5.5 *Protein synthesis – the heart of the clock?*

Protein synthesis appears to be a requirement for other circadian clocks too. Phase-dependent phase shifts in the circadian photosynthesis rhythm of the alga, *Acetabularia* (Fig. 10.5), can be produced with pulses of either anisomycin or cycloheximide (cf. §10.4); and in the circadian glow rhythm of *Gonyaulax* (Fig. 10.4) with cycloheximide (Dunlap, Taylor & Hastings, 1980). In *Euglena*, the phototactic rhythm is slowed by cycloheximide. Cycloheximide may have a dual mode of action. It has an early effect on the *Gonyaulax* rhythm, believed to be due to perturbation of the ion regulating system, and a late effect that may be due to inhibition of protein synthesis (Walz & Sweeney, 1979).

Inhibitors of protein synthesis in prokaryotes, none of which have yet been found to show circadian rhythms, are ineffective on rhythms in eukaryotes, suggesting that the eukaryotic ribosome is the important site. The requirement for protein synthesis prompts the idea that RNA synthesis may also be required. Unfortunately most of the attempts to block RNA synthesis have simply resulted in abolishing the rhythm, because the effects of the blockers were not reversible. A reversible RNA synthesis inhibitor with minimal side effects is therefore needed. DNA-dependent RNA synthesis does not seem to be important in the clock mechanisms for *Acetabularia*, since enucleated cells continue to have a clear photosynthesis rhythm, and blocking extra-nuclear RNA synthesis with rifampicin likewise does not stop the clock.

11.5.6 *Membrane-based clocks?*

Although the results indicate that protein synthesis is important for proper clock function, there is little evidence to show how protein synthesis actually contributes to the clock. Action by specific proteins on the control of intracellular ions is suggested. There is substantial evidence to support the involvement of ions (see §11.5.4) and ion transport in circadian clocks, including the effects of ethanol, various ionophores (valinomycin and A23187), and ions (potassium and lithium). A membrane model has been proposed (Njus, Sulzman & Hastings, 1974) to account for these effects. It is compatible with the limit-cycle oscillator idea and provides an explanation for the temperature compensation exhibited by clocks (§2.2.4); it is also compatible with present ideas on phytochrome (§7.5). It is not an explicit model, however, so a direct test is difficult.

No other model has been put forward to show how proteins, ions and energy contribute to the clock, but recent advances such as the genetic mutant–biochemical approach (§11.5.1), the dissociated avian pineal cell cultures (§11.5.2), and the current refinements in chemical perturbation experiments are evidence that persistent and innovative inquiry will yield the circadian clock mechanism.

This work was supported in part by National Science Foundation grant BNS11154. I thank Alice Jacklet for helpful comments, Thea Hotaling for assistance and Linda Welch for the typescript.

11.6   Further reading and key references
Books and review articles are indicated by asterisks

Binkley, S., Riebman, J. & Reilly, K. (1978). The pineal gland: a biological clock *in vitro*. *Science*, **202**, 1198–201.

*Brady, J. (1969). How are insect rhythms controlled? *Nature* (*London*), **223**, 781–4.

*Brady, J. (1974). The physiology of insect circadian rhythms. *Advances in Insect Physiology*, **10**, 1–115.

*Brady, J. (1979). *Biological Clocks*. Studies in Biology, No. 104. London: Edward Arnold.

Deguchi, T. (1979). A circadian oscillator in cultured cells of chicken pineal gland. *Nature* (*London*), **282**, 94–6.

Dunlap, J., Taylor, W. & Hastings, J. W. (1980). The effects of protein synthesis inhibitors on the *Gonyaulax* clock. I. Phase-shifting effects of cycloheximide. *Journal of Comparative Physiology*, **138**, 1–8.

Edmunds, L. N., Jr. (1976). Models and mechanisms for endogenous timekeeping. Chapter 8, in Palmer, J. D. *An Introduction to Biological Rhythms*. New York, San Francisco, London: Academic Press.

Eskin, A. (1979). Circadian systems of the *Aplysia* eye: properties of the pacemaker and mechanisms of its entrainment. *Federation Proceedings*, **38**, 2573–9.

Feldman, J., Gardner, G. & Denison, R. (1979). Genetic analysis of the circadian clock of *Neurospora*. In *Biological Rhythms and Their Central Mechanism, Naito Foundation*, ed. M. Suda, D. Hayaishi & H. Nakagawa, pp. 57–66. Amsterdam: Elsevier/North-Holland Biomedical Press.

*Hastings, J. W. & Schweiger, H. G. (Eds) (1976). *The Molecular Basis of Circadian Rhythms*. Berlin: Report of the Dahlem Workshop.

Hudson, D. & Lickey, M. (1980). Internal desynchronization between the identified circadian oscillators in *Aplysia*. *Brain Research*, **183**, 481–5.

Inouye, S. & Kawamura, H. (1979). Persistence of circadian rhythmicity in a mammalian hypothalamic 'island' containing the suprachiasmatic nucleus. *Proceedings of the National Academy of Sciences, U.S.A.*, **76**, 5962–6.

Jacklet, J. W. (1974). The effects of constant light and light pulses on the circadian rhythm in the eye of *Aplysia*. *Journal of Comparative Physiology*, **90**, 33–45.

*Jacklet, J. W. (1978). The cellular mechanism of circadian clocks. *Trends in Neuroscience*, **1**, 117–19.

Jacklet, J. W. (1980). Protein synthesis requirement of the *Aplysia* circadian clock, tested by active and inactive derivatives of the inhibitor anisomycin. *Journal of Experimental Biology*, **85**, 33–42.

*Konopka, R. J. (1979). Genetic dissection of the *Drosophila* circadian system. *Federation Proceedings*, **38**, 2602–5.

*Lickey, M. E., Block, G. D., Hudson, D. J. & Smith, J. T. (1976). Circadian oscillators and photoreceptors in the gastropod, *Aplysia*. *Photochemistry and Photobiology*, **23**, 253–73.

Lickey, M. & Wozniak, J. (1979). Circadian organization in *Aplysia* explored with red light, eye removal and behavioral recording. *Journal of Comparative Physiology*, **131**, 169–77.

Njus, D., Sulzman, F. & Hastings, J. W. (1974). Membrane model for the circadian clock. *Nature (London)*, **248**, 116–20.

*Page, L. (1981). Localization of circadian pacemakers in insects. In *Biological Clocks in Seasonal Reproductive Cycles*, ed. B. K. & D. E. Follett, pp. 113–24. Bristol: John Wright.

Pittendrigh, C. S. & Daan, S. (1976). A functional analysis of circadian pacemakers in nocturnal rodents: (V) Pacemaker structure: a clock for all seasons. *Journal of Comparative Physiology*, **106**, 333–55.

*Rusak, B. (1979). Neural mechanisms for entrainment and generation of mammalian circadian rhythms. *Federation Proceedings*, **38**, 2589–95.

*Rusak, B. & Zucker, I. (1979). Neural regulation of circadian rhythms. *Physiological Reviews*, **59**, 449–526.

Sokolove, P. & Loher, W. (1975). Role of eyes, optic lobes, and pars intercerebralis in locomotory and stridulatory circadian rhythms of *Telegryllus commodus*. *Journal of Insect Physiology*, **21**, 785–99.

Truman, J. (1974). Physiology of insect rhythms: (IV) Role of the brain in the regulation of the flight rhythm of the giant silkmoths. *Journal of Comparative Physiology*, **95**, 281–96.

Truman, J. (1979). Interaction between abdominal ganglia during the performance of hormonally triggered behavioural programmes in moths. *Journal of Experimental Biology*, **82**, 239–53.

Walz, B. & Sweeney, B. (1979). Kinetics of the cycloheximide-induced phase changes with biological clock in *Gonyaulax*. *Proceedings of the National Academy of Sciences, U.S.A.*, **76**, 6443–7.

Zimmerman, N. & Menaker, M. (1979). The pineal gland: a pacemaker within the circadian system of the house sparrow. *Proceedings of the National Academy of Sciences, U.S.A.*, **76**, 999–1003.

INDEX

Note: most entries relating to particular organisms are given under their scientific names.

abscisic acid, 116
accuracy of timekeeping, 17
Acetabularia (unicellular alga), 166–7, 175, 186
Acronycta (knot-grass moth), critical day-length in, 68–9, 83
ACTH (adrenocorticotropic hormone), 124
action spectra, for phytochrome, 104, 108
adaptive advantage, of timekeeping ability, 3, 11–12, 28, 36
adrenal glands, endogenous rhythmicity in, 124–5
adrenal hormones, 124–5, 147
adrenaline, urinary excretion of, 147
adrenocorticotropic hormone, *see* ACTH
aestivation xiv, 101
agriculture, photoperiodism and, 98
alertness in humans, rhythm in, 143–4
algae, rhythms in, 35 *and see Acetabularia, Amphidinium, Dictyota, Gonyaulax, Hantzschia*
Ammospermophilus (ground squirrel), phase–response curve, 25
Amphidinium (dinoflagellate), tidal activity rhythm, 40
amplitude, xiv–xv
anaesthesia, rhythm in duration of in man, 155–6
anisomycin, 184–5
annual rhythms, *see* circannual rhythm
Anser (goose), 69
Antheraea (silkmoth), diapause timing, 95–6 (*see also* silkmoth)
Anthrenus (beetle), 78–9
anti-diuretic hormone, *see* pituitary gland
antigonadotrophin, of rodent pineal gland, 92–4
ants, sun-compass orientation in, 49–50, 57
aphids, seasonal polymorphism in, 66, 71–3, 80, 96–7
Apis, see bee
Aplysia (sea hare), eye clock of, 18, 20, 173–4, 179–80
  phase–response curve of, 183–5
Aschoff's rule, 27–8

ATP/ADP/AMP system, 160–4
auxin, 18
azimuth, xiv
  in entrainment, 20
  in orientation, 56–7

barnacles, non-endogenous tidal rhythmicity in, 36
beavers, free-running rhythm in arctic winter, 13
bees, sun-compass orientation in, 50, 56–7
  feeding timing, 30, 50
  marathon dancers' time sense, 56
behavioural rhythms, 131–6
bi-coordinate navigation by celestial cues, 52, 58
biochemistry of rhythms, 159–on, 184–5
bioluminescence rhythm, in *Gonyaulax*, 19, 164–6
birds, *see also Anser, Branta, Junco,* kestrel, *Parus,* quail, rook, sparrow, *Sterna, Sturnus, Sylvia*
  dawn chorus by, 28
  magnetic orientation in, 59
  migration of, *see* migration
  photo-neuroendocrine control of reproduction in, 90–1
  photoreceptors in brain of, 69, 90–1
  pineal hormones and circadian rhythms in, 91, 135
  time-compensated celestial orientation in, 50–5, 58–9
body-temperature rhythm in man, 124, 127, 144–8, 150–3
  in jet-lag, 152–3
  in shift work, 153–4
Bombyx (silk moth), diapause timing, 66, 95–6
brain
  neurosecretory cell rhythm in *Drosophila,* 123
  pars intercerebralis and optic lobes, in insect rhythms, 176–7, in insect photoperiodism, 95–7

brain (*cont.*)
  photoreceptors of birds in, 69, 90–1
  photoreceptors of insects in, 95, 97, 176
  primary clocks in, 138–40
  see also optic lobes, pineal gland, raphe
    nuclei, suprachiasmatic nuclei
Branta (Hawaiian goose), 69
Brassica, 114
bud dormancy, 166
Bünning's hypothesis, 72, 74–5, 107

calcium, excretory rhythm of, 125–6; ion
    effects in clocks, 185
CAM, *see* crassulacean acid metabolism
Canavalis, leaf-movement rhythm, 12–13
Cannabis (hemp), 65
carbon dioxide
  fixation, 166–71
  production, 127–8
Carcinus (shore crab), tidal rhythm, 35–9
celestial orientation, and circannual rhythms,
    59–60
  see also moon-compass, star-compass,
    sun-compass
cell cultures, circadian rhythms in, 122, 138
cell-division rhythms, 17, 121–2, 165
cell membranes, 114–15, 168, 186–7
cells
  circadian rhythms in, 121–2, 138, 164
  clock mechanisms in, 4, 180–7
central nervous system
  circadian change in excitability, 136
  and circadian rhythms in responsiveness,
    131, 133, 135
  and control of gated rhythms, 131, 134
  see also brain
central *versus* peripheral control of
    behaviour, 133–5
Centrostephanus (sea urchin), lunar spawning
    rhythm in, 42
Chenopodium
  energy metabolism in, 163–4
  phytochrome in, 108–9, 111
chitin, *see* cuticle
chloride, excretory rhythm, 125
chlorophyll, 104, 109, 167 (*and see*
    photosynthesis)
chrono-pharmacology, chrono-therapy, 156
circadian 'gate' in developmental rhythms,
    129–30, 135
circadian organisation, 138, 143, 174–80
circadian period, free-running, 5, 27
  in diurnal and nocturnal animals, 28, 30
  in humans, 17, 145–8, 152
circadian rhythms (*see also* under specific
    functions)
  as basis for photoperiodic timing, 72–7,
    88–9
  as endogenous oscillators, *see* oscillators

entrainment of, *see* entrainment
  evolution of, 11–12
circadian time (CT 'hours'), 23, 76
circalunar rhythms, 42–7, 140
circannual rhythms, and migration, 43,
    59–60
  and photoperiodism, 77–9, 81
circa-semilunar rhythms, 42–5
circatidal rhythms, 33–6
  entrainment of, 36–41
  modulated by circadian rhythm, 35, 39–42
  physiological control of, 140, 173
clocks, biological, 1–4
  concepts of, 4
  different types of, 71–4, 79–81
  fast and slow, in entrainment, 27–8
  hierarchical arrangement of, 139
  literature on, 5–6
  mechanism of, 160–6, 173–4, 180–7
  models for, 74–5; external coincidence,
    75–7, 80, 107; internal coincidence, 77,
    80, 108
  nature of, 69–70
  as oscillators, 4–5
  sites and coupling of, 174–80
  '*the* clock' and primary clock concepts, 6,
    138–40, 179
Clunio (intertidal midge), adult emergence
    rhythm, 46–7
cockroach
  circadian rhythms in, 11, 19
  cuticle deposition rhythm in, 127–8
  optic lobes and circadian control, 20, 135,
    138, 176–7
  phase–response curve, 25–6
Colias, 74
compass, *see* sun compass, star compass,
    moon compass
consciousness, 136
continuously consulted clocks, 55, *and see*
    time sense
Convoluta (turbellarian), 39
corals, fossil rhythms in, 11
corpora allata
  cellular rhythm in (*Drosophila*), 123
  in diapause control, 95–6
corpora cardiaca secretions, 95–6
corticosteroids, urinary excretion of, 143,
    145, 147
coupled oscillators, 18, 77, 139–40, 146, 149,
    174
coupling mechanisms, in circadian clocks,
    139, 174–5, 179–80
cows, effects of lengthened winter days on,
    98
Crangon (brown shrimp), swimming rhythm,
    39–40
crassulacean acid metbolism (CAM), 167–70
crayfish, retinal sensitivity rhythm, 26–7

crickets, optic lobes and circadian control, 138, 176
critical day-length (or photoperiod), xiv, 67–9, 83, 106
crustaceans, *see especially*: *Carcinus, Crangon, Eurydice, Excirolana, Talitrus*
cuticle, rhythm of deposition in arthropods, 126, 127–8
cycloheximide, 182, 186
cytokinins, 116

dawn, *see* sunrise
dawn chorus, 28–9
dawn and dusk oscillators, 77, 149, 179
day-length effects, *see* photoperiodism
deer, breeding season of, 84, 86
destruction, *see under* phytochrome
desynchronisation of circadian rhythms, in humans, 149–52, 179
  as cause of pathological conditions, 156
developmental (gated) rhythms, 129–31
diapause in insects, xiv, 66–9, 94–6
  hormone, 96
  and temperature effects, 95
Dictyota (brown alga), gamete discharge rhythm, 42
diel rhythms, xiv
diurnal animals, 28
DL propranolol, 116
dormancy, in plants, xiv, 102
Drosophila, phase responses, 25–6
  cellular rhythms, 123
  mutants with non-24-h rhythms, 181
  pupal eclosion rhythm, 16, 19, 74, 130–1
  temperature compensation, 19
drugs, and circadian timing, 19, 128, 155–6
dual role of phytochrome, 108
dusk, *see* sunrise

ecdysone, 95–6, 124
eclosion, rhythm, 74, 129–31, 134–5, 176–7; circannual, 79; lunar, 42
eclosion hormone, 131, 135, 177
electro-encephalogram (EEG), *see under* sleep
emergence rhythm in insects, *see* eclosion
endocrines (*see also* under hormones)
  and circadian rhythms, 122, 131, 138, 177
  and photoperiodism, 86–98
endogeneity of rhythms, xiv, 3, 12, 16, 35, 41
energy charge, and ATP rhythmicity, 164, 166, 167
energy metabolism rhythms
  in animals, 127, *and see* metabolic rhythms
  in *Chenopodium*, 163–4
  in fermenting yeast, 160–3

entrainment
  of circadian rhythms, 13, 18–20, in man, 146–9
  of circatidal rhythms, 36–41
  fast and slow clocks in, 27–8
  in jet-lag, 151–3
  light as dominant stimulus in, 20, 139–40, 151
  limits to, 19, 30, 149
  phase responses in, 23–7
  photoreceptors in, 21–2
  by seasonal photoperiod changes, 78–80
  of semilunar rhythm, 45–6
enzymic rhythms, 30–1, 122, 161–on, 181–2
epidermal cells, *see* cuticle
equinox, xiv, 18
'escapement' concept in biological clocks, 5–6, 183
Euglena (protozoan), 17, 186
Eunice (palolo worm), lunar spawning rhythm, 42
Eurydice (sand-beach isopod)
  circatidal rhythm in, 35–9
  semilunar rhythm in, 43–4
evolution of biological timekeeping, 11–12, 28, 67
Excirolana (sand-beach isopod)
  circatidal rhythm in, 39–42
  semilunar rhythm in, 43–5
excretory rhythms, 124–6 (*and see* under urine)
exogenous rhythms, xv, *and see* endogeneity
external coincidence model in photoperiodism, 75–7, 80, 88, 107–8
eyes, rhythms in light sensitivity in, 26–7
  as light meters in entrainment, 21

fat-body rhythm in *Drosophila*, 123
feedback systems as oscillators, 160–3
'florigen', hypothetical flowering hormone, 70, 116
flowering in plants, photoperiodism and, 65–6, 70–3, 101, 107, 111–2
fly, *see Protophormia, Sarcophaga*
follicle-stimulating hormone (FSH), 86–7, 90–1
free-running rhythms, xv, 7, 13, 28, (in man) 145 (*and see* circadian, circatidal, circannual)
frequency, xv, 18–19 (*and see* period)
FSH, *see* follicle-stimulating hormone
Fuchsia, 112

Gammarus (estuarine amphipod), swimming rhythm, 45
gating, and gated rhythms, xv, 78, 129–31, 135
geese, breeding seasons of, 69, 83
genetics of clocks, 30, 46, 164, 181
gibberellins, 116

Glaucomys (flying squirrel), 20;
   phase–response curve, 25
Glossina (testse fly), 29, 127–8, 131–3
Glycine (soy bean), 66, 72–4
glycolysis, 160
GnRH, *see* gonadotrophin
gonadal function in birds, and migration, 60
gonadotrophin-releasing hormone (GnRH),
   and vertebrate photoperiodism, 87–91
Gonyaulax (dinoflagellate), temperature
   compensation, 19; phase–response
   curve, 25–6
   coupled circadian rhythms in, 121, 175
   metabolic inhibitor effects on, 186
   rhythmic bioluminescence in, 19, 164–6,
   186
goose, 69, 83
gramicidin, 116, *and see* ionophores
growth hormone, episodic secretion of, 124

hamster, see *Mesocricetus*
'hands' of the biological clock, 5–6, 74, 183
Hantzschia (diatom), rhythm of vertical
   migration in sand, 40
hibernation, xv, circannual rhythm of, 78
high frequency rhythms, 4–5, 160–3
homeostasis and circadian rhythms, 18
homing, *see* bi-coordinate navigation
hormones
   and circadian rhythms, 122, 131, 138,
   176–7
   connecting different clocks, 139
   controlling gated rhythms, 134 (*and see*
   eclosion)
   episodic secretion of, 86, 124
   and photoperiod (in animals) 86–98, (in
   plants) 70, 116, (in insects) 95–7
   see also ACTH, ecdysone, eclosion h.,
   'florigen', FSH, GnRH, 5-HT, juvenile
   h., LH
horse, breeding season in, 84–5, 98
hour-glass mechanism as a 'clock', xv, 7, 53,
   58, 108
   as damped circadian oscillator, 80
   in photoperiodism, 71–3, 79–80
5-HT, *see* serotonin
humans
   circadian rhythms in: anaesthesia, 128,
   155; behaviour, 131, 143–5; body
   temperature, 144–on; pain thresholds,
   155; sleep–wake cycles, 17, 143–on, 118,
   152
   desynchronisation of circadian rhythms in,
   149–52, 179
   electro-encephalograms of, during sleep,
   136–7
   entrainment of circadian rhythms by
   zeitgebers, 146–9
   excretory rhythms in, *see* urine
   jet-lag, 151–3
   medical aspects of circadian rhythms in,
   155–6
   shift work, 153–5
Humulus (hop), 65
Hyoscyamus, 72, 104, 114
hypothalamus
   and circadian rhythms, 124
   and photoperiodic control in birds, 90–1;
   in mammals, 87, 92–4
   see also under suprachiasmatic nuclei, and
   retino-hypothalamic tract

inheritance, of timekeeping ability, 3, 11, 30,
   33, 46, 181
insecticides, sensitivity rhythms, 128–9
insects (*see also* under: *Acronycta*,
   Antheraea, *Anthrenus*, aphids, bees,
   Bombyx, *Clunio*, cockroach,
   Drosophila, *Glossina*, locusts, *Ostrinia*,
   Pectinophora, *Povilla*, *Protophormia*,
   Sarcophaga)
   circadian rhythms in, 11, 19, 123, 127,
   135, 176
   diapause in, *see* diapause
   gated rhythm in eclosion of, 129–30, 135
   mortality of, and circadian timekeeping,
   17
   optic lobe control of circadian timing in,
   127, 135, 138, 176–7
   photoperiodism in, 68, 71–5, 83, 96
   photoreceptors in brain of, 69, 95, 97
internal coincidence model in
   photoperiodism, 77, 80, 108
internal desynchronisation, 149–52, 179, *see
   also* rhythm splitting
ionophores, 116, 166, 185–6
ions in clock mechanisms, *see* calcium,
   lithium, potassium, sodium, and
   ionophores

jet-lag, 151–3
Junco (snow bird), photoperiodism in, 66
juvenile hormone (in insects), 95–6

Kalanchöe, 16, 71–2
   crassulacean acid metabolism in, 169–71
kestrel, rhythmic feeding in, 29
kidney, excretory rhythms by, 124–6, *see
   also* urine

Lacerta (lizard), temperature compensation,
   19
latitude, and critical photoperiod, 68–9, 83
leaf movement rhythms, 12–13, 28, 115,
   171
   and photoperiodic timing, 28, 43–4, 73–4,
   115
learning, in circadian rhythms, 30–1, 50

Lemna (duckweed), photoperiodism in, 108–9, 115–16
Leptinotarsa (Colorado beetle), 95–6
Leuresthes (grunion fish), lunar spawning rhythm, 42
LH, *see* leuteinising hormone
light
  adjustment of circadian rhythm by intensity of, 20, 139–40
  intensity, daily cycle of, 20, 109
  and models for photoperiodism involving entrainment, 65, 77
  phase responses to, *see* phase–response curves
  photosynthetic and photoperiodic roles of, 65
light compass, *see* sun compass
light dominance, 112, 114
limit cycle oscillators, 14, 19–20, 183
limits to entrainment, 19, 30, 149
lithium ions, effects on clocks, 116, 186
locomotor activity
  circadian rhythms in, 23–4, 54–5, 128, 131, 173
  semilunar rhythms in, 43–5
  tidal rhythms in, 35–40
locusts, 126–7
Lolium (grass), 101, 109, 112–14
long-day/short-day responses, 66, 84–6, 101, 106, 112
luciferase, of *Gonyaulax*, 165–6
luminescence, *see* bioluminescence
lunar rhythms, 42–7
luteinising hormone (LH), in vertebrate photoperiodism, 86–9, 91, 124

magnetic field of earth, and orientation in birds, 59
Malpighian tubules, 126
mammals, *see*: *Ammospermophilus*, cows, deer, *Glaucomys*, horse, humans, *Mesocricetus*, mice, *Microtus*, rabbit, rat, rodent, sheep
  circadian rhythms in, 23–5
  hormonal control of photoperiodism in, 92–4
  photoperiodic time measurement in, 88–90
  photoperiodism in, 84–8
  (*and see* suprachiasmatic nuclei)
man, *see* humans
masking effects, in circadian rhythms, 124, 144–5, 153
mechanical disturbance, entraining circatidal rhythms, 39
medical aspects, of circadian rhythms, 155–6
Megoura (aphid), photoperiodism in, 71, 73, 80

melatonin, rhythmical secretion by pineal, 91–4, 122, 178
membranes in clock mechanisms, 91, 105, 114–16, 163–4, 166, 168–70, 186–7
Mesocricetus (hamster), phase–response curve, 25
metabolic inhibitors, and circadian clocks, 166, 184–5
metabolic rhythms, 122, 127–8, 160–4 (*see also* CAM)
mice, 17
  phase–response curve, 25
  rhythms in sensitivity, to alcohol, 156; and ouabain, 128
Microtus (vole)
  breeding season, 85
  phase responses, 23–4
migration of birds, 50–2, 60, 66, 84
  gonadal state, and direction of, 60, 66
  migratory restlessness in, 50, 52, 60
  sun-compass orientation in, 50–8
Mimosa (sensitive plant), leaf movement rhythm, 171
Mirabilis (four-o'clock plant), rhythm precision in, 18
moon, effect on tides, 33–4
moon-compass orientation, in *Talitrus*, 57–8
moonlight, entrainment of *Clunio* rhythm by, 45–7
  reason for leaf movement rhythms, 28
morphogenesis, 129 (*and see* photomorphogenesis)
mortality, in non-24-h entrainment, 17, 77
moths, *see under* insects
moulting, 45, 60, 78, 83–5, 94 (*and see* eclosion)
Mus (house mouse), *see* mice
mutants for rhythms
  in *Drosophila* emergence and locomotor activity, 181
  in *Neurospora*, for conidial formation, 164, 181

NADP rhythm, 160, 163, 167
Nasonia (parasitic wasp), photoperiodism in, 96
NAT, *see* pineal gland in birds
Nauphoeta (cockroach), phase–response curve, 25–6
navigation, *see* sun compass
neap tides, xv, 33–4
Nephrops (lobster), circadian rhythm in, 40
neural rhythms, 134, 173–4, 179
Neurospora (fungus), spore discharge rhythm, 164, 181
Nicotiana (tobacco), 66
night-break (night-interruption) experiments on flowering in plants, 70–1, 72–3, 106–7, 111

night-break (*cont.*)
    on induction of diapause in insects, 71–5
    on testicular growth in birds, 90
night-length, importance in photoperiodism, 70
nocturnal animals, 11, 28
noradrenaline, 182
nucleus, role in clock mechanisms, 166–7, 182, 186

oestrus cycles, 86
optic lobes, and circadian rhythms in insects, 127, 135, 138, 176–7
orientation, *see* sun compass
oscillators
    biological clocks as, 4–5, 80
    coupled oscillators, 18, 77, 139, 174–80
    'dawn' and 'dusk', 77, 149, 179
    endogenous nature, xiv, 3, 12, 16, 35, 41
    homeostasis and, 18–20
    as limit cycles, 14, 19–20, 183
    precision of, 17–18, 28
    principles of, 14–16
    self-sustained, 14, 16, 143
Ostrinia (corn-borer), 73, 95
oxygen-consumption, *see* metabolic rhythms
oxygen-production rhythms, 35, 166–71
ouabain, circadian rhythm in sensitivity to (mice), 128

P_{fr}/P_r, *see* phytochrome
pacemakers, *see* oscillators, clocks
pain, rhythmic threshold in, 155–6
Palaemon (intertidal prawn), circatidal rhythm in, 40
Paramecium (protozoan), mating rhythm, 121
pars intercerebralis, *see* brain
Parus (tit), photoperiodism in, 84; singing, 30
Passiflora (passion flower), rhythm precision in, 18
Pectinophora (bollworm), 71, 74–5, 128–9
Perilla, flowering in, 102
period, xv
Periplaneta (cockroach), temperature compensation, 19
Pharbitis (morning-glory)
    induction of flowering in, 72–3, 101, 103
    phytochrome in, 107, 110–11
phase, xv; phase advance/delay, 23–6; photo-inducible phase (ϕ_i), 75–6, 107
phase–response curves (PRC), xv
    to pulses of light: in diapause induction, 75–7; in entrainment of circadian rhythms, 23–7; in entrainment of circatidal rhythms, 40–1
    to various agents, in *Aplysia* eye rhythm, 184–5

phase shift, xvi, *and see* phase–response curve
Phaseolus (bean), temperature compensation, 19
pheromone release rhythm in moths, 133
photo-inducible phase (ϕ_i), 75–6, 88, 107
photomorphogenesis, controlled by phytochrome, 102, 112, 114
photoperiodism, xvi, 65–9, 83–98
    in animals, 83–4, 97–8
    and circannual rhythms, 77–9, 81
    clocks in, *see under* clocks
    critical photoperiod in, 66, 67–9, 83
    in insects, 94; for aphid polymorphism, 96–7; for diapause, 70–1
    and leaf movements to avoid moonlight, 28
    neuroendocrine mechanisms (birds) 90–1, (mammals) 92–4
    night-break experiments in, 70–1, 72–3, 90, 106–7, 111
    in plants, 65–6, 70–3, 102–16 (*and see* phytochrome)
    refractory period in, 81, 85, 98
    time measurement in vertebrates, 88–90
    in vertebrate reproduction, 84–8
photophase, xvi
photophil, 72
photoreceptors,
    circadian rhythm in sensitivity of, 27, 133, 135
    in entrainment of circadian rhythms, 21–2, 69, 139, 174, 176, 182
    non-retinal, *see* under brain
    in photoperiod perception, 69, 90–1, 95–7, 139
    phytochrome in leaves of plants, 69–70, 102
photorefractoriness, 81, 85, 98
photosynthesis, rhythms, in, 11, 165–7
phytochrome (P_{fr}/P_r), xvi, 69, 102–3, 107, 114–16
    absorption spectra of, 104
    action via circadian rhythms and membranes, 114–16
    changes in sensitivity to, 114
    chromophore in, 103
    in circadian rhythms, 115
    destruction or reversion of, 104–7
    detection and measurement, 104–5
    dual role, 108
    in floral induction, 107–114
    hypothesis for mode of action of, 107, 112
    interconversion of P_{fr}/P_r, 104–7
    in membranes, 114–16, 186
    in metabolism of Crassulaceae, 164, 169
    in PEP-carboxylase rhythms, 169
    in photomorphogenesis, 114

phytochrome (*cont.*)
in photoperiodic physiology, 102–6
as photo receptor in plants, 101–3
problems concerning, 109–12
rhythmic interconversion in, 114
Picea (spruce), 112
Pieris (cabbage butterfly), photoperiodism in, 67–9
pigeon, homing, 45
pineal gland in birds
circadian rhythm in *N*-acetyl transferase (NAT), 122, 181–2
controlling circadian timekeeping, 138, 177–8
isolated cells' rhythmicity, 181–2
and photoperiodic responses, 91, 135
photoreception by, 90, 182
pineal gland in mammals
innervation of, 92
melatonin rhythm in, 92–4, 182
and photoperiodic responses, 92–4
pituitary gland, 124–5
plankton rhythms, 11
plants, *see especially*: *Canavalis, Chenopodium, Kalanchöe, Lemna, Pharbitis, Phaseolus, Xanthium*
Platynereis (polychaete), circalunar rhythm in, 42
Plumbago, 102
polymorphism, *see* aphids
population rhythms, 42, 131
populations of coupled oscillators as clock mechanisms, 4, 18, 77, 139–40, 146, 149, 174
Portulaca, 112
potassium ions
effect on *Gonyaulax* clock, 166
excretory rhythm of, 125–6, 147
in membrane-based clocks, 115, 166, 186
phase responses of *Aplysia* eye clock to, 184–5
Povilla (mayfly), lunar emergence rhythm in, 42
PRC, *see* phase–response curve
precision of oscillators, 17–18, 28
pressure, entrainment of circatidal rhythm by, 38
prokaryotes, circadian rhythms not found in, 186
prolactin, episodic secretion of, 124
propranolol (DL), 116
protein synthesis
and the *Aplysia* eye clock, 184–5
and the *Gonyaulax* clock, 166, 186
as heart of the circadian clock, 186
required for pineal clock in birds, 182
prothoracic glands of insects, 123–4
prothoracotropic hormone (in insects), 95–6

Protista: *see Acetabularia, Euglena, Gonyaulax, Hantzschia, Paramecium, Tetrahymena*
protocerebrum, photoperiodic clock of insects, 95, 97
Protophormia (blowfly), sensory rhythm in, 133–4
puromycin, 185

Q_{10}s, *see* temperature coefficient
quail
breeding season of, 85–6, 89–90
photoreceptor in brain of, 90–1

rabbit, retinal sensitivity rhythm, 26–7
raphe nuclei in brain stem, and sleep, 137
rat, suprachiasmatic nuclei in, 20–2
reaction speed of humans, rhythm in, 144
REM, *see under* sleep
resonance experiments on photoperiodism, 72, 77
respiratory rhythms, *see* metabolic rhythms
responsiveness, behavioural, 131–3, 135, 144, 155
retina, variations in sensitivity of, 26–7
retino-hypothalamic tract (to suprachiasmatic nuclei), 22, 69, 90–2
reversion, *see under* phytochrome
rhythm splitting, 77, 149, 179
ribosomes, in circadian clocks, 186
rifampicin, 186
RNA synthesis
and the *Gonyaulax* clock, 166
and pineal clock in birds, 182
rodent (*see also Ammospermophilus, Glaucomys, Mesocricetus, Microtus, Mus*, rat)
pineal gland and reproduction of, 92–3
sleep EEG patterns, 137
suprachiasmatic nuclei and rhythm control, 138
rook, breeding season of, 85

salinity, entrainment of circatidal rhythm by, 38–9
salivary gland cells, circadian rhythm in (*Drosophila*), 123–4
Samanea, leaf movements in, 18
Sarcophaga (fleshfly), phase–response curve, 25–6
induction of diapause in, 67, 73, 75–7, 84
SCN, *see* suprachiasmatic nuclei
scorpions, 21, 26–7
scotophase, xvi
scotophil, 72
seasonal responses, *see* photoperiodism
self-sustained oscillator, *see under* oscillators
semilunar rhythms, 42–7

Sempervivum (house leek), induced to flower in winter, 65
sensitivity rhythms, 26–7, 128–9, 133–4, 155–6
serotonin (5-hydroxytryptamine, 5-HT), 137–8, 181, 184
sheep, breeding season of
  photoperiodism and, 84, 86–7, 98
  sleep EEG patterns, 137
  suprachiasmatic nuclei and, 94
shift work, and circadian rhythms, 153–5
short-day responses, *see* long-day
silkmoths, brain in circadian timing, 176–7, *and see Antheraea, Bombyx*
singularity point, of an oscillating system, 16
skeleton photoperiod, xvi, *and see* night-break experiments
skotophase, xvi
skotophil, 72
sleep
  adaptive function of, 29
  deprivation of, and circadian rhythms, 144–5
  EEG patterns during (in mammals), 136–7
  episodic nature of, 124, 136
  induced by serotonin, 137–8
  rapid-eye-movement sleep (REM) and dreaming, 136–7
sleep–wake rhythm, 121, 143
  adaptive function of, 29
  and body-temperature rhythm, 125, 128, 146–50
  free-running, in man, 29, 143–5, 148, 151
  in jet-lag, 153
sodium, excretory rhythm of, 125–6
solstice, xvi, 33–4
sparrow
  photoreceptor in brain of, 90
  pineal gland of, 138, 177–8
spontaneous activity, 131–3
spring tides, xvi, 34
star-compass orientation, 58
starling, *see Sturnus*
Sterna (sooty tern), circannual breeding rhythm, 43
stomatal rhythms, 11
strawberry, flowering in, 112
Sturnus (starling)
  circannual rhythm in, 81
  feeding arrhythmicity, 16
  sun-compass orientation in, 50–5
subjective day/night, 23–6
sun-compass orientation, 49–on
  and bi-coordinate navigation ('map and compass'), 52, 58–9
  from polarisation pattern of sky, 56
  time compensation in, 50–6
sunrise and sunset
  light changes at, 20, 23

in photoperiodic timing, *see* external coincidence
as zeitgebers, 14, 16, 26, 53, 77, 179
suprachiasmatic nuclei (SCN)
  in circadian timekeeping, 22, 124, 135, 137–8, 178–9, 182
  in photoperiodic timekeeping, 91–4
Sylvia (warbler), circannual rhythms and orientation in, 58, 60
synchronisation, *see* entrainment

Talitrus (strandline amphipod)
  circadian rhythm in, 40
  moon- and sun-compass in, 56–8
  semilunar rhythm in, 43–5
Talorchestia (sand-beach amphipod), 39
temperature
  coefficient (Q_{10}), xvi, 19, 126
  and diapause of insects, 95
  entrainment by, in circadian rhythms, 19; in circatidal rhythms, 36–8; in semilunar rhythms, 47
  and photoperiodism, 84, 107
  rhythms in, *see* body temperature
temperature compensation, in biological clocks, 4, 19, 78, 84, 126, 186
territorial occupancy, by diurnal and nocturnal animals, 28, 30
Tetrahymena (protozoan), cell division, 121
tidal phenomena, 33–4; *see also* circatidal rhythms
time-cues, *see* zeitgebers
time sense, 49, 50, 56
tissue cultures, circadian rhythms in, 122
tissue rhythms, 122–7
tonoplast, *see* vacuole
transients, unstable cycles in phase-shifted rhythms, xvi, 15
trout farms, manipulation of day-length at, 98
tuber formation, photoperiodic control of, 102, 116

Uca (crab), entrainment of tidal rhythm, 39
unicellular organisms
  circadian organisation in, 174–5
  circadian rhythms in, 121–2
  and see under Protista
urine, circadian rhythms in
  amount excreted, 125–6
  concentrations of constituents, 125–6, 143, 145–7

vacuole in Crassulaceae, role in malic-acid rhythm, 167, 169–70
valinomycin, *see* ionophores
vole, *see Microtus*, kestrel

water, effects on plant clocks, 115

water excretion, in urine, 125–6
water turbulence, entrainment by, in
 circadian rhythms, 39
 semilunar rhythms, 45–7

X-rays, rhythm in sensitivity to, 128–9
Xanthium, flowering in, 101, 104, 107

yeast, rhythmic glycolysis in, 160–3

zeitgebers (environmental entraining signals),
 xvi, 13–14, 175
 daily correction of endogenous rhythms
 to, 17
 see also entrainment
zeitgedächtnis, xvi, 49, 50, 56
Zonotrichia (white-crowned sparrow), 84–5,
 88
zugunruhe (migratory restlessness), xvi, 50,
 52, 60